GLORY DESCENDING

GLORY DESCENDING

Michael Ramsey and His Writings

Douglas Dales, John Habgood,
Geoffrey Rowell and Rowan Williams

WIPF & STOCK · Eugene, Oregon

Wipf and Stock Publishers
199 W 8th Ave, Suite 3
Eugene, OR 97401

Glory Descending
Michael Ramsey and His Writings
By Dales, Douglas and Habgood, John
Copyright©2005 SCM
ISBN 13: 978-1-5326-5317-9
Publication date 3/13/2018
Previously published by Canterbury Press, 2005

Contents

Acknowledgements ix
About the Contributors xi
Abbreviations xii
Preface xiii
Introduction xv
Michael Ramsey – a Biographical Outline xxii

Part One A Michael Ramsey Reader

1 The Word of God 3
2 The Cross 34
3 The Lord of Glory 57
4 The Body of Christ 97

Part Two Reflecting on Michael Ramsey

Michael Ramsey: Man of God 139
John Habgood

Living through Dying: Suffering and Sanctification in the 151
Spiritual Theology of Michael Ramsey
Douglas Dales

The Christian Priest Today 163
Rowan Williams

Theology in the Face of Christ 176
Rowan Williams

Michael Ramsey, Transfiguration and the Eastern Churches 188
Geoffrey Rowell

The Lutheran Catholic 211
Rowan Williams

'One Body': the Ecclesiology of Michael Ramsey   223
    Douglas Dales

Part Three Epilogue

True Glory   241
    Rowan Williams

'Made like Him': Transfiguration in the Spirit   245
    Douglas Dales

Bibliography   251
Index of Biblical Quotations   256
Index of Names   259
Index of Subjects   260

In grateful memory of Joan, Lady Ramsey

+

*Neque enim quaero intelligere ut credam,
sed credo ut intelligam.*

(St Anselm – Proslogion)

Acknowledgements

Sincere thanks are due to SPCK for permission to quote from *Canterbury Pilgrim*, *Canterbury Essays and Addresses*, *The Christian Priest Today*, *Holy Spirit* and *The Gospel and the Catholic Church*; also to Zondervan for permission to quote from *Be Still and Know*. Thanks are also due to SLG Press for permission to quote from *The Christian Concept of Sacrifice*, and *Jesus the Living Lord* and their other publications; also to Taylor & Francis Ltd for permission to use the article ' "One Body": The Ecclesiology of Michael Ramsey', which was first published in the *International Journal for the Study of the Christian Church*, March 2005. It has not been possible to trace permissions to quote from Michael Ramsey's other published works, all of which are now out of print, but all quotations have been fully attributed.

About the Contributors

Douglas Dales is Chaplain and Head of Religious Studies at Marlborough College, Wiltshire. He is the author of *Glory: The Spiritual Theology of Michael Ramsey*, published by the Canterbury Press, and numerous other titles.

John Habgood was Archbishop of York from 1983 to 1995 and was previously Vice Principal of Westcott House, Cambridge; Principal of Queen's College, Birmingham; and Bishop of Durham. He has written extensively in the field of religion, science and ethics.

Geoffrey Rowell is the Bishop of Europe. He was Chaplain of Keble College, Oxford, from 1972 to 1994. His many published works include *Flesh, Bone, Wood* and *Come, Lord Jesus*, published by the Canterbury Press, and he was a co-editor of *Love's Redeeming Work: The Anglican Quest for Holiness*, published by Oxford University Press.

Rowan Williams is the Archbishop of Canterbury. He was previously Dean of Clare College, Cambridge, and Lady Margaret Professor of Divinity at Oxford. He has written numerous academic and devotional books, including *Arius*, published by SCM Press, and *Ponder These Things*, and *The Dwelling of the Light*, published by the Canterbury Press.

Abbreviations

BS	*Be Still and Know*
CEA	*Canterbury Essays and Addresses*
CP	*The Christian Priest Today*
CTP	*Canterbury Pilgrim*
DA	*Durham Essays and Addresses*
FC	*The Future of the Christian Church*
FFF	*Freedom, Faith and the Future*
FM	*F. D. Maurice and the Conflicts of Modern Theology*
GC	*The Gospel and the Catholic Church*
GG	*The Glory of God and the Transfiguration of Christ*
GT	*From Gore to Temple*
GW	*God, Christ and the World*
HS	*Holy Spirit*
IC	*Introducing the Christian Faith*
JP	*Jesus and the Living Past*
RC	*The Resurrection of Christ*
SS	*Sacred and Secular*

Preface

This book is intended to be a companion to *Glory: The Spiritual Theology of Michael Ramsey*, published in 2003 to commemorate the centenary of Michael Ramsey's birth on 14 November 2004. The introduction gives an overview of why he was such a significant figure in recent Church history, and why his memory is still so cherished by Anglicans and others.

The first part is a reader drawn from all his writings, which constitute a remarkably consistent body of spiritual theology and teaching. It is rooted in the Bible and readers are urged to delve into the Scriptures that Michael Ramsey loved so deeply, that were the wellspring of his ministry, prayer and teaching. This part is also designed to be a companion to the Christian liturgical year, and so to be a resource for anyone preaching or teaching. The passages are referenced so that a new generation may be prompted to read and study the books that he wrote.

The material selected has been edited, and in places abridged in the interests of coherence and clarity; archaisms have been removed where necessary; and the language made more inclusive for modern ears. The principle has been to make accessible and immediate the essence of his thought while indicating the context in which it is to be found; breaks within extracts are not indicated, however. Michael Ramsey used to speak of Christianity as experiencing 'a living past speaking to a living present'. His is not just a voice from the past, but a prophetic call to holiness and faith in our own times, which are not far removed from his.

No Church can flourish without prayer and a deeply rooted belief that is intelligently wrought, and clearly and compassionately expressed. The spiritual theology of Michael Ramsey could prove to be a foundation for a new era of integrity and confidence for Anglican Christianity in its doctrine, ethics and witness throughout the world. These passages, which emerge from his many writings like a seam of gold, demonstrate that he was a true spiritual father.

I am grateful to the Archbishop of Canterbury for his constant kindness and encouragement. It is very good to be able to include as the second and third parts of this book the lectures and sermons given by him, and by Lord Habgood and Bishop Geoffrey Rowell, to mark Michael Ramsey's centenary at Cuddesdon, Lambeth, Durham, York and Cambridge, together with those that I was able to deliver in New York and Canterbury and elsewhere. Warm thanks must go to Bishop Michael Marshall and Dr Charles Miller for their part in organizing these. Thanks must also go to Mrs Christine Smith, the publisher, for initiating this reader, and for her wise help and support, and also to Canon Donald Allchin for his friendship and inspiration.

This book is dedicated to the memory of Joan, Lady Ramsey, whose love supported Michael Ramsey in all that he did, and whose prayers and gracious kindness blessed many lives.

Douglas Dales
Marlborough
Feast of St Anselm, 2005

Introduction

Michael Ramsey, who died in 1988, was born in 1904. The celebration of his centenary has prompted renewed appreciation of him in England and America as one of the most remarkable spiritual leaders of the last century. Most of his early ministry was spent in theological learning and education, in Lincoln, Durham and Cambridge. But in 1952 he became Bishop of Durham, and shortly after in 1956 he was made Archbishop of York. His time as Archbishop of Canterbury, from 1961 until 1974, spanned one of the most troubled periods in the life of post-war English society, and also in the Church of England. Despite domestic preoccupations and confusion in the life of his own Church, he moved ecumenical dialogue between the Anglican Church and the Roman and Orthodox communions into a new and decisive phase, while giving leadership to attempts to unite Anglicans and Methodists in England. Much of his energy also went into fostering the life and unity of the Anglican Communion throughout the world.

On the challenge of being a priest among the demands of public life, he once quoted with evident sympathy some words of St Gregory the Great, the apostle of the English, whom he greatly revered:

> Holy men go forth like lightning, when they come forth from the retirement of contemplation to the public life of employment. But they would freeze too speedily amid their outward works did they not constantly return with anxious earnestness to the fire of contemplation.

Like his great and beloved predecessor, St Anselm, Michael Ramsey entered his duties from an inner fastness of prayer; and his own anxious earnestness to return there was seldom absent for long.

Yet to those who met him, or came to know him well, there always seemed a hidden depth and warmth of sanctity that still leaves a deep impression upon the memory. His contribution to the life of the Church that he loved to dearly was inward as well as outward. In the long perspective of history, it may well be this inner spiritual legacy that marks Michael Ramsey out as a true saint of the Church of God.

Sanctity

Michael Ramsey himself had a very clear sense of what makes a person a saint: the capacity 'to make God real', a phrase he often used. He did not see a saint, however, as a perfect person, for the whole of Christian experience is a becoming, a perfecting by the Holy Spirit. But like St Gregory the Great, he perceived in a saint 'perfection in imperfection', the sign of divine presence and remaking in love. The path to this living sanctity is, however, the way of the Cross. He believed, and knew from his own experience, that only as people follow the call of Christ along the path of 'living through dying' do they discover the meaning of God's love, and come to share in the glory that is revealed in the suffering face of Jesus Christ.

This path of suffering love is not just an individual matter, however: it is the secret of the Church's whole life as the Body of Christ. The sacraments of Baptism and the Eucharist point to this mystery, setting before Christians that which they are called to become by the grace of God. The existence of saints, hidden or revealed, within the life of the Church, in all its diverse expressions, is the pre-eminent sign of its reality and unity, rooted as it is within the eternal life and love of God.

The spiritual writing of Michael Ramsey, derived from more than fifty years of active ministry as a Christian priest and teacher, provides a rich and fascinating insight into how the acceptance of the call of God to holiness transforms a person's vision and understanding, and how the call to ministry is a participation in the self-giving sacrifice of Christ. For one of the most striking things about him was his sensitivity. He was by nature a shy person, and someone who had at times been deeply hurt. His spiritual formation at Cuddesdon, near Oxford, was a crucible of suffering, which left its mark on his whole response to the gospel. It made him deeply compassionate in his approach to individuals, and to situations of cruelty and conflict at home and abroad. His stand on human rights was anchored in an alert sympathy that was fine-tuned by pastoral contact with people across the world, and by a deep life of prayer.

The most direct and immediately accessible of his spiritual teaching concerned prayer. In his well-beloved book, *The Christian Priest Today*, he gave searching and inspiring direction to those called to the ministry of the Church. Towards the end of his life, his little book, *Be Still and Know*, encapsulated his whole approach to the spiritual life. Both these books remain of abiding worth today.

Embedded in his other writings are many glimpses of his inner life of prayer, and of his sense of the presence and love of God as Father in his relationship to human beings. To meet Michael Ramsey was to sense his deep friendship with God, and his personal devotion to Jesus Christ. The heart of his spiritual life and vocation as a priest was essentially simple. Like St Anthony in the desert, it could truly be said of him that 'to see you, father, is sufficient'.

His simplicity was his hidden spiritual strength, for, to his mind, God is by nature simple. This did not make him blind to the complexities of life and its moral issues, or to the frequent sense of inner confusion that marks the slow growth in spiritual life. But his trust in God was strong, often wrought out of real pain and difficulty. In the end his was a faith unshaken because it had on occasions been deeply shaken. He sometimes spoke of this: 'For me, the struggle is not between faith and unbelief so much as within faith itself.' He believed that it was possible, however, to achieve 'peace in the heart of conflict', and that this was one of the gifts of Christ's Resurrection. The lives of those who are truly Christian, and also truly human, testify to this miracle: 'for just when the problem of evil oppresses us, they assault us with the challenge of goodness'. This is an important message for today, and it is close to the spirit of the New Testament. To pray is to become rooted in the reality of God, and to become an embodiment of his suffering and saving love in each precise human situation where a person is set. But this is not just an individual stand: this spiritual integrity, while rooted in God, is found within the hidden reality of the one Church, of human beings of all races who are in union with Christ crucified and risen.

Church unity

Michael Ramsey believed profoundly in the unity of the Church of God. He was himself heir to Congregational as well as to Anglican Christianity. As his own spiritual life developed, his debt to Orthodoxy and also to certain strands of Roman Catholicism deepened. Behind his energetic ecumenical leadership as Archbishop of Canterbury lay a remarkable vision of the spiritual meaning of the apparent divisions within the Church's life. He believed that the unity of the

Church is already a reality in union with that of Christ himself, but that its apparent divisions mirror the damage within humanity caused by sin over many ages. He asserted this in his first book, *The Gospel and the Catholic Church*, which was remarkable for its prophetic insight, and depth of understanding of the Church's hidden life and unity.

Michael Ramsey believed that the recovery of the Church's unity, and its proper expression, is therefore an inner as well as an outer task. Christians are called, in the depths of their own hearts, to respond to and participate in the prayer of Christ 'that they all may be one'. This is the work of prayer, 'to put love in where love is not', and so to enable the Spirit of Christ to reach out into the wounds of humanity through suffering and compassionate prayer. This urgent intercession should drive the quest for true unity among Christians. This is a momentous vision and vocation, for as an unknown early Christian writer once put it: 'As the soul is to the body, so the Church is to the world.'

The Bible

Michael Ramsey was a highly able person with a first-class mind. His capacity to express Christian truth simply and deeply was remarkable, and was the result of much thought and learning, tested by prayer and pastoral care of others. He was greatly concerned with the intellectual and moral integrity of theology, and spent much of his academic energy engaged in study of the Bible, and especially of the New Testament. During his youth, his interpretation was somewhat unfashionable in its historical approach, and towards the end of his life he again found himself out of step with certain currents of contemporary theology. To some extent he swam against the tide.

The Bible lay at the heart of his study and teaching, and also of his prayer. He was confident that it is the place where the mind of God engages with the hearts and minds of men and women, and that its essential message is direct and consistent. All of it spoke for him of Jesus Christ, revealed in the Gospels as the Word of God. One living mind of the Holy Spirit breathes through its pages, and therefore worship and prayer can open its mystery as well as study and teaching. *Lex orandi, lex credendi* – Christian thought and prayer come together in understanding and contemplation of the Bible. He did not think that there should be any separation between these two modes of approach.

The Incarnation holds the key to understanding the Bible: for if He who is the Word of God, and exists from all eternity, became one with us in our human nature, then His self-communication through all the long ages of the Bible could not be separated from its human expression in the history that its pages record. Prayerful study of the Bible can open the doors of the heart and of the mind to the immediacy of His living presence and the fullness of his love. Michael Ramsey's approach to the Bible was catholic in its reverence and vision, but critical in discerning the historical context and mode of its expression. His sense of humour and irony always safeguarded a fundamental sanity in his whole approach to theology.

Authority

As Archbishop of Canterbury, Michael Ramsey found himself in a place of great moral and spiritual authority at a time when all such authority was increasingly subject to much criticism and even mockery. He was fully aware of the long history of the heirs of St Augustine of Canterbury, and of the peculiar difficulties of wielding authority within a Church comprising such diverse spiritual and historical traditions within a free society. Yet he believed deeply in the essential unity of Anglican Christianity, and was eager to encourage its development throughout the world. Often his vision in this area seemed to be more appreciated outside England than within it. He himself had sensed the call of God to the ministry while in the Church of the Transfiguration in New York in 1925, and this always gave his love of the Anglican Church, and of the American Episcopal Church in particular, a largeness of heart that people cherished whenever they met him on his travels across the world.

Michael Ramsey was himself a person of Evangelical origins but of Catholic formation. Although he was often critical of much that passed for 'liberal theology' before and after the Second World War, he was of a liberal instinct, the heir of Charles Gore and Liberal Catholicism as well as William Temple's Christian Socialism. His contacts with Orthodoxy, and more particularly with Roman Catholicism as it came to be moulded by the spirit of Vatican II, inevitably raised questions in his mind about the exercise of spiritual authority within the Anglican Communion, and about its own significance and integrity. His courage and willingness to examine the inheritance of which he was trustee and leader found expression in the deliberations of ARCIC on these very issues. Behind this determined initiative lay his own friendship and affinity with Pope Paul VI, whose episcopal ring he treasured as a unique gift to the end of his life.

He returned again and again to the teaching of St Gregory the Great, who defined primacy as becoming 'the servant of the servants of God'. Michael Ramsey frequently drew attention to the significance of Jesus washing his disciples' feet in John 13, and revealing the heart of his relationship with his Father in his prayer in John 17. In words he often liked to quote from St Augustine of Hippo: 'Proud man could only be saved by the humble God.' Herein lies the key to the exercise of authority within the Church.

Contemplation

One of the most remarkable aspects of his spirituality was its openness to other Christian traditions. His Nonconformist roots were not disregarded when he became an Anglican as a student at Cambridge; but his formation within Anglican tradition was Tractarian, the work of Eric Milner-White as much as of Cuddesdon. He later said that he owed most of his theological integrity to the teaching of Charles Gore, and he certainly regarded William Temple with love and awe. But he also made great friendships with many Orthodox Christians through the Fellowship of St Alban and St Sergius, and the impact of this did much to enrich his love of the New Testament with a living sense of the Fathers and of the communion of the saints. This is most apparent in his numinous book, *The Glory of God and the Transfiguration of Christ*. His strong historical sense enabled him to appreciate in a living way the long line of English saints, from Bede and Anselm, through the mystics of the fourteenth century to the great Anglican divines of the Reformation, Hooker and Andrewes, and to the Oxford Movement.

His own inner vocation as a contemplative Christian followed closely the spirit and teaching of St John of the Cross, whose writings were with him to the end of his days. He used to say that without this sense of the communion of the saints, of the living past feeding a living present, he could not have sustained his ministry as Archbishop of Canterbury. His constant concern was that Anglican Christians should draw life, confidence and hope from their own spiritual roots, and live faithful to the inheritance of which they were both trustees and beneficiaries.

Michael Ramsey stood for the holiness of God in all the costly challenge of its loving power. He once tried to communicate his vision of its impact within a human life in these words, which unwittingly described so much that was true of himself:

> The saint is one who has a strange nearness to God, and makes God real and near to other people. His virtues do not make him proud, for he is reaching out towards perfection far beyond them, and is humbled by this quest. His sins and failings, which may be many and bitter, do not cast him down, however, for the divine forgiveness humbles him and humbles him again. He shares and bears the griefs of his fellows, and he feels the world's pain with a heightened sensitivity; but with that sensitivity he has an inner serenity of an unearthly kind, which brings peace and healing to other people. This strange blending of humility, sorrow and joy is the mark of a saint; and through him God is real and near.'

Michael Ramsey
– A Biographical Outline

1904 Born in Cambridge on 14 November
1927 First-class degree in Theology at Cambridge; ordinand at Cuddesdon, Oxford
1928 Ordained as curate of St Nicholas, Liverpool
1930 Sub-Warden at Lincoln theological college
1936 Published *The Gospel and the Catholic Church*
1937 Senior curate at Boston, Lincolnshire
1939 Vicar of St Benet's, Cambridge
1940 Canon professor of theology at Durham
1942 Married to Joan Hamilton (Lady Ramsey)
1950 Regius professor of Divinity at Cambridge
1952 Bishop of Durham
1956 Archbishop of York
1961 Archbishop of Canterbury
1966 Meeting with Pope Paul VI in Rome
1974 Retired to Cuddesdon
1977 Moved to Durham
1986 Moved to Bishopthorpe, York
1987 Moved to St John's Home, Oxford
1988 Died on 23 April: buried at Canterbury Cathedral on 3 May
1995 Death of Lady Ramsey: buried at Canterbury Cathedral on 17 February

Part One
A Michael Ramsey Reader

I

The Word of God

APPROACHING THE BIBLE

The season of Advent begins the Christian year and bids us think again of the coming of Jesus Christ, the Word of God, into human history. This immediately leads us to consider the integrity and purpose of the Bible as containing the Word of God. Here Michael Ramsey is a sure guide, being through and through a biblical theologian, for whom the study of history, theological reflection and thought, and the life of prayer were inextricably one. In this he saw himself within a long Anglican tradition to which he often drew attention.

Christ is also the Wisdom of God, the key to understanding all truth. Michael Ramsey was confident that theology should be in dialogue with other disciplines of thought, and that neither the Bible nor Christianity had anything to fear from critical inquiry. The Old Testament provides the context in which the hidden coming of the Word of God is disclosed, seeking his people in love, judgement and forgiveness. Michael Ramsey also drew attention to the coming of God to those of other faiths, commending a reverent appreciation and respect for them, which should govern all dialogue about Christ himself.

The suffering of Jesus is the key to discerning the pattern of God's salvation throughout the Bible, both in the Old Testament and in the New. His death on the Cross was the supreme sacrifice for sin that redeems men and women, and that fulfils the whole sacrificial tradition of the Old Testament. In the process the language of sacrifice in all its facets is metamorphosed in the pages of the New Testament.

The suffering of Jesus is also the key to beginning to understand the nature of divine judgement, another theme of Advent. Michael Ramsey was unequivocal in his teaching about this, recognizing the tragic truth about the nature of the fall of human nature, the challenge posed to the pride and will of men and women by the humility of God revealed in Jesus, as well as the risk of final refusal by them of God's love.

Advent looks forward to the coming of God's kingdom and to the reality of heaven: it is a season of solemn joy. Michael Ramsey saw the Resurrection as the key to understanding the unique character of the Gospels, and indeed of the entire New Testament. The life and teaching of Jesus, seen in the light of his death and Resurrection, gives to all the writing of the New Testament its mysterious dynamic and saving power.

The Bible is therefore the place where the mind of God engages the hearts and minds of those who seek him and will listen to him. The New Testament becomes the threshold by which men and women may enter the eternal reality of his kingdom. The Gospels remain central, for in them Jesus Christ may be seen and loved as the fullness of God expressed in the miracle of his human person.

The authority of the Bible

The Bible is the sacred book of the Christian Church, but it would be wrong to infer from its exalted place in every form of Christianity that Christianity is a religion of the Book. The central fact of Christianity is not a book but a person – Jesus Christ, described as the Word of God. The books of the Old Testament came to have authority within the Church because Jesus Christ set the seal of his own authority upon them, and interpreted them as preparing the way for himself. The books of the New Testament came to have authority because the Church recognised in them the authentic testimony of the apostles to Jesus Christ. It is this relationship of the books to a person that makes them very different from a collection of oracles itself providing the basis for a religion. Indeed both in Judaism and in Christianity, the religious belief in and experience of revelation preceded the making and the canonisation of the holy books. In both the Old and New Testaments, therefore, the collection of sacred books was not the basis of the belief in divine revelation, but its consequence.

The conviction in the Church that Jesus Christ was himself the Word of God (John 1.14; 1 John 1.1) rested on the belief that there was in Jesus the divine utterance, not only in his teaching and message, but in himself: the Word and the person were one. Furthermore, the Word, who was made flesh, had himself been 'in the beginning with God', at work in the creation of the world, and in giving life and light to human beings. Thus, in a sense hard to describe yet decisively perceived, the scriptures of the Old Testament not only prepared the way for Christ, but also revealed him, as the Word of God, now incarnate in him, who had been at work from the beginning.

('The Authority of the Bible' 1b, 6b)

Inspiration and understanding

Although the Church confirmed the canon of the New Testament, it was not thereby conferring authority on its holy books. Rather it was acknowledging these books as possessing authority in virtue of what they were; and it was an authority supreme and divine. The concept of inspiration was applied to them not by intuitive criteria so much as on the principle that where there is divine authority it is from the Holy Spirit. The fathers thought of inspiration as a form of special possession by God's Spirit. Although this was the dominant idea, it is very significant that often the fathers pleaded for leaving room for the rationality and human volition, the thought and literary methods of the individual writers of the scriptures.

The hearing of the Word of God in the Bible today, and the pursuit of critical historical study of it are in no way incompatible therefore. It is necessary to reject the idea that a firm faith implies repelling from the mind the questions raised by historical criticism: for the faith of a Christian is faith in God who is the giver of the scholar's quest for truth, who sets out in search of it as one who knows not whither he or she is going. It is required of faith that it does not deny the spirit of inquiry; but it is required also of the spirit of inquiry that it does not cling to prejudices as to what God can or cannot do in the sovereign activity of his Word. For the synthesis of faith and criticism is but one aspect of the larger problem of divine grace in its relationship to human freedom.

('The Authority of the Bible' 8b, 11a)

Spirituality and theology

It is my belief that the understanding of the history and theology of Christianity cannot properly be separated from the study of Christian spirituality. What is the character of the Christian life? What is the nature of Christian saintliness? How far is it linked with a response to the historical givenness of the gospel, and to the divine self-giving in history? These are questions of supreme significance, and a good deal of contemporary discussion ignores them.

(JP 4)

Past and present

Two misconceptions can bring confusion into discussion of the 'pastness of the past'. One concerns the nature of the Christian Church. For the Church is not merely a series of generations of Christians, each encased in its own setting of time and culture. It is rather a community of experience reaching across the generations, so that the language and symbolism that it uses can evoke the past in a way that strikes a chord in the experience of the present. The other misconception is to understand the relationship between the past and the present in predominantly cerebral terms: for the question is not only whether certain ideas of the past can fit the intellectual outlook of the present, but whether the past can speak to us now as human beings with our sin and our guilt, our hopes and our fears.

(JP 19)

The ethos of Anglican theology

There is a distinctive witness to be borne by Anglican theology out of the depths of its own tradition. Biblical theology is in an unsatisfactory state and it cannot be naively invoked as the solution for everything. There is a task here for Anglican theology, by keeping alive the importance of history, in the manner of its great divines of the past; also by strenuous attempts to relate Biblical revelation to other categories of thought in the contemporary world, by striving to integrate doctrine with spirituality in the life of prayer, and by presenting the Church as the effectual sign of the supernatural in the midst of the natural order. No less is it necessary to avoid imbibing uncritically the assumptions of contemporary ecumenism, but rather to meet them with something deeper, if less immediately popular, drawn from an appeal to Scripture and tradition. Our eyes must be helped to distinguish between a synthesis that is superficial and a synthesis that is surely grounded, between arbitrary liberalism and genuine liberality, between facile comprehensiveness and true theological coherence. For the theological coherence that Gore or Temple exhibited came not from a quest for tidiness but from a vigorous wrestling with truth for its own sake. Without such coherence the Church's moral witness will appear as piecemeal moralizing, and the majestic unity of the Church's faith will be too faintly made visible.

(GT 169–70)

The Bible and the Church

The canon of Scripture sets forth the historical redemption and the one Body. The scriptures of the old Israel of God are still the books of God's people, and they become the Bible of the new Israel, which knows itself to be the messianic people, the inheritor also of the promises of God. The new people of God uses the scriptures as Christ has taught, and finds within them the age-long plan of God that the Messiah should suffer and die, and so redeem his people. 'The Son of Man goes even as it is written of him' (Mark 14.21; cf Luke 22.37; 1 Peter 1.11). The apostles in the earliest days of the Church expounded from the scriptures how Isaiah spoke of his death, and David of his resurrection (Acts 2.25–8, 8.32–3; cf 1 Peter 2.21–4). From this redemption there springs 'a chosen race, a royal priesthood, a holy nation, a people for God's own possession' (1 Peter 2.9). Christians find the scriptures made intelligible by two themes: the redemptive death and rising of Christ, and the calling of a redeemed race. When later to the books of the old covenant the Church gradually added the books of the new covenant, the same themes were still dominant in the new canon – the redemptive acts of Jesus, and the redeemed people of God. To understand the Bible, therefore, it is necessary to share in Christ's death and resurrection, and to become a member of his people.

(GC 61)

The nature of Christian truth

Jesus Christ is not only the Way and the Life: he is also the Truth (cf John 14.6). The Church, which is his Body, is commissioned to teach the truth. How shall the Church know where to find what is true, and then so assimilate it as to proclaim it with authority? It is not enough, and it may even be misleading, simply to assert that truth is found in the Bible and in the Church. We must ask, 'what is this truth that has created both the Church and the Bible?' For truth is uttered in God's redemption through Christ, and men and women learn the truth through repentance as well as through intellectual processes, and they apprehend the truth in their life as well as in their thinking. God's truth is not an abstract value to be contemplated: it is active to save in Christ. In the New Testament crucifixion, truth and the life of holiness are all linked; and divine wisdom is set forth in the death of Christ, in direct contrast to human wisdom, and as the negation of the wisest ideas in the world (cf 1 Corinthians 1.18–23). Christians who are brought into the wisdom of the crucified are also led on to the life of wisdom in the Spirit.

The range of this wisdom is as wide as the whole world, for the whole world, created by God, becomes intelligible in the light of the crucifixion, wherein the character and method of divine authority are disclosed. For Christ who redeemed men and women is also he who created the world, and in him all things shall be summed up. The fellowship that shares in his death and resurrection shall be led by the Holy Spirit truly to interpret all life and history. This work of interpretation involves all the activities of the human intellect and every part of science, art and research. Yet the process of true knowledge is not by these activities alone. For there are secrets to the meaning of the world, which are unlocked through a knowledge that is linked with the life and love of the human community which shares in the Cross: a knowledge which grows through the building up of the one Body in love (cf Philippians 1.9; Ephesians 4.13). Christian knowledge and Christian love lie close together, and Christian theology is not only a detached exercise of intellect: it is the life of the one Body in which truth is both thought out and lived out.

The Church proclaims the wisdom of God, set forth in its very essence in the crucifixion of Jesus Christ. It is a wisdom learnt only when men and women are brought to a crisis of repentance, and to the resulting knowledge of self and of God. The wisdom of the Cross seems at first to deny the wisdom of the Spirit of God in the created world: it scandalises the human sense of what is good and beautiful. But Christians, who have first faced its scandal, discover in the Cross a key to the meaning of all creation. The Cross unlocks its secrets and its sorrows, and interprets them in terms of the power of God. Hence 'orthodoxy' means not only right thinking but also right worship – 'true glory' after the Biblical meaning of the word for glory – *doxa*. For life and thought and worship are inseparable activities within the Body of Christ.

It follows then that the Church can never be said to have fully apprehended the truth. Rather truth is the divine action that apprehends the Church. Dimly it understands what it teaches. For the more the Church learns of God, the more it is aware of the incomprehensible mystery of His being, in creation, in transcendence, and supremely on the Cross. The Church's perilous office of teaching is therefore inseparable from the Church's worship of the mystery whereby it exists.

(GC 120–6)

Other faiths

Greater involvement by the adherents of the world's religions with one another is bringing to an end the isolationism that used to prevail. Christians should find themselves approaching other religions with reverence and humility. Taught by the prologue of St John's gospel (John 1.1–18), they know that in other religions there is truth and goodness derived from the light that lightens every human being. At the same time they believe that Jesus is the perfect revelation of God, the fulfilment of all that is true, the final Word. Christians will witness to this only if their concern is less to promote Christianity as a system, than to show Christ and to find Christ in others. A missionary should bring Christ to those of other faiths while being alert to finding Christ there. Thus they may come to acknowledge as Lord and Saviour Christ who has already been among them.

(HS 125)

The meaning of the fall

Adam stands as a symbol of human privilege and catastrophe. God is the Creator and humanity is made in God's likeness with immense power in relation to nature, and with the responsibility of using that power for God's glory. The intuition remains that the human sinful predicament is grim, in the abuse of nature and the perversion of civilization, an impasse that is irremovable without God's costly deliverance. In our very different modern context, Christianity may still draw from the Bible the essence of belief in God, with the gospel of the death and resurrection of Christ as its climax.

(JP 22)

The nature of divine judgement

Where is God, and what is He doing? Recall a biblical doctrine too often forgotten, that of divine judgement. When people and nations turn away from God's laws and prefer the courses dictated by pride and selfishness to the path dictated by conscience, calamitous results follow. God is not absent from the contemporary scene: He is present in judgement through the catastrophes that follow human wilfulness. In the words of the psalm: 'He gave them their heart's desire, and sent leanness into their souls' (Psalm 106.15). God is not dead: God is here, in judgement; and as His judgement is accepted and felt, so in the same moment may His loving kindness and mercy be found – 'My song shall be of mercy and judgement' (Psalm 101.1). Let it be remembered, however, that divine judgement falls first upon God's people, the Church; for St Peter reminds us that 'judgement begins at the house of God' (1 Peter 4.17). The Church shows the message of divine judgement to the world as it sees God's judgement upon its own life and begins to mend its ways.

This recovery of the doctrine of divine judgement is a direct appeal to biblical truth. But let the appeal be to the *whole* of the biblical concept, adumbrated in the psalms and maturely gathered up in St John's gospel. The supreme act of divine judgement is the coming of Christ: 'this is the judgement, that the light has come into the world, but people loved darkness rather than the light because their deeds were evil' (John 3.19). It must be in the figure of Jesus crucified and risen that we present both divine judgement and divine mercy. I see no other way of bringing the themes of sovereignty, power, compassion, and judgement home to our contemporaries except in terms of Jesus, in whom all these divine actions are focussed.

(CP 22–5)

The inspiration of the prophets

The prophets lived within a divine kingdom in history made by God, and they had the unique office of being sent by God to proclaim that kingdom. The uniqueness of the Bible as inspired lies in the uniqueness of biblical history as the history of the kingdom of God in the midst of the world. As Israel was what no other people was, and as Israel's history was as no other history, so the books that God bade men in Israel write for a testimony to His kingdom are what no other books are. Such is the special character of the Bible. Biblical history is therefore the crux of F.D. Maurice's theory. Upon the uniqueness of this history the special character of scripture rests.

Today Maurice may help us, for he foreshadows the synthesis that we are seeking. The Bible is the book of the divine kingdom: it yields its secrets only to those who share its faith, and yet by the reality of its own human element it vindicates the role of the historical critic. Its climax is the gospel; but the gospel stands upon the foundation of the creation, the covenant with Noah, and the giving of the Law to Moses. As we are redeemed into the family of the Son of God, so we are enabled to perceive beneath our catastrophic world a foundation of which the same Son of God is the maker and builder.

(FM 85, 97)

The Suffering Servant

In fulfilment not only of particular passages in the Old Testament (e.g. Isaiah 53; Psalm 22 etc.) but of the whole Passion of Israel which the Old Testament contains, Christ's death was the act of divine power which broke the forces of evil and set up God's Kingdom among men and women. While the final interpretation is in St John's gospel, where the Passion is portrayed as an act of victory and glory, the same fact is implicit in the more realistic record of St Mark, where the humiliations of the Messiah are the disclosure of the power of God.

For through the lonely death and the resurrection which seals its triumph, and the gift of the Spirit of him who died and rose, there is created a new people of God, the Church, in which the gospel of God is proclaimed. It is still God's purpose to unite humanity through a people, and this people does not mean a loose collection of believers in Jesus, but a new nation to which the characteristics of Israel – the vine, the temple, the bride – are now applied, and which has the same sense of being one race, brought to birth by the creative act of God. The Church is God's people still, but there are two great differences: this race is drawn from any and every earthly nation, whether Jew or Greek, male or female, slave or free (Galatians 3.28). Secondly, this new race does not find death and suffering to be its baffling problem. For by the Messiah's death it has been created and made a people unto God.

The Church exists because he died. That which had been the cause of despair, tension and offence throughout the history of Israel in the Old Testament – the suffering of righteous ones – has become the centre of the Church's being. Jesus the Servant has become the 'light to lighten the Gentiles', because the Servant has suffered and has identified himself with the death of all human beings (Hebrews 2.9; John 12.32; Ephesians 2.13–14). In his death the Church now rejoices, worships and shares: for the death of Jesus is the centre of its existence, of its worship, and of the way of unity, which it offers to men and women. It seems that Christ creates the Church by dying and rising again, and that within him, and especially within his death and resurrection, the Church is actually present. We must search for the fact of the Church not beyond Calvary and Easter, but within them. For Jesus Christ, in his solitary obedience, *is* the Church. It is indeed a paradox that the death of Jesus, an event of utter isolation from human existence, should become the means of fellowship between human beings and God, and also between each other.

(GC 18–21)

Sacrifice in atonement

Sacrificial images from the Old Testament, by being fulfilled in Christ, are blended together in the New Testament and their meaning is transformed. Thus Christ is both the pure victim offered as a cleansing sacrifice, and the unholy scapegoat bearing human sin. It is a paradoxical combination, yet he is never more the one than when he is the other, since the love whereby he offers his pure obedience to the Father is the self-same love whereby he bears human sin and shame. The Cross demonstrates divine justice, because it issues in the actual deliverance of humanity from evil into the world-to-come. Christ bears our penalty, but does so in such a way that the death that is penal is also sacrificial, resulting in the acceptance of his shed blood in the resurrection. The resurrection is therefore the climax of sacrifice, in that the sacrificial blood of Christ is accepted and made available in all its cleansing power. But this is only another way of saying that the resurrection is the beginning of new creation.

(GT 57)

The ethos of the letter to Hebrews

Among the writings of the New Testament, the letter to the Hebrews often seems very remote from us in its language and its cultural setting. But it can speak to us still with a powerful message about the things that are not shaken. The imagery of holding on to a reality which is unseen can mean much amidst the meaningless chaos of the world which we do see. The theme of faith as seeing one who is invisible may mean much to some to whom the Pauline or Johannine imagery of

Christ-in-us may be puzzling. So too the message that security is not to be found in any of the world's structures can evoke a response in these times, with the warning against identifying Christianity with any one of its cultural forms in this world. Finally, while the response of our prayer is 'through the veil' of heaven itself (cf Hebrews 10.19–20) and Christianity is uncompromisingly otherworldly, it is never a flight from that sacrificial existence in this world, where Christians worship and have fellowship with one another. It is in the Christ-like and the sacrificial life that reality is to be found.

(BS 60)

Resurrection and the New Testament

The earthly ministry of Jesus was remembered, handed down and taught, never as a self-contained biography, always as a part of the gospel of God, whose climax was the Passion and the resurrection. The words and deeds of Jesus were narrated with the light of the resurrection upon them. For the first Christians lived in a double perspective: the risen Jesus at the right hand of God, and the Jesus of Galilee and Jerusalem. It is from this double perspective that all the apostolic literature was written. For the early Christians, the gospel without the resurrection was not a gospel at all.

In the case of St John, he points his readers beyond history to the eternal significance of Jesus, but he as often brings them down to earth again with his sudden reminders of the stark historical facts. But he will not let them rest in history, for history cannot reveal God, or be understood, unless it points men and women beyond itself. Nor will he let them rest in an unhistorical mysticism; for the risen Christ, interpreted by the Paraclete, is known only by those who will believe and treasure the historical events wrought in the flesh of Jesus.

The apostles knew that in the resurrection of Christ, another world had come, and that they were already its citizens; and they summoned men and women to enter it with them and to claim it as their own. The old world continued with its contradictions and its sufferings, but by the Cross and resurrection these very contradictions and sufferings could be transformed into things fruitful and creative wherein, by faith in Jesus crucified, the power of God might be found. There was no escaping from the hard facts of this world. Rather did their membership within the world-to-come enable them to see the realities of this world with the light of the Cross and the resurrection upon them; and to know that their own tasks were but the working out of a victory that Christ had already won.

(RC 7, 12, 15 and 33)

The meaning of miracles

To Charles Gore, the Incarnation was inherently miraculous, and the miracles accompanying it stood attested by good historical evidence, unless blind prejudice against the miraculous gave bias to an historian's mind. Miracle was to him the vindication of the freedom of the living God, intervening to restore a created world wrecked and disordered by sin. In moving words Gore used to speak and write about how hard he found it to believe in the love of God in the face of the tragedies of the world. He could not find that love within the world's natural processes. It was in the transcendental actions of God's freedom, such as the resurrection, that Gore could feel that God's love was apparent, coming to the rescue. This accounted for the vehemence with which Gore contended for miracle in some of the controversies of his time: it was a doctrine affecting the very roots of his faith. Gore concluded on historical grounds that the evidence for both the virgin birth and the resurrection from the tomb on the third day was overwhelmingly strong, and that only dogmatic prejudice against the miraculous could cause anyone to reject it.

(GT 21 and 79)

THE INCARNATION

Belief in the full reality of the Incarnation lay at the root of Michael Ramsey's worship and faith. He was heir to a strong tradition about the centrality of this doctrine within Anglicanism that he associated particularly with William Temple and Charles Gore. He emphasized again and again, however, the fragile human reality of how God became a human person, stripping Christmas and its message of any sentimental or romantic notions. The birth of Jesus was a hard reality, moving in its simplicity and love, being the hidden outpouring of the whole goodness of God himself.

The mode of the Incarnation demonstrates the self-emptying (kenosis) of God in the person of Jesus, an act of perpetual self-restraint and self-giving that runs like a golden thread throughout the whole gospel story until his death on Calvary. Its very human context, and the supreme trust placed in Mary and Joseph by God, indicates the depth and extent of divine identification with human existence. This has profound ethical implications for every aspect of human relationships, asserting the essentially loving character of both God and human beings.

Christmas is the focus of Christian worship, expressed in the canticle 'the Gloria', which itself takes up the song of the angels at the birth of Christ. Jesus himself is seen as one who, in his whole life and self-offering, fulfilled the destiny of human beings to worship God in spirit and in truth. The sacrifice of Jesus must be seen therefore in the light of this dynamic of worship, by which the invisible glory of God became manifest in the perfect human life of one who was the eternal Son of God.

The story of Christmas and the proclamation of the gospel are fraught with paradox and pain, and to some extent this is marked by the feasts in the Church that surround the birth of Jesus: notably the martyrdom of Stephen, the first to die for his allegiance to Jesus, and in his suffering to glimpse a vision of the heavenly Son of Man. The evangelist, St John, also stands close to Christmas as the one who saw deepest into the mystery of the Word made flesh. Then there is the sordid murder of the children of Bethlehem, a human atrocity bred out of cruelty and fear. In England, the commemoration of the murder of Thomas à Becket in the cathedral at Canterbury reminds us that our own Church is not unmarked by the suffering of the Cross. The feast of Circumcision reminds us also that Jesus was born into a specific religious and racial tradition, that of the Jews, to whom Christianity owes the deepest gratitude, love and respect.

Christmas

Today the joy of Christmas shines in a world that is darkened by sadness. How real are the gifts of human goodness, nonetheless: they are gifts from the God of Bethlehem who is their source; for God who took human flesh in the stable is God from whose store of love humanity's gifts of love are drawn.

The stable is a symbol of Christ's poverty. The characteristic that gave him the title poor was his *simplicity*. He did without many of the things that people crave for. None did he criticise more severely than those who hankered after more and more possessions and who were preoccupied with money. The worth of a person's life, he insisted, does not consist of possessions, for piling things up does not increase worth. People matter more than things, as people have an eternal destiny. Those who do not fuss about their standard of living and their luxuries are freer to love one another, to serve one another and to enjoy one another. Christ became poor, and he chose the way of simplicity; and if we follow him he promises us riches of his own, riches of happiness and brotherhood shared with one another and with him.

How did Christ become poor? By coming to share in the limitations, frustrations, and hard realities of our human life, our pains and sorrows, and even our death. The imagery of Christ's riches and his poverty is a vivid picture of the Incarnation; but it is another thing to grasp its moral message and to live by it, the message of simplicity and self-sacrifice. Christ gave himself to us to enable us to give ourselves to one another: that is the message of Bethlehem to a world in trouble.

Come to Bethlehem once again: see the stable – see the child. Knowing that he is God made man, knowing that he who was rich has become poor for us, let us kneel in the darkness and cold that is the symbol of our blind and chilly human hearts, and say in a new way: 'yours is the kingdom, the power and the glory forever'.

(CTP 74–6)

The mind of Christ

Fellowship – *koinonia* has a divine root, springing as it does from the incentive of God's love, the mind of Christ and the fellowship of the Holy Spirit (cf Philippians 2.1–7). The mind of Christ is defined as that of one who sees his divine status as an opportunity not for grasping but for pouring himself out and taking on the role of a servant. No phrase is more telling than 'the mind that you have in Christ', for to act divinely is not to grasp, but to pour self out. That is the secret of the Incarnation, and it is no less the secret of fellowship. Such indeed is the Christian way.

(HS 76)

The worship of God in Christ

In the Old Testament a person's duty of worship was inherent in their human nature. Because the human person is made in God's image and after His likeness, he or she has an affinity with God, which requires that they give glory to God and not to themselves. But the meaning of human worship is bound up with the relationship with creation.

Human beings are set over the rest of God's created works as God's deputy, and in the praise of God human beings represent the creation. Creation becomes articulate in and through the worship offered by human beings.

The perfect act of human worship is seen only in Jesus, the Son of Man. He alone made the perfect acknowledgement upon earth of the glory of God and the perfect response to it. On the one hand the prophetic revelation of the glory of God is summed up in him, as he is himself the glory of which the prophets unknowingly spoke (cf John 12.41). On the other hand the ancient sacrifices are fulfilled in him as he, both priest and victim, makes the reasonable offering of his will in Gethsemane and on the Cross. In Christ the praise of God, the wonder before God, the thirst for God, the zeal for God's righteousness, which fill the pages of the psalms, find pure and flawless utterance. In him too human contrition for sin, and for the sin of the whole human race, finds its perfect expression: for the sinless Christ made before God that perfect acknowledgement of human sin which no sinful human being can make.

Risen and ascended, the Son forever glorifies the Father; and in this glorifying, which was from all eternity, the human nature, assumed in the Incarnation, now shares. The Johannine doctrine of the glorifying assists our understanding of the concept in the epistle to Hebrews of Christ as our great high priest. Christ's priesthood belongs, as does his sonship, to the eternal world: forever Son, he is also forever our priest. Priesthood means offering, and in the Son there is forever that spirit of self-offering, which the sacrifice of Calvary uniquely disclosed in the world of sin and death. The sacrifice of Calvary has been wrought once for all; but now Christ the high priest 'ever lives to make intercession for those who draw near to God through him' (Hebrews 7.25). He has entered 'into heaven itself to appear now before the face of God for us' (Hebrews 9.24). Though Calvary can never be repeated, Christ is forever with the Father in that character of self-giving and self-offering of which Calvary was the decisive historical expression. In the ascended Christ there exists our human nature rendering to the Father the glory which human beings were created to render. Whether we speak of this as the presence of our high priest before the Father's face, or as the glorifying of the Father by the Son, who was made man and died for us, the essential meaning is the same.

In union with its heavenly Lord, the Church on earth worships, looking back to what he did once on Calvary, and looking up to what he now is with the Father. It is worship in Christ and through Christ.

If it is called a worship of sacrificial offering, it is so because it is through Christ who is our high priest: 'through Jesus let us continually offer up to God the sacrifice of praise, the tribute of lips that acknowledge his name' (Hebrews 13.15). If it is called a worship of glorifying, it is so because it is through Christ, who glorifies the Father: 'when we give glory to God, it is through Jesus Christ that we say "Amen"' (2 Corinthians 1.20).

(GG 91–5)

Worship in the Church

God's glory in creation is not forgotten but enhanced in the worship of Him as redeemer. In truly catholic worship the joyful access of Christians to their Father, and the thankfulness of Christians to their Saviour, are interpenetrated by the adoration offered by the creature to the Creator. Herein is that blending of action and passivity, of movement and rest, which belongs to the tradition of worship within the Catholic Church.

Within the Church the scriptures of Israel are retained as Holy Scriptures, for they are now seen to speak of Christ and of his glory. Among these scriptures the psalms have a special place. They are the voice of God's people, worshipping God as Creator, king and redeemer, and praying for victory over enemies that are no less deadly because they are spiritual, subtle and unseen. The psalms are also the prayer book of Christ himself. In his own use of them, their words of adoration, supplication and self-committal were brought to their perfect end, even unto the end (cf Mark 15.34; Luke 23. 46). Using the psalms in the name of Christ, the members of his Body make their own the prayer of their head.

At the heart of the Church's glorifying of God there is the new rite of the Eucharist. Here the Church is united to the glory of Christ on Calvary and in heaven, and finds the focus of the glorifying of God by all created things. The food that they receive is the life of Christ laid down in godward offering: the glory that they are given is the glory by which Christ glorified the Father. Thus the Eucharistic worship of the Church is on its godward side a participation in Christ's glorifying of the Father, and on its manward side a receiving of Christ's glory – the glory of the Cross. Inasmuch as it is a showing-forth of Christ's death (1 Corinthians 11.26), it recalls the glory of Calvary. Inasmuch as it is a sharing in the Body of Christ and in his blood (1 Corinthians 10.16), it unites those who partake with the glory of Christ as he now is – risen, ascended and glorifying the Father. Inasmuch as it uses God's gifts of bread and wine and brings them to be blessed, it is a glorifying of the Creator by giving back to Him of His own created gifts. Inasmuch as it points forward to the coming of Christ again (1 Corinthians 11.26), it is an anticipation of feasting with Christ in the world to come, when we shall behold with open face him whom we now perceive by faith.

Inasmuch as the glory is the glory of the Father and the Son in the bond of love, which is the Holy Spirit, the Eucharistic gift of glory to the disciples is tested in their unity. The Pauline 'we being many are one bread, one Body, for we all partake of the one bread' (1 Corinthians 10.17) is tested in the Johannine, 'the glory which you gave me I have given to them: that they may be one, even as we are one' (John 17.22). The new covenant in the blood of Christ is inseparable from the new commandment of mutual love as the manifestation of Christ's own love (John 13.31–5). Hence the common life of Christian fellowship is not only a witness to the glory, but is itself the glory of the Father and the Son shown forth to the world in the Church. Without this common life, *ichabod* – the glory is departed.

(GG 97–9)

Proclaiming the glory of Christ

The preaching of the glory of Christ, if it is guided by the New Testament use of the word *doxa*, has at its centre the resurrection with the Cross as its prelude. It leads men and women to see the significance of the ministry and teaching of our Lord with the light of Calvary and Easter upon them. The preaching will appeal to the affinity between the gospel and human beings created in the divine image, and its preachers will commend themselves 'to every person's conscience in the sight of God' (2 Corinthians 4.2). But the warning of St Paul must be heeded also: 'If our gospel is veiled at all, it is veiled only for those on the way to destruction; their unbelieving minds are so blinded by the god of this passing age that the glory of Christ, who is the image of God, cannot dawn upon them and bring them light' (2 Corinthians 4.3–4). It is not to be thought that the gospel can be made simple or attractive to the worldly and impenitent, and any attempt to make it simple or attractive to them may well corrupt or distort it.

For it has been wisely said that 'the simplicity of the gospel lies in the simplicity of the moral issues it raises, and not in the ease with which its teaching can be explained to the careless or hardened'. Our Lord's injunction to let our light so shine before others that they may see our good works and so be led to glorify God as Father (Matthew 5.16) does not mean that a programme of good works can commend the gospel by meeting people's ideals at their own level, without any challenge to the assumptions upon which those ideals often rest. The fellowship of the Church can indeed manifest the glory of God to the consciences of men and women; but it does so not by providing something for impenitent human beings to like and admire, but by being a fellowship so filled with God Himself that their conscience is pierced by God's love and judgement. Thus the gospel of the glory of God is always very near to human beings, and yet always very far from them: near, because the divine image is in every human person and the gospel is the true meaning of the human person; far, because it is heard only by faith and repentance, which overthrow all human self-glorying.

(GG 99–100)

THE MINISTRY OF CHRIST

The feast of the Epiphany recalls the coming of the wise men to see Jesus, his baptism, and his first miracle. In the weeks that follow, up to the beginning of Lent, we think again about the ministry of Jesus, how it unfolded: the pattern of his miracles and the content of his teaching. Central to all that he did was his proclamation of the nearness and nature of God's kingdom. Bringing God near to people so that awareness of him would transform their lives, their values and attitudes: this is very close to the heart of the genius of Jesus as teacher.

His miracles worked hand in hand with his teaching, for they were mainly acts of purposeful and sometimes hidden compassion, which also demonstrated truths about God's relationship with human beings. Some of course, like the Feeding of the 5,000, directly revealed that he was the awaited Messiah; but these also contained disturbing indications of the fate of the Messiah. If his miracles were works of love, they posed a choice and their meaning was not at the time fully evident.

The key to the Messiahship of Jesus lay in his relationship with God as Father. In their different ways each of the Gospels conveys the sense that Jesus revealed something that was eternally true about the nature of God. From this there flowed the deep concern of Jesus with individuals and his refusal of any mass following. The scope of his com-

passion reached to the very edges and depths of society, setting an example that would define the lives of those who followed him. For the depth of his own identification with humanity, in all its suffering, weakness and sinfulness, pointed to the supreme miracle of compassion, his death on the Cross.

The kingdom of God

Nearness to God and trust in His providence will remove fear from your life; and being without fear you will be without those sins that have fear as their root. For God forgives all of us, however terrible our behaviour may have been, however undeserving of His forgiveness we may be. God has forgiven us so much that living near to God within His kingdom we shall find ourselves forgiving others instead of being resentful towards them, because we are just reflecting the nearness of God towards whom our lives are being lived. Such is the righteousness of a Godward relationship, and this is rooted in an attitude of childlike dependence and receptivity towards God.

Now in many ways the ethical teaching of Jesus is terribly hard, and sometimes it is so because Jesus gives such stern calls to sacrifice and renunciation. But this can be very joyful too if it is part of being near to God, and God Himself is our constant reward. But the greatest difficulty of the ethical teaching of Jesus is not, I would say, his stern calls to renunciation nearly so much as his insistence on the generosity of God's giving to us. It demands that we shall be utterly humble, utterly childlike, and utterly receptive. It is this that is the hard thing that Jesus demands we shall follow: that we shall be humble enough to receive goodness and righteousness that is all God's gift and never our achievement. For the kingdom itself means God ruling in human hearts and wills.

(Jesus the Living Lord 4–5)

The miracles of Jesus

The miracles in the gospels partly revealed Jesus for what he was, the Messiah, but also partly baffled people because they were bound up with a righteousness and a glory that were seen to involve the Cross. The belief of the disciples, first in the Messiahship of Jesus and ultimately in his divine lordship, was their response to the impact upon them of Jesus himself; and within this impact the miracles had their place as satellites to the sun. The cardinal miracle was and is Jesus himself. For unless the ultimate devotion to him as divine was idolatrous, he was the unique breaking of the divine into history and nature. He was the miracle: and the particular miracles showed, to those with discerning faith, various aspects of his meaning and his claim.

Meanwhile, none of the good Creator's gifts lie outside the Creator's use of them for His children's good. But this good, lived out as it is in the everyday context of earthly life, is a good of a more than earthly concern. Down to earth as the supernatural may be, it always relates to a world beyond. As do the miracles recorded in the New Testament: not for nothing does one of the apostolic writers call them 'the powers of the age to come' (Hebrews 6.5). So too do the people whom Christendom calls saints. It so describes them not just because they are good or do good, but because there is in them a humility, an other-worldly touch, which helps to make God and heaven real and near.

(*CEA* 48 and 50–1)

The intercession of Jesus

The intercession of Jesus means his ceaseless presence with the Father in heaven. He is with the Father, not as begging the Father to be gracious, for from the Father graciousness ever flows. He is with the Father as the one who died for us on Calvary, with the Father with a life that is ever the life that died. He is also with the Father as one who was tempted as we are, and who bore our sins and our sufferings; and he is with the Father as the focus of our hopes and desires. To approach the Father through Jesus Christ the intercessor is to approach in awareness of the cost of our redemption, by a sacrifice made once for all and a victory once accomplished, a sacrifice and victory that are both past history and ever present realities. It is this that enables and characterizes our response to God through Jesus Christ.

(*BS* 54)

The heart of love

Amidst the vast scene of the world's problems and tragedies you may feel that your own ministry and witness seems so small, so insignificant, so concerned with the trivial. But consider – the glory of Christianity is its claim that small things really matter, and that the small group, the very few, the one man or woman or child are of infinite worth to God. Let that be your inspiration. Consider our Lord himself. Amidst a vast world with its vast empires and events and tragedies, our Lord devoted himself to a small country, to small things and to individual men and women, often giving hours of time to the few, or to the one man or woman. For the infinite worth of the one person is the key to the Christian understanding of the many. You will never be nearer to Christ than in caring for the one man, the one woman, the one child. His authority will be given to you as you do this, and his joy will be yours as well.

(CP 42)

The comings of Christ

Watch and be ready for the Lord's coming. Think of your ministry or Christian life as a series of comings of Christ; then the more you learn not to be taken unawares, the more you can love his appearing. How does he come to us? In times of grief and disappointment he comes. Just when you begin to be oppressed, you find that your nearness to his grief is the supreme fact: you are near his Cross again, and you are taken out of yourself. In times of joy in your life or ministry he comes; and just when you are tempted to be pleased with your own success, you find that his joy is the supreme fact, and it makes an enormous difference. In times of complacency or unfaithfulness he also comes; and in your sudden painful awareness that all is not well with you, he is near in judgement and forgiveness.

When the master of the house comes, what does he do (cf Luke 12.35–46)? We would expect him to sit down and refresh himself, and tell his servants to wait on him. But no: the Lord waits on them. So our Lord always comes to us in order to serve us; and it is for us to let him do so. Occupied as we are in our life and ministry with serving him and other people in his name, we have to face the sharpest test of our humility, which is our readiness to let him serve us. For he never comes to us without longing to serve us: 'Jesus, who served the apostles by washing their feet: serve me often, serve me daily, in washing my motives, my ambitions, my actions. "Cleanse me from my secret faults" (Psalm 19.12).' By your humility you will prove that the authority entrusted to you is really Christ's; for Christ is your servant.

Let him serve you in the frequent cleansing of motive, ambition and action; and then your authority, possessed in his name, will be wielded always with the humility that is his.

(CP 64–7)

One world

Christianity teaches us that when we have troubles of our own we see them aright when we see them as part of the wider, vaster troubles of humanity as a whole, and when we remember that there are parts of the world where sufferings are so great that our own can scarcely be called sufferings at all. We in this country are not starving, we are not very poor; we have a high standard of living and we have many luxuries. So try to picture those who have a few mouthfuls for their families to eat every day: just a few mouthfuls. Again and again I find the apostles in the New Testament bidding Christians to think of the greater conflicts, the greater hardships of their brothers and sisters in other lands. We are, we really are, members of one another.

While, however, we are pressing for peoples and governments to adjust their sights to a Christian vision and to the obligations that arise, we find the voice of Christ speaking to our own consciences. Am I ready for a simpler way of life, ready for standards less affluent than we have had in the past? Do I myself care enough to be doing all I can in the service of the hungry? Do I care in a way that really costs me?

We may picture Jesus today weeping over many cities, towns, villages, and countries: some with their poverty and hunger, some with their wealth, their power, and their complacency. The tears of Jesus unite our world and show us how bound in a bundle we are. Jesus would have us share in his grief, and if we are his followers we shall not wish it otherwise. But those who share in the grief of Jesus are admitted to a share also in his joy: his joy over one sinner who mends his or her ways, his joy over every cup of cold water given to a child who is in need, his joy over every act of true service to his heavenly Father and to his human brothers and sisters (cf Matthew 25.31–46). We shall not ask: 'Who is my neighbour?' (Luke 10. 29f) My neighbour is Christ, and Christ is everywhere.

(CTP 158–9)

Going to the Father

The life of Christ is described by St John as being all the way a journey to the Father. 'I go to the Father': these words are a haunting refrain throughout the story as he goes his way to the Father, through the lifting up on the Cross to glory. But the journey to the Father was at every moment a journey deeper and deeper into humanity with its sin, its sorrow and its death. And nowhere was Jesus more utterly with the Father's glory than when bearing the world's darkness and dereliction on Calvary he cried out that he was bereft of God. Towards heaven, towards the world's darkness: these were but two facets of the one journey and the one Christ.

(SS 76)

DISCIPLESHIP

Lent comes round each year to give us time and opportunity to review and renew our own Christian life and discipleship. We are called to follow Christ, and to imitate him in his faith and prayer and in his service of others. How Christ-like is our life becoming? How central is our relationship with God? Do we give enough time in prayer to the eternal purpose of our lives?

This is difficult in the face of the speed of modern life and the fact that many fundamental Christian values now run counter to the direction of our society. Michael Ramsey was very honest about the nature and difficulties of belief and faith; but he was also fearlessly demanding in the way he used to call people to a renewed repentance and discipleship.

Central to his spiritual teaching and pastoral guidance was the call to confession in order to renew Christian commitment and to deepen life in Christ. The heart of the gospel is repentance, a complete change of attitude and values that takes a lifetime to accomplish at the hand of God. Confession means opening the whole person to the love and judgement of God, as it is revealed to us in Jesus Christ. For there is no true discipleship without cost.

Love of God and love of others go hand in hand: and it is often here that repentance and renewal are most difficult. Michael Ramsey firmly believed that marriage and family life were central to the life and well-being of the Church, and of individuals within it. He also had great sympathy and respect for monastic life, encouraging it within the

Church of England, and seeing it as embodying many of the distinctive values of the kingdom of God in a way that could change lives.

Peace in the heart of conflict

I have been through nearly all my life as a believing Christian, but that does not mean that I have found belief easy. Christian faith has been for me a constant process of wrestling, of losing and finding, of alternating night and day. Faith is a sort of adventurous conflict in the midst of which certainty deepens. When certainty passes, as it does for me, into a sense of peace and serenity, it is nonetheless a costly peace, a peace in the heart of conflict.

The one doctrine of Christianity that is never obvious or easy is the doctrine that God is love. The sensitivity of a Christian to human suffering prevents any facile statement or acceptance of the proposition that God is loving. Indeed belief that God is almighty and all-loving is strained for a sensitive Christian until he or she passes on to see the divine way of dealing with suffering in the Cross of Christ. There the answer comes: it is an answer not speculative but practical, for it is an answer valid only when the spirit of Christ crucified has been translated into human lives – lives that show what can be made of suffering in terms of heroic saintliness. Such lives are faith's most powerful witnesses, for just when the problem of evil oppresses us, they assault us with the challenge of good. The message that God is love will never be made convincing by facile statements, but only by Christians who share in that love in the spirit of Christ crucified.

(*Problems of Christian Belief* 7–8)

Modern secularism

There is the widespread idea that human beings are competent by their own powers to organise their own progress and happiness. It is a strange idea, inasmuch as the world is deeply divided and unable to rid itself of terrible weapons of destruction. Yet the idea is there because men and women do not sit back and ask themselves the question *quo tendimus* – where are we heading? Instead they press on absorbed in the use of their powers and their fascination with them. The mind that enjoys its own creations in discovery, technology, and in the organization of human welfare can become too busy and absorbed to question human competence and destiny. Hence in the midst of mature human intellectualism there is pride and insensitivity to the Spirit of God, which creates what we call 'modern secularism'.

There is the tendency for modern people to live in a whirl with their minds overcrowded. There are so many more things nowadays to think about, and so many impressions entering the mind in rapid succession, while there are still only sixty minutes in each hour and only twenty-four hours in each day. Hence the minds of men and women tend to lose their freedom and become ruled instead by the flux of impressions and sensations. I sometimes think that in the circumstances of the modern world an important part of our Christian asceticism needs to be the discipline of the mind to secure its freedom, just as much as the discipline of the body.

There is, as a result of this loss of touch with God, a deep frustration and fear, often subconscious and always divisive in its effects upon the human soul. Is not the considerable over-emphasis upon sex due less to any increase in the power of sexual impulses than to the urge to escape frustration by the sense of achievement that sexual adventure can provide? I agree with those who say that frankness and openness about sex is to be desired, as it is one of the Creator's good gifts. But the obsession with sex denotes in part a flight from frustration, and in part also a severance of the bond that unites sex and the other elements in personality, which all together find fulfilment in marriage and the family.

It is when the Creator is forgotten that His gifts and creatures are allowed to dominate and to become ends in themselves. So it is that technology, or money, or comfort, or sex can rule human beings, instead of having their true place, which is to be ruled by human beings for the glory of God. We now have a society where men and women, mature in their powers of mind and spirit, often lose their freedom, and lose their way to God.

(CEA 23–4)

The role of the Church

What then is the role of the Church? It is commissioned by the Lord to be living in the midst of the world a life that is Godward in worship and adoration, and a life that is in the service of men and women by carrying the gospel of God to them. Thus the Church's life, Godward and towards humanity, is a constant rhythm of coming and going, of detachment and involvement.

When the Church fails it is because the spirit of the world in one way or another invades it, as its historians often point out. For every member of the Church has a double existence of flesh and spirit, being still a member of the created world where sin is rampant, and also a member of the divine order of the resurrection. Today, it seems to me that the spirit of the world has invaded the Church in a very distressing way by the disease of mental and spiritual overcrowding. There are so many things that the Church must apparently do. As the Church engages with a world that is ever more and more complex, it finds itself engaged on too many fronts: what follows? One result is that amidst this faithful doing by the Church of all this hard work there is the overcrowding of the Church's mind and soul. So it is that we who belong to the Church succumb to the world's characteristic disease of being dominated by the flux of time, and of losing the power to consider (cf Luke 10.38–42).

(CEA 146–7)

Christian vocation

The particular vocation of a monk or nun to poverty, chastity and obedience, is but one form of the vocation that every single Christian receives at Baptism: to be poor in spirit, to be pure in heart, and to be obedient to the Lord Jesus Christ. This vocation belongs to each one of us, and it bids each one of us search our hearts before our Lord 'who loved me and gave himself for me' (Galatians 2.20). Thanking and praising God for all His mighty deeds, we pray that he will raise up His power and come among us for our sanctification and for the winning of souls.

(CEA 155)

The grace of repentance

How often does someone say to a priest, 'I want to be sorry for my sin, but I find that I cannot be: I want to confess my sins, but I do not know how!' The fragmentary movements of penitence in the soul too often become stifled as soon as they are born, whether by lethargy which cannot face sorrow at all, or self-pity which misdirects it. Then the wise pastor or evangelist has to show that we cannot sorrow for our sins as we should: there is only Christ's perfect sorrow for them, and our sorrow is learnt from him, and received by us as a tiny fragment of his. Repentance and forgiveness are by grace alone: for there is not only the grace of Christ who pardons us, there is also the grace of Christ who is at our side in our contrition and confession, making it with us and for us, as *Christus totus in nobis* – Christ totally one with us.

(GT 48–9)

Confession and reconciliation

The forgiveness of God is costly. It does not mean a declaration that sin does not really matter much: it is rather an act which affirms the divine hatred of sin and invites us to share in that repudiation at the moment when God's own compassion flows into us. Calvary tells of the cost of God's forgiveness and of the character of our sin as selfishness and pride, which wound our relationship to God. By the depth of their realization of what penitence and forgiveness mean, Christians are helping a deeper holiness to arise in the life of the Church.

The Anglican Church allows us a wise liberty. We are free to confess our sins in prayer to God, sure that if our confession has been careful and complete the forgiveness of God comes to us. There is no doubt of that. We are also free, if we are so drawn, to confess our sins in the presence of a priest, who will give us sacramental absolution in the name, and by the authority, of Jesus Christ. Those who freely choose this latter way do so because it is thorough and at times rather painful, and they feel that both thoroughness and pain are not amiss; and there is also the joyful decisiveness of sacramental absolution. Far from being the intrusion of a priest between the soul and God, absolution makes vivid the decisiveness of divine forgiveness in word and act.

Repentance – *metanoia* – is the turning of the mind, and with the mind the imagination, affections and will, away from sin and self, and towards God. It is within our act of turning to God that self-examination happened. We look towards God in gratitude for His loving-kindness, towards Jesus in his death for our sins, and then towards our own true self in what it is meant to become. The examining of our conscience must be thorough; but it will not be introspective, for it will be mingled with looking up towards God and exposing ourselves to Him. But the preparation will have to be thorough: it is not just a matter of naming those sins that seem to be big or that worry us especially: it is necessary to confess all the ways in which our attitudes and actions have been contrary to the way of Christ. That is what is important: it is a confession of the whole self: and those attitudes and actions which we may sometimes think to be small may be a decisive part of the self's orientation. Preparation for this sacrament, however, is also preparing to receive the grace of absolution, in the presence of Jesus who absolves us. For absolution is a real encounter with Jesus, who died for us and now lives, and we prepare to meet him in his holiness and compassion. Sacramental confession can be a meeting with Jesus as wonderful and decisive as meeting him in Holy Communion.

The ministry of reconciliation is part of the life of a reconciled and reconciling Church. This means a Church aware that it owes its own existence to the reconciliation of the Cross, and has its worship ever deepened by that awareness. It means also a Church which prays for the world, with the question, 'who is my neighbour?' ceaselessly in heart and mind and outgoing action. Within this reconciling prayer and action is Christian concern about relations with people of other races and religion, about poverty and hunger in the world, about cruelty and injustice, and about weapons of destruction. Within the confession of our sins there will be included sins of attitude, complacency or idleness of thought. We are not sinning if we are unsure of the answers to hard questions: we are sinning if we do not think or care. All this is part of a renewed ministry of reconciliation in the life of the Church.

(BS 108–11)

The great commandment

With the hope of heaven in the heart giving true perspective to present existence, human beings are set to serve God within the world that God has created. With this world they are utterly involved, and their service of God is always through the world and not apart from it. Human relationships are the stuff and substance of human worship of God. The first priority, however, is the enjoyment of God for God's sake, in whom is the perfection of all that can be perfect; an enjoyment that can never be selfish as it is outgoing love responding to outgoing love. God can never be treated as if He were the means towards ends greater than Himself. But because God is righteous there is no true worship of Him that is not immediately reflected in the love and service of others in society. Our love and service of them, however, will be saved from being patronizing or possessive, as in our doing of it we are humbled by God's love and forgiveness, and by our knowing that God's glory is the goal of all that we are trying to do.

(*CTP* 57)

The family

We who are Christians believe that the family is part of God's scheme of things. When men and women take part in the procreation of children they have the wonderful privilege of sharing in God's creation of human life, and they are called to do this in God's way. God's way means that procreation takes place not just anyhow, but by a man and a woman who are joined together in a lifelong union, a union in which they give themselves to one another until death parts them. That is the atmosphere of love and stability into which, in God's design, children are born. Having been born into a family, they are loved, cared for, and protected, and they grow up in the freedom and discipline of mutual love and care for one another. So when children go out and take their part in the world, their role in their own family is not left behind but lasts as a permanent part of their lives. For the happiest families are not introverted and wrapped up in their own circle, but are outgoing as part of a wider community. For us who are Christians there is no substitute for bringing men and women and children to the knowledge and love of God, and it is this that gives to the family its deepest meaning and strength.

(*CTP* 168–70)

Monastic life

The vows of monastic life to poverty, chastity and obedience mean the total acceptance of the call of God and are a gift from God: they are accepted 'by faith alone' and 'by grace alone', for the glory of God.

There was perhaps never a time when monastic life was more significant in Christendom and in the world than today. For today there is the love of pleasure, self-pleasing, wilfulness, and the belief that life is best with no authority at all; and it is against this that the call to obedience in monastic life is so very significant as a witness to the truth of God. Today the love of money, the spirit of getting and grabbing is widespread, and against that the joy of poverty in

Christian vocation is so very significant. Today too, lust and self-expression, and self-expression as an unthinking ideal, are widespread, and against this the call to the beauty and joy of chastity is very significant also.

As to the life of a religious or monastic community, here its stability and its permanence have a telling and divine meaning. Human life flits these days from one excitement to another, from one novelty to another, a little of this and little of that, and bondage to the passing moment is widespread. Hence witness to God is borne by the stability of a Christian home and a Christian marriage – 'those whom God has joined together let no one put asunder' – as a union of lives 'until death us do part'. A similar witness to God is borne by the stability of a religious community. It stands for the permanence of the vocation of its members; but it stands also as a witness to things that are not shaken, to truths and ideals that are not of any one age of Christian history, but that reach across the centuries: a ladder set up whose top reaches to heaven.

Laborare est orare, orare est laborare – to work is to pray and to pray is to work (St Benedict). Prayer is itself the work of a religious community, and service of the world is itself prayer, offered to the most high God on the world's behalf. This means apartness, like the apartness of our Lord in the desert, praying and fighting on behalf of us all, on behalf of the whole human race. It is apartness by being with God; but always on behalf of the human race with its sins, its joys, and its sorrows. All Christian apartness must be real and costly just as nearness must be real and costly too. The door of prayer towards heaven, towards the heart of God, is always a door of love into the world of human needs. For the ladder of Christian prayer not only reaches to heaven: it rests most firmly on earth; more than that, it unites heaven and earth very closely, because the ladder is Jesus himself, our incarnate Lord.

(CTP 65–8)

What is Christianity?

Christianity is Jesus Christ alive in the world, in the Body whose members are his servants, slaves, brothers and sisters, friends, and priests: people who know, however, that these images are only fragments of the truth and wonder of their relationship to him. As we discover new ways of serving Christ and of expressing our Christian fellowship in the community around us, we shall find new and enhanced meaning in Christianity's central rite: for the sacrament of the Eucharist is for all time our sharing in Christ's Body broken in death. If the faults and sins of Christians, including our own, and the failures of Christian institutions often make us feel that we are stumbling in the dark, we shall not be afraid. It is after all, the darkness of Calvary and the light of Easter, which are still the conditions of the Christian life, whose foundation is Jesus Christ.

(FFF 38)

* * * * * *

2

The Cross

THE PASSION

Passiontide and Holy Week bring us very close to the heart of the Christian mystery, and close also to what was most distinctive and demanding about Michael Ramsey's spiritual teaching, for his vocation to the priesthood was forged in a crucible of intense personal suffering, and in the darkness of those days it would seem that he glimpsed something real and near of the suffering presence of Christ that marked his life. His own sensitivity and reflective temperament made him tender towards the sufferings of others throughout his whole life and ministry.

His first book, The Gospel and the Catholic Church, *expressed the outcome of these formative experiences, rooted in a sure academic grasp of the New Testament. At the time and subsequently it was regarded as prophetic and profound. It proved to be the very foundation of the rest of his ministry and teaching over many years. Towards the end of his life he once said that when he looked back on these first writings, he realized that 'through the experience of the years I believe them to be true not only as an academic conclusion but as a fact with which we live'.*

This 'fact' he used to sum up in the phrase 'living through dying': what did he mean? First, that God was in all that happened to Christ and in all that he accomplished and endured. Jesus reveals the extent of divine humility and self-restraint in God's dealing with wayward human beings at all times and in all places. What is true of God the Creator, his self-effacement, is also true of God the loving re-creator of men and women.

Secondly, 'living through dying' also means standing with Christ in the face of suffering, evil and death, and not running away. It means dying to self, as Jesus predicted. For it is in the darkness that the light shines brightest, and the whole principle of Christ's life was one of self-sacrifice. Christians are called to embrace this way with all its challenge and cost, thus sharing in the death and Resurrection of

Jesus. To this the great sacraments of Baptism and the Eucharist point; for Christ and his Cross pose a present and final choice to each person.

Die to live

I suggest to you that as the Cross and the resurrection were the spearhead of the gospel's relevance and potency in the first century, so they can be also for our contemporary world. Ours is a world full of suffering and frustration: of what significance to it is Jesus who lived and died nearly two thousand years ago? The answer is chiefly this: that in the death and resurrection he shows not only the way for human beings, but the true image of God himself. Is there, within or beyond our suffering and frustrated universe, any purpose, way, meaning, sovereignty? We answer, yes, and the death and resurrection of Jesus portray this purpose, way, meaning, and sovereignty as living through dying, as losing self to find self, as the power of sacrificial love.

To commit oneself to this way is to be near to the secret of God's own sovereignty, near to the power, which already wins victories over evil and that will ultimately prevail. This is the point at which Jesus can be shown to be near to our own world; and when he is found to be near at this point, then his life and teaching are found to have their compelling fascination. For through his life and teaching there runs the principle, 'he who exalts himself shall be humbled, and he who humbles himself shall be exalted' (Luke 14.11). Throughout the life and teaching of Jesus there is a strange blending of authority and humility. Here, I suggest, is the point of impact of the old story of Jesus upon our new world: *die to live*. Here too is the meaning of the Church, and the meaning of apostolic ministry: 'always bearing about in the body the dying of Jesus, that the life also of Jesus may be manifested in our body' (2 Corinthians 4.10).

(CP 32–3)

The meaning of the death of Jesus

Christ's death is, first of all, the deepest point of the Son of God's identification of himself with men and women, and of his entry into the stream of human life. If he is near to them in the joyful contact of his ministry in Galilee, teaching, healing and blessing, he is nearer still as he goes to the Cross. Remote from all the superficialities of life and society, Christ enters by way of the Cross into nearer and nearer contact with the grim human realities of sin and createdness and death. For death is not merely a physical fact: it has a moral meaning since it marks and declares the sinfulness, createdness and fragility of humanity, which is gripped by sin and so falls short of the glory of God (Romans 3.23; 5.14 and 21). The New Testament writers know human nature, for all its achievements, as a dying creature confronted with the boundary and fear of death; and death sums up the truth about human nature when it is seen in the light of the eternal God.

Now into this death the Son of God came, tasting both the fear of death and the fact of death and the moral meaning of death (Hebrews 5.7). He bore it as the consequence of human sin, identifying himself with sinful men and women. The hard phrase of St Paul, 'Christ was innocent of sin, yet for our sake God made him one with human sinfulness' (2 Corinthians 5.21), finds its best commentary in the cry of dereliction from the Cross (Mark 15.34). For our Lord enters so deeply into the meaning, the pain and the darkness of a race cut off from God by sin, that he seems momentarily to lose his vision of the Father; and he is never more the brother of men and women, never more entirely one with us, than in this cry of dereliction. In Galilee he is indeed near to men and women, but the full meaning of sin before God was not disclosed. On Calvary he is near to them in death, which sums up and reveals what human nature is, a creature and sinner before God. He came in order to die, so as to be truly human: going the way all men and women must go. His coming to die did not mean the negative act of a suicide seeking self-destruction, however, but rather the positive act of one whose love embraces human beings and all that is theirs, saying, 'Where you go, I also will go' (Ruth 1.16).

(GC 21–3)

The self-sacrifice of Christ

The death of the Lord means also the laying down of self and the abandonment of all its claims. Throughout his life his will was wholly submitted to the Father's will, and he lived and died not as pleasing himself but as losing his will and his whole being in the Father and in humanity (Mark 14.36; cf Romans 15.3). His selfhood was so laid down that his power and authority centre in his humiliation. Such is the impression of the earthly life of Jesus in the gospels. But this self-abandonment does not belong to the earthly life alone, for it is the expression in history of the self-giving of the eternal God. St Paul makes it clear that the first and great act of humiliation is the act by which the Son of God was made man (Philippians 2.5–7). Thus before the humiliations of the Messiah in his life and death upon earth, there is the divine self-emptying by which he came and was sent. For St Paul the Incarnation is in itself an act of sacrifice than which none is greater: Christmas is as costly in self-giving as is Good Friday. Only the crucifixion is the deepest point of the divine self-giving, which entered history at Bethlehem, and which begins in heaven. For 'there was a Calvary above which was the mother of it all'.

St John's gospel unfolds this eternal love of God, expressed in the sending of the Son into the world, and in the self-giving of the Son to the point of death; and it shows also how this truth is the basis of the Church. The narrative points us both to Christ in the flesh and also to the eternal truth, which his flesh reveals. Christ is depicted throughout his life upon earth as living, speaking and thinking in utter dependence on the Father. This dependence of the Son means that the Son finds in the Father the centre of his own existence, and it implies a relationship of death to himself as himself. The Son has nothing, wills nothing, and is nothing of himself alone. His self has its centre in another; and this attitude and action of the Son in history reveals the character of the eternal God, the mutual love of the Father and the Son. This divine love now enters the disciples of Jesus, so that they may share in the self-negation and in the unity within God Himself.

Here then is a complete setting forth of the meaning of the Church: the eternal love of the Father and the Son is uttered in Christ's self-negation unto death, to the end that men and women may make it their own and so be made one. This unity, in a word, means death: death to the self as self, first in Christ and then in the disciples. This is the ground and essence of the Church, for God's power is manifested in self-emptying love; and to be made a man, to die and to be buried is of the power of God no less than is the creation of the world. For in the nothingness of death and the tomb there is a love so mighty that Christ now lives and fills all things. St John draws the death and resurrection so closely together that one is the inevitable divine sequence of the other. To him the Cross is not a defeat needing the resurrection to reverse it, but rather a victory so decisive that the resurrection follows quickly to seal it, so that the lifting up on the Cross and the exalting into heaven hardly seem separate.

Christ died to self, morally by the will to die throughout his life, actually by the crucifixion. He died alongside human beings as a man, coming by water and blood. God raised him, and in his death and resurrection the fact of the Church is present. For as he is baptized into human death, so men and women will be baptized into his death; and as he loses his life to find it in the Father, so may they, by a true dying to self, find a life whose centre is in Christ and in their brethren. 'One died for all, therefore all died' (2 Corinthians 5.14): to say this is to describe the Church of God.

(GC 23–7)

Christ dwelling in us

The death and resurrection of our Lord happened once and can never be repeated. The deed was done in history, yet it is the entry into human history of something beyond history, which cannot be known in terms of history alone. 'The time is fulfilled, and the Kingdom of God is at hand' (Mark 1.15). But this event, born in eternity and uttering the voice of God from another world, pierces deeply into our order of time, so that the death and resurrection of Christ were known not only as something external, but also as something *within* the disciples who believed. That is the meaning of the Church: 'Christ within you, the hope of glory to come' (Colossians 1.27). Not only did the crucifixion make possible the giving of the Spirit, but the life bestowed by the Spirit is a life of which crucifixion is a quality, a life of living through dying (cf John 7.39; 1 Corinthians 2; Galatians 3.1–2 and 5.22–4; Romans 8.16–17). For in every place where Christians are found, they dare to assert that Christ is in them, and that their relation to Him is not only a memory of a past event, but the fact of a present indwelling. The presence of the Spirit mediates the presence of Christ himself, so that to be 'in the Spirit' is to be 'in Christ'.

By the power of the Spirit, who brings the self-giving of God into a Christian's life, the self-centred nexus of appetites and impulses is broken, and human life is brought into a new centre and a new environment, Christ and his Body. The response of faith has preceded the receiving of this divine action, and the response of faith is continually needed in order to appropriate it: for baptism, like the Incarnation and the death of Christ, is a real action of God who recreates. The best commentary (cf Romans 6.2–11) is to be found in the saints, whose hidden life has been the response to the fact of their baptism.

Thus Christians look back to the death and resurrection of Jesus in whom they first believed, and they receive the Spirit of him who died

The Cross

and rose again, knowing as a result the dying and rising as a reality within themselves. As a result they are led to think both of Christ and of themselves in a new way (cf 2 Corinthians 5.14–17). Men and women are identified with Christ's death in such a way that they no longer consider themselves as separate and self-sufficient beings, but as centred in Christ who died and rose again. If they used to think of Christ as an isolated human figure, they now think of him as the inclusive head and centre of a new humanity in which the new creation of God is at work. The implication of this is far-reaching: Christ is defined not as the isolated figure of Galilee and Judea, but as one whose people, dead and risen with him, are his own humanity. Thus the fact of Christ includes the fact of the Church. This is not a novel speculation added to the original gospel: it springs from the gospel. The gospel record is unintelligible apart from the Messiah's death, and that death is spiritually unintelligible unless the disciples share in it. For by sharing in it through the baptism of the Spirit they and all believers know the death and resurrection as a present reality. Thus when St Paul describes the Church as the 'Body' of Christ and the 'fullness' of Christ, he is describing facts inherent in the Messiah's work from the beginning. 'One died for all, therefore all died': to know this is to know 'the Church which is his Body, the fullness of him that fills all in all' (Ephesians 1.23).

(GC 28–34)

The love of God or self-love?

Jesus is divine: his death is thus a symbol of universal significance. It is a symbol of the clash between the perfect love of God and the sinfulness of the *whole* human race – Peter, John and Paul as well as Caiaphas, Judas and Pilate. It is a mirror of humanity in its pride with which it wounds the love of God. Hence in every age human consciences have seen in the mirror of the Passion of Jesus *themselves*. Notice how each of the characters in the story portrays a familiar human attitude: these are the attitudes and actions, then and now, which drive nails into the love of God. Is it not awful to think about? The details of the scene may not actually fit the details of our own actions; but they do symbolise what happens within our hearts. We too choose the worthless and reject the perfect, for my will must be enthroned in my own little castle, and all else but my will must be driven out. Again, is it not awful?

(IC 50)

THE EUCHARIST

On Maundy Thursday, we commemorate the giving of the Eucharist at the Last Supper, and Jesus washing his disciples' feet. The Eucharist lay at the heart of Michael Ramsey's own spirituality. His devotion and way of celebration made a profound and lasting impression on many people. For him it was the gateway to holiness and heaven, a living link with the time of the gospel, and a loving bond with God, Father, Son and Holy Spirit.

He believed that the Eucharist provides a master key to interpreting the whole of the New Testament in all its various strands. It is also the very heart of the Church's continuing existence in every generation, and in every part of its worldwide life. The Eucharist therefore demonstrates the underlying unity of the Church and affirms it.

The Eucharist constitutes life in Christ by the power of the Holy Spirit. It entails participation in the mystery of the dying and rising of Jesus in all its pain and glory. Costly preparation and careful liturgical celebration are indispensable for sensing the hidden life of holiness that is offered to us in this sacrament, which should stand as the heart and focus of personal prayer.

The Eucharist reveals the great and eternal sacrifice that lies at the heart of God, which was demonstrated once for all upon the Cross. Through it there flows the life of the Resurrection, the drawing of time into eternity, the union of a living past with a living present of worship and joy.

The Last Supper

Jesus is with the twelve apostles at supper on the night before his crucifixion. On the next day he is to die the death, which is the perfect offering of himself to the Father in the obedience of loving sonship. The death on Calvary was an event external to the disciples, and it is external to us too. But Jesus wills that his death shall somehow become *within* us. He gives the sacrament, so that he who offers himself to the Father on Calvary will be himself the food of our souls within: thus united with him and nourished by him we may offer ourselves in him and through him. For he who gave himself on Calvary, gives Calvary to us, that we may give back our all to him.

(*IC* 73–4)

The Eucharist

The meaning of the Eucharist is to be found not only in the Last Supper but also in the light of the whole language of worship in the New Testament. The meaning of Christ's actions is determined by the whole meaning of his life and work, and the interpretation of the institution of the Eucharist depends upon the whole interpretation of his ministry. For if Jesus was merely a prophet and teacher, then his solemn actions on the night before he died might only have a meaning limited to that time and place. But if he is the Messiah proclaiming the Kingdom of God, then his action in setting up the new covenant in his blood has a significance reaching far beyond his own life and death.

The giving of a covenant implies at once the creation of a people, a new nation that looks back to the Lord's death as its origin and bond of unity, just as Israel looks back to the Exodus, the deliverance from Egypt. The disciples, however, will not only form a nation created by Christ's death: by eating the bread and drinking the cup they will be brought within his death. In an unutterable way they partake of it: it is no longer only an event outside them; it becomes something within them to feed and transform them. The Lord's words and actions were his final unfolding of the meaning of his death, and in them the whole meaning and power of that death were present. The disciples were brought within the death; his dying is become their food.

The climax of God's mercies in history is the death of Christ, in which God's whole work in the world and in Israel is summed up and fulfilled. This climax is set forth in this 'newer rite'. By sharing in the broken bread and the blood outpoured, the disciples find interpreted both the crucifixion, and the whole divine creation whose secrets the crucifixion unlocks. By this rite, Christ invests his death with its meaning for all humanity; by it he declares the power of this death in terms of redemption, and also its place within God's creation. Standing at the central point in the New Testament, the Eucharist is interpreted in the light of the whole gospel, for in it the truth of the phrase 'through Jesus Christ' is focussed. Thus in all Christian thinking about the Body of Christ, the Eucharist and the Church are inseparable.

The discourse in John 6, following the Feeding of the 5,000, teaches that the power of Jesus to feed and to give life is derived from the Father. The Incarnation and the Eucharist reveal the truth about the Father and the Son: for behind the life, the death, the feeding, there is the eternal relation of the Father and the Son, which the life, the death and the feeding reveal. In this earthly action the truth of the eternal God is learnt and becomes active to save the souls and bodies of men and women. Furthermore it is in the power of the ascended life and of the Holy Spirit that Christ will feed them with himself: his words, works and sacraments are to be understood in the light of his completed work and his ascended life. All these stupendous truths, and nothing less, lie behind the Eucharist and are focussed within it: the flesh of Jesus; his death, resurrection and ascension; the Father, the Son and the Spirit. His flesh must be eaten, for here is history and tangible reality. Yet history and reality have their significance in what lies beyond them. Like the Incarnation itself, the Eucharist is the breaking into history of something eternal, beyond history, inapprehensible in terms of history alone. To this no one comes unless it is given by the Father.

Underlying the language of the New Testament about the Eucharist is something greater than language can express, which is recreating language, thought and worship. The rite has within it something that disturbs and causes change. For example, just as our Lord was set apart from humanity in the awe and isolation of his Passion so as to be nearer to them by his death, so the Eucharist came to be set apart from common meals in an awe and mystery, whereby its nearness to common human life was to be realised more deeply. The gospel, which moulded the structure of the Church, moulded also the form of the Church's worship. This worship is indeed the Divine Liturgy whereby the people of God share in the self-offering of Christ. The ever-deepening union of Christians with Jesus in his death increases their awe and wonder, and their sense of the great unknown that lies before them.

(GC 99–112)

Sacrifice in the Eucharist

Sacrifice is a figure of speech, which early Christians, familiar with Jewish sacrifices, could use as one among many images to describe the work of Christ. The essence of the old sacrifices was the offering of an animal's blood that represented its life: death was necessary to release the blood, but the essence of sacrifice was the offering of life. Now Jesus Christ was a priest who offered sacrifice in a sense far transcending the ancient imagery, and the epistle to Hebrews bids us think of his priesthood in two ways. Firstly, Christ's priesthood is an eternal fact about his heavenly life: he is 'a priest forever after the order of Melchizedek', and as the Son of God he forever possesses the character of one who gives his life utterly in love. His eternal priesthood and sacrifice are the eternal element of self-giving love within God, the element that St John describes as the eternal love of the Son for the Father, and of the Father for the Son.

Secondly, this eternal self-giving or priesthood is uttered in time and history in the life and death of the incarnate Son; and when it is expressed in a world of sin and pain, the life of sacrifice involves death and destruction. Nonetheless the essence of the sacrifice remains the giving of life, making it forever 'the life whereof the abiding characteristic is to have died'. Thus, priest eternally and priest on earth, our Lord is priest *now* in his relation to the Father, for ever giving to the Father as Son of Man a life of which the death once died in history is the revealing mark and character.

For Christians, our present access to the Father has been created by the Lord's sacrifice, and it is only through facing the Cross, with its disclosure of the awful realities of sin and of God's forgiving love, that men and women have free access to Him as His children. It is only by looking constantly to Christ's sacrifice that they can approach God aright and in his name. Hence the divine action to which Christians look, and which they commemorate both as a finished event in history and as an eternal reality in heaven, is an action whereof priesthood and sacrifice are scriptural descriptions. Christians look back to the sacrifice of Calvary, and they look up to the eternal sacrifice that it reveals.

Nor is this all, for as the glory and the name are realties outside Christians but also realities within them, so likewise is the priesthood of Christ. The Body of Christ shares in his priesthood, for in his Body he lives his life of utter self-giving in the midst of pain and sin (cf 1 Peter 2.9). Meanwhile Christ's presence in heaven is as a sacrifice, and in the Eucharist his presence cannot be otherwise. He is there as the one who gave himself on the Cross for them, and who now unites his people to his own self-giving to the Father in heaven. In words of St Augustine: 'It is shown to the Church that in the Eucharist which she offers, she herself is offered' (*City of God* 10.6). For it is still the Messiah who gives thanks and breaks the bread: and herein is summed up the life of the Church, the gospel of God, and the whole meaning of human life. Here therefore Christian doctrine, with the scriptures and the creeds, finds its true context: *lex orandi, lex credendi* – the law of prayer is the law of belief. For here is seen, in the words of the Creed, 'the communion of saints': that fellowship both of holy things and of holy people, united in Christ, by whom all things were made: *hagia hagiois* – holy things are for holy people.

(GC 113–19)

Spirit and life

'The words that I have spoken to you, they are spirit and life' (John 6.63). These words disclose the heart of St John's doctrine. Is eating the flesh of the Son of Man an incredible idea? Something as startling is to happen: the ascension of the Son of Man to heaven where he was before. But these happenings, both the feeding upon Christ and the ascension into heaven, belong to the life-giving Spirit, and without the Spirit they are nothing. The words of Jesus are spirit and life, for they are filled with the power of the Spirit, and they are life giving in their effect. What is being said here applies to the mission of Christ and to the gift of the Eucharist. Both involve flesh, the flesh of history and the flesh of material food; yet both are nothing without the Spirit's power.

(HS 96)

Parish communion

Although catholic and evangelical Anglicans may differ in their views of the relationship between our Lord's sacrifice and the sacrament, they are one in believing our Lord's sacrifice to be the great reality under whose shadow we worship. We dare to bring bread and wine, our work and home life, and ourselves, only insofar as we humble ourselves before the all-sufficient sacrifice of 'the Lamb of God that takes away the sins of the world'. Although the new tendency is to emphasize that Holy Communion is corporate, and to speak of 'our communion' rather than 'my communion', coming to the sacrament involves nonetheless a responsible act of individuals, and it is an act full of awe and dread. Holy Communion does unite a person with others, but at the same time it sets a person alone with the Lord at the hour of death and the day of judgement. The awe in the individual person's approach to Holy Communion, which characterized both Tractarians and Evangelicals of old, stands in marked contrast to the ease with which many of our congregations come tripping up to the altar week by week.

Happy are those whose churches are full of reminders that the Church on earth is a colony of heaven, and that those who are called to be saints have fellowship with the glorious saints already. May we never have a generation of worshippers unfamiliar with the canticles and the psalms! I am pleading that we should be careful about values that may be lost by over reliance upon the main parish communion. Above all, there is much to be learnt from the quiet, early celebration of the Eucharist. It keeps alive, and gives real place to, the *meditative* element in religion. It is the meditative element, which is desperately needed, and so often imperilled.

I give my warnings and criticisms. But I cannot end with these. I can only end with great thankfulness for the revival of Holy Communion in the life of so many parishes. In the long run it will be its own interpreter and teacher. For the supreme question is not what we make of the Eucharist, but what the Eucharist is making of us, as together with the Word of God, it fashions us into the way of Christ.

(DA 15–21)

Praying with the Church

The praying Christian is also part of the praying Church, however solitary he or she may be or feel. The praying Church means not only the local community or the church of a country or a generation, but rather the Holy Catholic Church of Christ, the people of God in all places and ages. Divisions of place and time, of culture, and of our unhappy separations may hinder but they do not destroy the unity in Christ of those who know their prayer to be in the Spirit of Christ. To say this is not to deny the solitude of individual Christians in the uniqueness in which the Creator made them. Rather may individual Christians draw from the liturgy of the worshipping Church a strength whereby his or her own prayer becomes more than ever their own in its depth, enabling them in turn to bring into the liturgy the offering of their own devotion.

The Eucharist is the supreme encounter between God and His redeemed people, through recalling the death of Jesus. Here His people feed upon Jesus, who died and rose again, and offer themselves to the Father in union with his own perfect sacrifice. Into this act each Christian brings the offering of their own prayer. From this act each Christian draws divine strength into their own prayer in times of quiet. It is greatly to be desired that those who care specially for liturgy, and plan it, should give much more care to the relationship between liturgy and personal prayer and meditation. If every spare moment within and around liturgy is filled with music and activity, much is lost in the linking of the liturgy of the Church to the meditative and contemplative aspects of Christian life.

Christians who are struggling with prayer, far from the visible support of a Christian community, will realise that they are never alone. Christians are praying in many parts of the world, sometimes in places where persecution and cruelty are rife, and their prayers are near to Christ. The recollection of that may strengthen the prayer of the lonely Christian. So too may the bringing into personal prayer of some of the forms of common prayer, a collect, a psalm, a hymn, as a link with the praying people of God. Some of the psalms especially make a wonderful link with the prayer of Jesus, and of his Church praying through the ages. Nor will the praying Christian forget that the prayers of the saints are near too. As we remember them we pray that our prayers may be helped by the prayers of other Christians who pray better than we do. If this is true of Christians praying on earth, how true it must be of the prayers of the saints, who are beyond the grave, and nearer to the holiness of God and the vision of God in His beauty.

(BS 78–9)

The humility of God

There, in the scene of the feet washing, is the sum of the whole matter. Take the scene, recall it, explore it, and dwell on it. God's glory is in it, the majesty of our Creator who humbles Himself towards us, His creatures. You worship Him, and you let Him serve you by cleansing you. Your conversion, the forgiveness of your sins when you have confessed them, is Jesus serving you and cleansing you as he wills. So, in consequence, your own service of humanity will be a service humble, unselfconscious, and unpatronising. It will meet the needs of humanity more deeply, since God has first been allowed to meet your deepest need.

(IC 94)

GETHSEMANE AND CALVARY

Good Friday is set apart for contemplating the Crucifixion of Christ and its meaning. This lay at the heart of Michael Ramsey's own approach to prayer and theology, as his description of Perugino's portrayal of the Crucifixion reveals. A reproduction of this picture hung on his study wall right to the end of his life.

The obedience of Jesus and its cost is the dominant note in each of the Gospel stories, and is echoed elsewhere in the New Testament. What is significant is what the character of this obedience reveals about the eternal relationship between Jesus the Son and God as Father. This becomes the key to the meaning of all Christian obedience. Michael Ramsey returned again and again to the prayer of Jesus described in John 17: this was a passage of fundamental importance in his mind and also in his prayer; for it gave deep insight into this relationship of obedience and love.

Contemplation of the Crucifixion also means participation in some measure of its suffering. The shadow of the Cross falls over the turmoil and pain of Christian discipleship in many different ways. It also poses a sharp challenge to the sinfulness and cruelty of the world today and in every age of history. But its impact is life giving to those who will accept that 'God was in Christ reconciling the world unto Himself'. An important sign of the impact of this reconciliation or atonement is a heightened sensitivity and compassion towards the sufferings of humanity.

The agony of Jesus

In the story of Jesus in the Garden of Gethsemane, instead of the unswerving obedience of Jesus to his Father, there is 'horror and dismay', and an agonising blending of shrinking and acceptance. This tradition is known also in Hebrews (5.7) and in St John's gospel (12.27). Jesus is depicted as one with us in our frailty, not indeed of moral weakness but of body and nerve, and also one with the Father in his power to turn every faculty towards the Father's purpose. Amidst his own agony, Jesus is still the pastor caring for his disciples, eager that they may be watching and praying to be saved from their own trial when it comes to them, as immediately it does. This theme of watching and praying recurs often in the early Church in connection with the crisis of the Lord's coming.

Jesus thus 'learned obedience' (cf Hebrews 5.7–10) in the sense of discovering the full meaning of what obedience to God involves. 'Being made perfect' does not mean becoming morally perfect. 'To perfect' has in the letter to Hebrews the special meaning of 'made fit for a particular role', in this case Christ's role of his heavenly priesthood. In St Mark's gospel, Jesus by his cry of desolation (Psalm 22.1) enters into the depths of a world alienated from God and His presence. But if Jesus is thus in the depths, it is divine love that has brought him there; and what St Mark depicts as desolation, St John will depict as glory.

(BS 24–5)

The prayer of Jesus in St John's Gospel

The theme of prayer in the name of Jesus comes into prominence in St John's gospel, and this is shown to be the prayer of those who are closely united to Jesus by the coming of the Holy Spirit, the Paraclete. It is thus after the death and resurrection of Jesus that the deepest prayer of the disciples is made possible (cf Romans 8). The prayer of Jesus to the Father is seen in this gospel as the expression in time and history of the Son's eternal relation to the Father, a relationship that is supremely revealed in the self-giving love of the Passion. While this teaching about prayer lifts us into an eternal world, it does so by confronting us with the particular time and place of an event on the hill of Calvary. In these ways we learn about prayer much that is distinctive in this gospel; but what we learn is rooted in the early tradition about the prayer of Jesus as his obedience even unto death.

After the discourse there comes the prayer of Jesus in chapter 17, appropriately titled 'the prayer of consecration', for at its centre Jesus consecrates himself to his death on behalf of the disciples. But the recurring theme of the prayer is 'glory': glory in the Passion, glory given to the disciples, glory in the goal of heaven. It is a prayer set in the context of an acute historical situation, the hour of the death of Jesus in Jerusalem. Yet within the prayer there is reflected the timeless converse of the Son and the Father in glory before the world began.

As the prayer in Gethsemane was in St Mark's gospel the decisive step toward the Passion, so in St John this prayer after the Last Supper is the decisive step of Jesus towards the completion of the journey to the Father that is his mission. The Cross is the event of glory: by it there is the revelation of eternal glory, and from it there comes the mission of the disciples empowered by the Spirit, their consecration in the truth, their sharing in the unity of the Father and the Son, and their coming to glory in heaven.

(BS 43; 47–8)

Three crosses

Christianity is concerned not just with one cross but with three. When our Lord was approaching the final crisis of his life on earth he foretold that three kinds of suffering lay ahead. There would be his own suffering with its climax in his death by crucifixion. It was a death as terrible as any can be. But it was a death, which his followers were one day to hail not only as shame and reproach, but also as victory and glory. That was the first Cross, which has become the supreme Christian symbol.

There would be also the suffering that Christ's own followers would experience. You remember how he said to James and John: 'Are you able to drink the cup that I shall drink?' (Mark 10.38). The disciples shrank from dying with Jesus, there and then on Good Friday. But through the years Christians have been called to suffer with Christ, some by dying as martyrs, some by facing persecution, and all by lives of self-sacrifice. Those who have readily suffered with Christ have found that Christ's peace and joy become theirs too in a wonderful way. As one of the apostolic writers said: 'If we suffer with him we shall also reign with him' (2 Timothy 2.11–3). That is the second Cross that Jesus foretold.

Then the third Cross: this would be the suffering of the world, which rejected Jesus Christ; the divine judgement when people and nations bring suffering upon themselves and upon their fellow human beings. When they reject the way of love that Jesus taught, and turn their backs upon the ceaseless appeals of God to their consciences, calamities follow. So the last loving appeal of Jesus to his people was mingled with forebodings of judgement. Where there is in this world selfishness, hatred, violence, cruelty, lust, there comes a cross of human suffering, dark and bitter, with none of the radiance of Calvary to lighten it. That is the third Cross that Christ predicted.

'This is the victory that overcomes the world – our faith' (1 John 5.4–5). Jesus died, Jesus rose again, and Jesus lives. He has called us who are Christians to follow him, to live in fellowship with him, and to share in his joy and his victory. That is the message of Easter. But it is not a message that tells us that suffering has ended. No, the Easter message has as its context the stark realities of our suffering world. Amidst these stark realities Jesus summons us to follow him, and he tells us that as we do so we are likely to have trials and pains in plenty, the trials and pains of the second of our crosses. But it will be different, different because we shall be with Jesus, and his joy and peace will be with us. We shall be working with Jesus to rescue the world from the third Cross, the Cross of judgement and alienation, of human selfishness and misery.

(*CTP* 160–1)

Perugino's *Crucifixion* (The Gallitzin Triptych in the Washington National Gallery of Art)

Perugino's picture of the crucifixion of Jesus is for me a great picture, because it wonderfully shows a large part of what Christianity means. Christ is seen suffering, suffering terribly: and yet in it there is triumph because love is transforming it all. We see the victory of self-giving love, of sacrifice. Nothing is, I believe, more characteristic of Christianity than the power, drawn from Jesus Christ, of bringing into the midst of suffering this outgoing love, with its note of victory, serenity, even joy. It is one of the most marvellous things in human life, that just when we are downcast by the problem of evil, the challenge of goodness hits us in the eye and overwhelms us.

Christianity makes a twofold attack on suffering in the world. Christians hate the sight of suffering in other people and do their utmost to free them from it. They throw themselves into the care of those who suffer in every way they can: the sick, the homeless, the hungry, and those who face persecution, injustice, or abominations like torture. But sometimes when suffering comes to a person and cannot be escaped, a Christian is called upon, in the spirit of Christ, to use it, transformed by patience, love, sympathy, and power, like Perugino's picture. Someone once said that Christ fought suffering in other people as if nothing could be made of it, but when it came to him he used it as if everything could be made of it. Meanwhile let us remember, what we sometimes complacently forget, that there are many people in our world, whose suffering has been far greater than ours – the homeless, the really hungry, and those treated with injustice. Then we are stirred again to renew our caring about the sufferings of our fellow men and women.

(*CTP* 127–8)

Atonement

Christ comes as the true sacrifice. He embodies ideal sacrifice as the joyful response of creature to Creator. In Christ humanity is seen recovering its true destiny of cleaving to the Father in a holy fellowship to that good end for which human nature was created. But we also see in Christ, God dealing with the tragedy of sin and suffering. In describing how Christ, by his death and rising again, overcame the tragedy of human sin, none of the particular images of sacrifice of themselves suffice. If we identify the doctrine of the atonement with any single one of them in isolation we get a totally inadequate presentation of Christ. The meaning of Christ's atonement lies in that blending of sacrificial images which he himself made: a life, death, resurrection and ascension which was both a pure offering and a victory over sin, and an act of loving obedience, and thereby the act of bearing the whole of humanity's penalty and calamity.

All of these are only completed by the actual effect, through the Holy Spirit, of the life, death and resurrection of Jesus upon the human situation. It is helpful to blend together the imagery of sacrifice with the imagery of glory in St John's gospel. I believe that although the images are different, there is at bottom a similarity in their meaning. Thus the sprinkling with the blood of Jesus means that the self-giving of Jesus in his death and rising again is the power that is able to cleanse us from sin by replacing sin in us by the spirit of Christ's own self-offering. I doubt if, in essence, that means something very different from the Johannine language: 'The glory you gave to me, I have given to them' (John 17.22). For the giving by Christ to us of his glory means nothing other than that the self-giving love, evident in his life, death and resurrection, is given to us to be the life-giving principle of our own lives.

(The Christian Concept of Sacrifice 7–8)

THE SIGNIFICANCE OF SUFFERING

On Easter Saturday we confront the finality of suffering and death, as people do whenever they stand by the grave of someone they have loved. If that person has died tragically, the pain is doubly hard to bear. The inevitable question arises: why is there such suffering and dying in the world if God is a God of love?

Michael Ramsey had faced this question early in his personal life, and it coloured his whole approach to being a Christian and a priest. He was courageous in expressing the doubts and fears of many Christians and others, and did not think that being a Christian made it any easier to confront suffering and death.

The first response of a Christian towards suffering in others is compassion and identification with them, even at expense to oneself. This is a vital hallmark of anyone who sincerely seeks to follow the example of Jesus. But there come times when suffering cannot be overcome: what then? Here Michael Ramsey has wise teaching about the transfiguration of suffering, which he believed enabled people to experience the 'not yet' of Christianity, the mystery of how eternal life triumphs in the midst of the frailties of this life.

He is also frank about facing humiliations in life, and particularly in Christian ministry. Their impact and our response can brings us nearer to Christ in his humility and sufferings; and through them, as St Paul discovered, life may flow forth: for 'death is at work in us, but life in you'. This is the message and the mystery of the tomb of Jesus.

The meaning of pain

One of the many paradoxes of the New Testament is that there is a dying and rising still to be experienced, and the Church becomes the scene of dying and rising in every generation. There is first the struggle with sin in Christian life, and the battle with the 'ego' that still asserts itself. There is also the existence of pain and tragedy in nature and in the world, and here too Christians recognise the Passion of Christ. They do not fear the struggle, for pain has been used by Christ and has been given a new significance. Taught by him, Christians can use it for love, for sympathy and for intercession. It enables them to enter more deeply into his Passion, and it helps to wean them from any contentment with the present order of things with its false values. It also makes them 'members one of another' in a unity springing from the Cross, and pointing to a glory to be revealed.

Like Christ, the Church is sent to accomplish a twofold work in the face of human sufferings: to seek to alleviate, heal and remove them, since they are hateful to God; yet when they are overwhelming and there is no escape from them, to transfigure them and to use them as the raw material of love. So in every age Christians have fought to remove sufferings; but they have also borne witness to the truth that they can be transfigured, and so become the place where the power of God is truly known.

The Cross

The Church's unity in pain is very significant, for it is not only a unity by sympathy and imitation, but rather the unity of a single organism in joy and in sorrow. Suffering in one Christian may beget life and comfort in Christians elsewhere: 'So then death works in us, but life in you' (2 Corinthians 4.12). Thus the sorrows of Christians in one place may be all-powerful for Christians in another place.

(GC 40–1 and 46)

The 'not yet' of Christian experience

In two ways, the inner conflict with sin and the outer bearing of pain, the Church is a scene of continual dying. Yet it is the place where the sovereignty of God is known and uttered, and where God is reconciling the world unto Himself. Here life is given in abundance, and here the faithful discern the peace of the resurrection. For the reconciling work of God *is* the history of the Christian Church. Behind this history lies the redemption once wrought by God, the breaking of the eternal into the order of time. Before it there remains the 'not yet', since dying and rising are still to come; for the paradox of this 'not yet' runs throughout the New Testament. Christ is in us, yet his coming is in the future. The Church is here, yet the heavenly city has still to descend. Christians have died and risen, yet they must still die and rise.

The puzzle of this 'not yet' speaks of the inexhaustible and unimaginable character of God's purpose: He has redeemed us, but it is not yet manifest what we shall be. He has given Himself to us, but He has still more to give. This 'not yet' throws further light also on the meaning of the Church. It exists in faith and hope, in a hidden life in Christ, by a power that can never be known in terms of the world's ideas of progress. For it is the place where human personality is lost, yet found and enriched, and where all humanity shall be made one by the death and resurrection of Christ. It is in terms of that death and resurrection that the Church's history must be interpreted, and in its light the doctrines concerning the Church must be studied and understood.

(GC 41–2)

Transfiguration and suffering

Transfiguration is indeed a central theme of Christianity, the transforming of sufferings and circumstances, of men and women with the vision of Christ before them and the Holy Spirit within them. The language of vision and of transformation is found in the Pauline, Johannine and Petrine writings in the New Testament, and this language tells of Christian experience, which recurs throughout the centuries. The transfiguration of suffering is well attested in Christian life. Sometimes a person suffers greatly, and the suffering continues and does not disappear; but through nearness to Christ there is seen a courage, an outgoing love and sympathy, a power of prayer, a Christ-likeness of a wonderful kind. It is the privilege of a Christian pastor to be meeting these experiences and to be learning from them more than he or she can ever teach.

Circumstances are transfigured. Something blocks your path, some fact of life or person or obstacle, which is utterly thwarting and frustrating. It seems impossible to remove it, or ignore it, or surmount it. But when it is seen in a larger context, and that context is Jesus crucified and risen, it is in a new orbit of relationships; and while it still remains, it remains differently. Such is the transforming of circumstances: not by their abolition, but by the lifting of them into the orbit of the crucified and risen Jesus.

We are bidden to journey on, however, from the mountain of transfiguration to Calvary, and there to learn of the darkness and the desolation, which are the cost of glory. But from Calvary and Easter there comes a Christian hope of immense range: the hope of the transformation not only of humanity but of the cosmos too. The bringing of human beings to glory will be the prelude to the beginning of a renewed creation (cf Romans 8.18–23). Is this hope mere fantasy? At its root there is belief in the divine sovereignty of sacrificial love, a sovereignty made credible only by transfigured lives.

(BS 66–7, 69–70)

Humiliations

Let the griefs, pains and humiliations that come to you help you. You will hate them, as they always hurt. But they help you to be near to Christ, and you will be learning not to fear them. There is the pain of disappointment when some cherished plan has gone wrong, and you are inclined to be bitter and resentful: but let it help you to think more about Christ's pain and disappointment; then you are nearer to him and it becomes very different. There is the pain sometimes of opposition, or of misunderstanding, or even abuse perhaps, coming to you from other people: it can feel terrible, but again it can bring you near to Christ. What if it is a part of the discipline of Christ, which we profess to believe in?

There is also the pain that comes from our own mistakes coming home to roost. But that too can bring us back to the truth of our own inadequacies, and the greatness of Christ's forgiveness, to the decrease of self and the increase of him. These things are not things that we do or seek: they just come. They will come to you too. When they come, let them help you to be a little nearer Christ crucified; that is how we find the deep joy of priesthood and Christian life. You will come to know how truly the psalmist says: 'Thou of very faithfulness hast caused me to be troubled' (Psalm 119.75). Be ready to accept humiliations: they can hurt terribly, but they help you to be humble, and to be a little nearer to our humble and crucified Lord. There is nothing to fear if you are near to our Lord and in his hands.

(CP 58–9 and 80)

The obedience of humility

We are servants, called upon to obey. Has not the idea of obedience as a Christian virtue rather slipped out of our contemporary religion? We think much about the responses of faith, love, sonship, and friendship in our relation to God, or to our Lord. But *obedience*? We tend to think that it smacks of legalism, and not to dwell upon it. But it has an ineradicable place in the New Testament: Jesus was 'obedient unto death' (Philippians 2.8), and 'he learned obedience through what he suffered' (Hebrews 5.8). The apostle Paul describes himself as Christ's slave. It follows that besides our responses of faith and love, there are also our responses of obeying God in doing this or that because we believe it to be His will.

Where the will of God is there is God's presence and His peace, and where that will is obeyed there is pattern and harmony: for in His will is our peace. Therefore when duties are irksome and we say, 'Do I really have to do this?' or 'I cannot stick this for much longer!' we must remember that if God wills it, God's presence will be in it, and if He wills it this becomes our motive. We are to do it not just in the way we ourselves might have planned, for the 'how' is in God's hands. We must simply be ready to do this for as long as God wills that we should.

(CP 62–4)

St Paul

The living Christ to whom Paul now belongs is still Christ the crucified one, and he advances in the 'fellowship of his sufferings, being conformed unto his death' (Philippians 3.10). He is ever near to the Cross in his own conflict with sin, and in his bearing of sorrow, pain and humiliation when they come to him. In his bearing of the pains of others his knowledge is increasing of what Calvary meant and means. But in all this Paul is discovering that the risen life of Jesus belongs to him, and with it great rejoicing. Awhile perhaps it may be that the Cross is more apparent to him, and the risen life may seem to be hidden. But one day the secret that is already present will be made manifest, and in the resurrection that awaits him after death he will see again the risen Christ in whose life, though hidden, he has already shared.

(RC 95)

* * * * * *

3

The Lord of Glory

EASTER

The celebration of Easter is the centre of Christian liturgy and faith. But what is the nature of our faith in Jesus, risen and alive? Michael Ramsey taught that faith is an encounter with the living God with life-transforming effects. It is the wellspring of hope as well as the deepening of love, as the stories of the empty tomb in the Gospels reveal.

The Resurrection and Ascension of Jesus are the foundation for Christian belief in eternal life and in God's promise to each person of an existence with him beyond death: for he has taken human nature into God. Eternal life is an act of pure grace, however: there is nothing inevitable about it, for it means the recreation of each human person, held within the eternal love of God, out of the nothingness of death.

Faith in the Resurrection and Ascension does not evade the impact of the Cross, as St Thomas discovered, for faith means allegiance to Christ as Lord in his sufferings as well as in his risen life: 'they will gaze on him whom they pierced'. The Resurrection completely transforms the meaning of miracle, in the New Testament and also in Christian life as it is seen in the lives of the saints.

Faith

Easter says to us: have faith! Faith does not mean that we first try to see things in a coherent and intelligible shape and then conclude that God is true. Faith is more like when the women came to the tomb while it was still very dark, and they wondered who could move away the stone as it was very heavy: and look – the stone is gone! When things are very dark, when human possibilities are exhausted, when we are at the end of our tether, God acts. Easter defines for all time the character of Christian faith: human weakness, divine power; I can't, God can; I am weak, God is strong; I am a sinner, God forgives. Does this sound fanciful? It was such a faith that enabled the apostles to carry the gospel into a hostile world. It was such a faith that sustained Christian men and women again and again throughout the centuries. It is like a coin that is always on one side – frailty, penitence, death, and on the other side – power, forgiveness and life. Let the words of St John sound in our hearts today: 'This is the victory that overcomes the world – our faith' (1 John 5.4–5).

(CTP 161)

The nature of resurrection

The Creed reminds us that we should think first about the resurrection of the dead before we think about the life of the world to come. It is upon the resurrection that Christian hope is based, and resurrection belongs both to our present state as Christians and to our final destiny.

First, then, resurrection is a mighty act of God. Remember that in the New Testament the language used is not of Jesus rising, but of Jesus being raised by God. Jesus did not 'achieve' resurrection. Rather did he make himself nothing, and when all was dark, when human possibilities were exhausted, God raised him by a mighty act of His power. This truth about resurrection colours our whole understanding of human movement towards its goal, whether in this world or in the next. It is not that men and women, even under God's grace, get gradually better and better and so attain to saintliness here, and to heaven hereafter. Rather does the grace of God work surprises, turning defeats into deliverances, 'calling things that are nothing as though they are' (1 Corinthians 1.28), and acting beyond any laws of progress or expectation. We have no rights here, and no rights hereafter. Unprofitable servants at every stage, we know that the Christian life always has two facets: on the one side there is God who raises the dead, and on the other there is faith alone.

The resurrection of Jesus is the prelude to the resurrection of those who believe in him, and who are united to him by faith and baptism. It is through the doctrine of resurrection in the New Testament, with its double strain of something already realized and something 'not yet' that we approach the doctrine of heaven. Here let the word 'glory' guide us in our approach. It is one of the marvellous words in the Bible, for it tells of heaven and the last things, but it also tells of human nature and the first things. God created men and women in His own image in order that they might come to a perfect relationship with their Creator. It is a relationship of intimacy, love, and knowledge intermingled with awe and dependence because, for all the intimacy, the line between Creator and creature always remains. It is this blending of intimacy and dread dependence, of men and women reflecting the character of the Creator yet humbly ascribing everything to Him, which the Bible describes by the words 'glory' and 'glorify'. This is the secret of human existence and of its role in the created world, as it is the clue to human destiny. Heaven is its final consummation, for heaven is when human beings find themselves in the glory of their Maker.

(CEA 33–4)

The last beatitude

After the resurrection, there comes the last beatitude: 'Blessed are those who have not seen me, and yet believe' (John 20.29). Every one of us is included in this promise of Jesus. What is this faith in the resurrection that we can possess? It is unlike the faith of St Thomas, for it is not based upon touch or sight. Yet it is like the faith of Thomas, and it must always be like the faith of Thomas, in two significant ways.

First, an Easter faith that is true is always a faith that includes the wounds of Calvary. When Christ was raised from the dead, it did not mean that the Cross was left behind. Far from it, for the risen Christ is always the Christ who was once crucified. Cross and resurrection go together: Christian imagery and art have portrayed this throughout the centuries; for art and imagery convey deep truth. We can never know the risen Jesus and never serve him unless we face the reality of the Cross. We must repent of the sins that wound him, as our sins always do. We must still find him in those who suffer, as we go and serve him in them. Never can the notes of Calvary fade from the Church's songs of Easter victory.

The second way in which our faith must resemble that of St Thomas is that it must be a faith which says with him, 'My Lord and my God!' What a declaration that was! What are we saying when as Christians we declare, 'My Lord and my God?' *My God* – here is the great doctrine that Jesus is divine, and that without idolatry we may worship him as God of God, Light of Light, true God of true God. *My Lord*: here is an act of moral allegiance and obedience, the commitment of ourselves to a master and to a way of life. If we own Jesus as Lord we are setting ourselves to a practical allegiance, which again and again will be asking, 'What am I to do about this or that problem?' and 'Is Jesus the Lord of my attitudes, my values, my prejudices, my human relationships?' *My Lord and my God* – the ethics and the doctrine go together.

(CTP 26–7)

Miracle and resurrection

The resurrection of Jesus is far more than an example of human immortality: it is a victory uniquely won, and won in order that humanity might be enabled to share in Christ's resurrection. It does for us what we cannot do for ourselves. It is a miracle because it is the unique redemptive and creative intervention of God, interrupting the normal workings of historical cause and effect and of human sinfulness, and ushering in a new stage in the cosmic process.

A miracle may be called an event wrought by God, which does not fit into the hitherto observable laws of nature. It resembles in one way the actions of human free will that disturb the course of nature, and it resembles in another way the work of God's grace in human lives. Miracles are credible to those who, recognising the reality of human free will to distort the divine design, do not deny to the living God His own freedom in His work as redeemer. If the resurrection breaks what appears to be the law of nature, it does so in order to vindicate another and higher aspect of divine law. As a miracle, it is the disclosure of an order of being that is new, unknown, and transcendental: it unveils a new level of glorified human life. But the miracle of resurrection could only be made known to those who responded to the new level of spiritual existence that it disclosed.

There was in the resurrection of Jesus gentleness and restraint akin to that which was seen in his ministry and in the Passion. The silence and fear of the women at the tomb convey their own message; they tell, more than words can, of the overwhelming reality of the resurrection. The resurrection is not as other events in history: it is in truth the coming into the world of the life of the world to come. Meanwhile, without the resurrection the historian has the problem of Jesus, no less than the problem of the Church, to explain.

(RC 35–6, 40 and 76–7)

THE HOLY SPIRIT

Pentecost marks the culmination of Eastertide, preceded by the Ascension of Jesus. The reality of the Holy Spirit is a theme running through all of Michael Ramsey's writings, and he devoted an important book to this doctrine, shortly after his retirement. For him, the Holy Spirit was a living presence within a person, drawing them into the orbit of divine love and relationship.

Two of these passages were sermons he preached as archbishop in Canterbury Cathedral on the feast of Pentecost. In one he outlines what it means to describe the impact of the Holy Spirit as fire; in the other he indicates the cost of praying 'Come, Holy Spirit, fill now the hearts of your faithful people: and kindle within us the fire of your love.'

According to St John's Gospel, the giving of the Holy Spirit flowed directly from the suffering and death of Jesus on the Cross. Just as new human life is born in the middle of pain and travail, so renewed human life is won at great cost to God himself through the self-giving of Jesus. The gift of the Spirit is the pearl of great price, the harbinger of God's kingdom in the lives of men and women. The sign that this is so is the complete transformation of human attitudes and values over time, even to the extent that the love of enemies becomes decisive evidence of being filled with the Spirit of Christ.

Encountering God in the Spirit

In the New Testament, the Holy Spirit is sometimes described as the Spirit of God and the Spirit of Jesus. Yet to say only that the Spirit is the impact of God or of Jesus is to do less than justice to Christian experience; for the Holy Spirit was felt to be one who from within the lives of Christians makes response to Jesus and to the Father. It is here that the doctrine of the triune God begins to emerge, not only as a mode of divine activity but also as a relationship within the life of God Himself. In knowing 'the grace of the Lord Jesus Christ and the love of God and the fellowship of the Holy Spirit' (2 Corinthians 13.14), and in having access through Jesus 'in one Spirit to the Father' (Ephesians 2.18), Christians were encountering not only their own relationship to God, but also the relationship of God to God. When the Spirit cries within us '*Abba* – Father' and prompts us to say, 'Jesus is Lord', there is God within responding to God beyond. St John's gospel takes the further step of suggesting that the divine relationship, known in the historic mission of Jesus and its sequel, reflects the being of God in eternity. Here the key is found in St John's concept of glory. The glory of self-giving love in the Passion, and in the mission of the Holy Spirit, the Paraclete, is one with the glory of God before the world began.

(HS 119–20)

The fire of Pentecost

The power of the Holy Spirit is mighty, but intimate and personal too. The effects of God's actions are seen in human behaviour: the actions themselves, in minds, hearts and consciences are describable in symbol alone. On the day of Pentecost (Acts 2) a gale of wind was felt and tongues like fire were seen; but in the world of men and women throughout the centuries, what do wind and fire denote? What does *fire* tell us about the Holy Spirit?

The fire of the Holy Spirit enables you to see, and to see like a Christian, perceiving things as they really are in the eyes or mind of Jesus, perceiving people as they really are with the light of Jesus upon them; also perceiving meaning and purpose instead of shapeless confusion, perceiving what a Christian ought to be and to do. The Holy Spirit keeps the light of Jesus glowing within us: that is how we may see as Christians should see. Fire also gives warmth; so the warmth of the love of God within you can warm your heart to love Him in response. It means that the very love of God creates in us a love which is both our own and also His within us.

Light, warmth, and burning too: the Holy Spirit will burn us. If we are to have vision and warmth of love, we must be exposed to the pain of burning. All that is fearful, unloving, selfish, hard, must be burnt out of our existence, burnt to destruction, and to ashes. While we think we have some Christian insight and knowledge, and while we may think we have some warmth of love, there are within us impenetrable barriers of selfishness, pride and prejudice, which resist the grace of God and thwart the light and warmth of His Spirit. The Holy Spirit will burn his way through to the core of our being in the ever-painful process of disclosure and penitence, and of divine forgiveness. Only by such burning can our hearts be exposed fully to his warmth, and our minds be exposed fully to his light. There is no seeing and no warming without burning.

The Holy Spirit brings us sight, warmth and burning, and he does so as the Spirit of Jesus. The seeing becomes seeing through the eyes of

Jesus, seeing things and people less through our own spectacles of prejudice and more as Jesus sees them. The warming means the actual love that is in Jesus, crucified and risen, becoming our own. The burning is with the painful exposure that comes to those who find themselves in the presence of Jesus. It is the Spirit of Jesus who accomplishes the work of Jesus in us. Notice, however, that in all that he does, the Spirit is the Spirit of *koinonia* – fellowship. The first disciples only came to know the Holy Spirit as the one in whom they all shared, who created this fellowship among them. It is as he draws us into fellowship with one another, that the seeing, the warming and the burning of the Holy Spirit become our own. May he enable us together to see, to love and to burn.

(CTP 79–81)

Life in the Spirit

Christians are justified by faith, they have peace with God, they rejoice in hope, and they rejoice even in suffering, because the Holy Spirit has poured the love of God into their hearts. What is this love of God? It is the love made known in the death of Christ for the sake of the ungodly, and in that death the love of God Himself was commended to men and women. The event of the death of Christ not only enables the Christian life, it provides its continuing motive and interpretation: 'It is folly to attempt finding a shorter way to God, than that of closest contact with His own condescension in Jesus' (Von Hugel). But it is a costly thing to invoke the Spirit, for the glory of Calvary was the cost of the Spirit's mission, and it is also the cost of the Spirit's renewal. It is in the shadow of the Cross that, in any age of history, Christians pray: 'Come, Holy Spirit.'

(HS 131)

The cost of Pentecost

Today I would speak to you about the *cost* of the coming of the Holy Spirit. If we realize what the cost of the gift was and is to our Lord, we may better understand what it costs us to make his gift our own, and to let it have its true effect within ourselves.

Jesus is recorded as saying in his final discourse at the Last Supper: 'I will pray the Father, and He will give you another Comforter' (John 14.16). This gift, like other gifts of God, is an answer to prayer, in this case the prayer of Jesus. But what sort of prayer was it? The prayer of our Lord, which enabled the Holy Spirit to come to the apostles, and also to come to us, was not just the speaking of a few words to the Father. No, it was the total offering of himself to the Father's will and glory, the surrender of himself: that is the heart of the prayer of Jesus. So before the end of St John's account of the Last Supper there come the words of the 'high-priestly prayer' as we call it (John 17), when Jesus dedicates himself to his coming death. In the garden of Gethsemane and on Calvary there is the climax of the prayer and self-giving of Jesus, as he moves right into the darkness of evil and human tragedy. Such was the prayer of Jesus, the prayer of his self-sacrifice. From this prayer, from this self-sacrifice, there flows the gift of the Holy Spirit to the disciples.

Only from our Lord's crucifixion, does the power of the Holy Spirit, cleansing and life giving, flow to us (John 7.37–9 and 19.34). When Jesus comes to his disciples on Easter evening, as St John's gospel again records (John 20), he greets them and shows them the wounds in his hands and his side. It is immediately after showing them the wounds that he breathes on them and says: 'Receive the Holy Spirit.' It is from our Lord's complete sacrifice, from Calvary and Easter, that the Holy Spirit is given. The Cross and the Holy Spirit go together, for the Holy Spirit is the Spirit of Jesus, the Spirit of Calvary and Easter, the Spirit of self-sacrifice, the Spirit of losing life to find it. That is power like wind and fire and water. We recall that Jesus said that the Holy Spirit would glorify him; and now the Spirit brings to us the glory of Jesus, the self-giving love in which he lived and died and rose again.

Today we long to see spiritual renewal and revival. We hope for it, we pray for it, we work for it. But remember what it costs, to make such a prayer and to receive such a gift. For our prayer is a little sharing in the prayer of Jesus, and we must ask ourselves what this costs us, both in the giving and in the receiving.

(*CTP* 120–2)

The indwelling of love

Here indeed is a picture of what Christians were experiencing (Romans 5.1–8): a new access to God, forgiveness, inner peace, joy even in the face of suffering, the facing of a stormy world with hope. How has this come about? It has come about by the shedding of God's

The Lord of Glory

love into their hearts when the Holy Spirit was given to them. This means the love shown in the death of Jesus for the ungodly – the love of enemies. For it is by this historical reference that the experience is defined and understood. The history enshrined in the gospel did not only initiate this experience, it perpetually defines its character and inspires its renewal.

(JP 57)

TRANSFIGURATION

The Transfiguration occupied a central position in Michael Ramsey's theology and spirituality. If his first book was the foundation, then The Glory of God and the Transfiguration of Christ *was the framework for his thinking and writing for the rest of his life. For him, the key word was 'Glory', a word he pronounced in a very distinctive and memorable way, full of reverence and joy. The opening passage gives a glimpse of how he interpreted his own first encounter with its mystery while training to become a priest at Cuddesdon, near Oxford.*

The main delineaments of this, his greatest book comprise the rest of this section. It is a remarkable study of biblical language and its metamorphosis in response to the experience of God revealed ultimately in the face of Jesus Christ. It represents the amalgam of the influence of Cambridge biblical theology, notably that of Hoskyns, with Michael Ramsey's own experience of and sympathy towards Orthodox Christianity. It was composed during the Second Word War and is in part a spiritual response to that tragedy and to the challenges facing the Church as a result.

The section entitled 'Glory and the Christian Faith' is the central chapter of the book and may well have been written separately. It is a powerful epitome of his vision and thought. The last section, 'The Gospel of the Transfiguration', is the conclusion to the book and remains of abiding worth.

Climbing the holy mountain

It was here at Cuddesdon that the ideal of what it means to be a priest came vividly home to us. It was here that we faced the truth about ourselves before the Cross of Christ, and with the painful shattering of our pride discovered that we have no sufficiency of ourselves to think anything of ourselves. With memories solemn and searching there mingle memories light and ludicrous, since, for all the seriousness of the purpose which brought us here, we were human beings with our absurdities and our sense of the absurd. Learning to laugh at ourselves, we did not lack other things to laugh about. How should we, if the Christian life is indeed the knowledge of Him who is the author of laughter as well as tears?

Is it fanciful to see in what Cuddesdon meant a re-enactment of the story of the Transfiguration? We were withdrawn, faced with what Newman calls the 'two luminous realities – the soul and its Creator'. We were apart too as men climbing a mountain. The discipline was not easy for all of us: learning to pray is difficult; learning theology is difficult. But we were apart and climbing, because we believed that our Lord was so leading us. And he was leading us in order that he might give us, here on this sacred hill, a glimpse of his glory. Our study of the scriptures was done to the end that our Lord might show himself to us. In contrition, love and gratitude we were glad that we were here, and the conviction of the presence of God became very real to us. It was brought home to us here that our God is not only to be adored: He is a righteous God, to be heard and obeyed. We heard His voice, and so we came down from the mountain.

So now whatever new things we learn and do, let none of them blind us to our recurring need of withdrawal to the holy mountain. Yet I do not see this withdrawal emphasised in the life of our Church, or in the counsels of our Church in its search for divine wisdom under the guidance of the Holy Spirit: rather does it seem all too widely forgotten and imperilled. Today, however, we must ask for forgiveness, and for renewal in the climbing of the holy mount.

When our Lord went up to be transfigured, he carried with him every conflict, every burden, both of the days behind and the days ahead, to be transfigured with him. So when we go apart to be with Jesus in his glory, it is so that our frustrations, our pains, and our cares may be carried into that supernatural context which makes all the difference to them. These frustrations are not forgotten; they are not abolished; they can still be painful. But they become transfigured in the presence of Jesus, our crucified and glorious Lord. And when we have carried our frustrations up to our Lord in his glory, we find in the days which follow that he so generously brings his glory right down into the midst of our frustrations, saying: 'My peace I give unto you.'

With grateful hearts we shall soon be taking leave of this place, which means more to us than words can tell. But wherever we may be, we are still allowed to go apart by ourselves and to climb to where we

The Lord of Glory

may see the glory of Jesus. And if we are really trying to do this, he is at hand to change us by his Spirit into the same image from glory to glory.

(CEA 156–60)

'Glory'

'Can we rescue a word, and discover a universe? Can we study a language, and awake to the truth? Can we bury ourselves in a lexicon, and arise in the presence of God?'(Hoskyns). The word 'glory' is often on the lips of Christians, but they frequently have only a vague idea as to its meaning. Derived from the Bible, this word expresses in a remarkable way the unity of the doctrines of the Creation, the Incarnation, the Cross, the Holy Spirit, the Church and the world to come. In the Bible, the word 'glory', in Hebrew and later in Greek, is used to express a concept of the glory of God that is rich and complex in its final development in a way that is no less true of its early history.

(GG 5, 6, 10)

The glory of Sinai

The Priestly writer in Exodus has his own conception of the divine glory: the cloud appears at Sinai. It is seen in the camp of Israel only when the tabernacle has been completed, and it dwells continually in the tabernacle. By day it is seen as a cloud, by night as a fiery pillar. If it should be seen to be fiery by day, there unmistakably is the *kabod* – the glory. The cloud is not itself the glory, however, nor is it part of a set of storm phenomena, which together manifest the glory. Rather it is a covering, which conceals the glory that shines through from within it. It was at Sinai that this appearance first took place.

(GG 17)

The glory of God in the prophets

Perhaps Isaiah of Jerusalem had a decisive influence on the Old Testament understanding of God's self-revelation expressed in the Hebrew word for glory – *kabod,* as a result of the vision, which he saw in the Temple (Isaiah 6.1–4). The glory of the Lord is linked with His holiness; and if His holiness means a remoteness from all that is unrighteous, His glory is that union of sovereignty and righteousness, which is the essence of the divine character. Isaiah's words have significance for the revelation of God's glory that reaches far beyond the Old Testament, however, into the worship of the Christian Church. For in the liturgy of the Church the adoration of the divine glory in the words of the song of the Seraphim, 'Holy, Holy, Holy', immediately precedes the Eucharistic action, in which the glory of the Cross of Christ is set forth.

The post-exilic writer of the last part of Isaiah, however, pictures Jerusalem as the scene of the shining forth of the glory of the Lord to the nations (Isaiah 60.1–3). Here the idea of radiance has the greatest prominence. Indeed, in the glory of the Lord, radiance, power and righteous character are inextricably blended; and the word tells of a theology in which the attributes of God in Himself are inseparable from His attractiveness and saving activity in the world. Israel's knowledge of God's glory has its corollary, however, in Israel's obligation to reflect God's character in care for the poor and the naked (Isaiah 58.7–8).

(GG 13–14)

The glory of the God of Israel

There is unity in diversity in the doctrine of the glory of God in Israel. There is unity because from very early times the conception of the *kabod* or glory was linked with Israel's faith in a righteous and sovereign God. There is diversity also because the faith of Israel did not drop down in a neat pattern from heaven, but was wrought in the ups and downs of a turbulent history. In fact nowhere are the tensions of biblical theology greater than in the doctrine of the divine glory. But in these tensions lies hidden the paradox of the theology of the Old Testament: 'Am I a God at hand, says the Lord, and not a God afar off?' (Jeremiah 23.23). Always in tension, these contrasted aspects of the divine glory find their true unity when the Word, by whom all things were made, became flesh and dwelt among us: for the glory of Bethlehem and Calvary is the glory of the eternal God.

(GG 21–2)

Glory in the Septuagint

The writers of the Septuagint, the Greek version of the Old Testament written in Alexandria, were faced with the need for a Greek word to translate the Hebrew *kabod:* they used the word *doxa.* By so doing they gave it a sense totally different from its original meaning in Greek literature. No word in the Bible has a more fascinating history. That a word, which originally meant human opinion or reputation, should come to express the greatest theological ideas both of the Old and of the New Testaments is one of the most striking instances of the impact of theology upon language. Flexible in its ability to express every aspect of the divine glory – *kabod,* and every Hebrew word akin to it, the word *doxa* also served to translate the Aramaic word *Shekinah,* meaning God's indwelling among His people. So it was that these two separate conceptions came to be fused together by Greek-speaking Jews: thus the Septuagint sets the imagery of glory, tabernacle and the dwelling of the Lord in a composite pattern. This pattern was familiar to later Greek-speaking Jews at the time of the apostles, and it lay to hand for the Christian Church to build upon.

(GG 23–6)

Glory in the New Testament

In every aspect of divine glory expressed in the New Testament, the person of Jesus Christ becomes the dominant fact. In so far as *doxa* means the power and character of God, the key to that power and character is found in what God has done in the events of the gospel. In so far as *doxa* is the divine splendour, Jesus Christ is that splendour. In so far as a state of light and radiance awaits the Christian as his or her final destiny, that light and radiance draw their meaning from the presence and person of Christ. Hence new possibilities of language emerge: for such is the place of Jesus Christ in relation to the divine glory, that it is possible to speak of 'the glory of Christ', and by those words to mean no less than the glory of God Himself.

It follows that the word *doxa* reflects and expresses the pattern of apostolic faith. This faith has as its groundwork the glory of God in creation, in nature and in the history of Israel; it has as its centre the glory of God in the birth, life, death and exaltation of Jesus; and as its goal the participation of humanity and of all creation in the eschatological glory of the Messiah. Thus creation, redemption and eschatology form a single pattern; and to separate them is to render each of them unintelligible, and to distort the theology of the apostolic age.

(GG 27–8)

The glory of the Son of Man

The picture of the Son of Man in glory is no novelty (cf Daniel 7 and Psalm 8). Yet the novel element in our Lord's use of it is unmistakeable: 'the Son of Man must suffer'. For it is by a road of suffering that Jesus must enter into the glory, which the Father has in store for him as Messiah, King and Judge. He is the one through whose heavenly glory, and preceding suffering, the Kingdom of God comes. In the latter part of St Mark's gospel the sayings of Jesus disclose this twofold picture: the Son of Man suffering, and the Son of Man in glory. Side by side with this theme is the challenge to the disciples: if they will suffer, they too will share in the glory (Mark 10.32–45).

Later in the New Testament, the eschatological use of the word 'glory' is renewed in the teaching of the apostolic Church; but meanwhile the event of the resurrection has wrought a decisive change. Jesus has been exalted into the radiant light of heavenly glory; and in the conviction of his lordship, as raised from the dead and now in heaven, the apostles await with certainty his coming to receive his followers into glory with him. Thus the imagery of glory expresses realities that reach beyond itself: yet at the centre of these realities is Jesus Christ himself.

Hence the apostolic writers are not concerned to elaborate their description of the heavenly glory, but to emphasize that Jesus Christ himself is its centre. It was his resurrection that begat their faith, and it his appearing that awaits them. Epiphany, apocalypse, manifestation – the appearing of the divine light, the disclosure of the divine secret, the coming before men's eyes of Christ – these are the things which Christians await, with the conviction that what the future will bring is the consummation of a past event and also a present possession. Nor is it otherwise with the glory: as they worship Jesus the Lord who has been exalted into it, and as they look for the day when it is made visible, they come to realize that is has been disclosed to them in him, and is already near to them.

(GG 30–5)

Glory in the teaching of St Paul

To St Paul the glory of God is the character and power of God, known in creation, in providence and in history (Romans 1). There is indeed in the thought and language of St Paul a fusion between a certain conception of light and radiance and a view of glory as the power and character of God in redemption through Christ. Neither aspect of St Paul's thought can probably be excluded from the pregnant phrase: 'the glory of God in the face of Jesus Christ': here we seem to be at the heart of St Paul's doctrine (2 Corinthians 4.3–6).

Because God is 'the God of our Lord Jesus Christ, the Father of glory', St Paul knows that he lives in a world where the decisive act of salvation has already been wrought, where suffering itself is being transfigured, where 'neither death nor life, nor angels, nor principalities, nor things present, nor things to come, nor height, nor depth, nor any other creature shall be able to separate us from the love of God which is in Christ Jesus our Lord' (Romans 8.38–9). Even as a prisoner, with the prospect of death before him, he is sure that the sovereign power of God is working out the purpose of His will, with the praise of His glory as the goal.

(*GG* 47–50)

Vision and transformation in St Paul

The Christians have before them a mirror, Christ, in whom the glory of God is reflected. Looking at this mirror they see the glory not in the far distant future, but already among them. So St Paul claims that to see the glory is a present possibility, but the perfect vision will be only when our transformation is complete (1 Corinthians 13.12). For as we see the mirrored glory we are changed, and the sovereignty of the Spirit makes this changing possible. What sort of changing is this? It is into the likeness of Christ that we are being changed, a transformation of the essential person (Romans 12.2). This change is from glory into glory. There is no despair, for glory is a present possession: but there is no complete contentment, for a far greater glory is the final goal.

The glorification of Christians is no pious mysticism, however. It is a matter of conflict and struggle in human flesh and blood: from first to last it is realized by faith. It includes the imitation of Christ in outward actions (1 Corinthians 11.1), and the formation of Christ in the inward person (Galatians 4.19). It involves the continual rejection of the standards and values of this present age, in order that the will of God may be discerned (Romans 12.2).

This often means a life such as the present age may not deem to be glorious in the least. St Paul tells us what this life in glory meant for the apostles: they were 'pressed on every side, yet not crushed, perplexed yet not to despair, persecuted yet not forsaken, smitten down yet not destroyed, always bearing about in the body the dying of Jesus so that the life of Jesus may be manifested in our mortal flesh' (2 Corinthians 4.8–10). But amidst these conflicts they discovered the true relation between 'a light affliction' and 'an eternal weight of glory' (2 Corinthians 4.16–18). The glory is thus hidden from the world, and, in a measure, hidden from Christians who are already beginning to participate in it. But at the appearing of Christ it will be unveiled. They have made Christ's life their own: but it is a hidden life in God.

(*GG* 53–5)

The ethos of the Fourth Gospel

The fourth evangelist records the story of the ministry, passion and resurrection of Jesus with the conviction that the glory of God was manifested throughout these events. Hidden from those who did not believe, it became apparent to those within the circle of faith. The Transfiguration is omitted, for the glory belongs not to any isolated episodes but to the story as a whole; and it will be suggested that in several ways the tradition of the Transfiguration has left its mark upon the thought and language of the writer: for this gospel is indeed the gospel of glory.

The prologue of the gospel (John 1.1–18) declares that the manifestation of the glory of the Son of God is the climax of the activity of the Word, who was in the beginning with God, who created all that exists, and who gave life to the whole creation, and light to the human race. The event cannot be torn from its cosmic context. The glory, which the disciples saw in Galilee, Jerusalem and Calvary, is the glory of him who created the heavens and the earth, and who made himself known in the redemption of Israel. All that is learnt of the glory of God from the Pentateuch, and the psalmists, prophets, wise men and rabbis, and from the light that lightens every human person, is both fulfilled and outshone in the glory of the Word-made-flesh.

Neither in history nor in eternity has Christ a glory that is of himself alone, however, for in revealing his own glory he reveals the glory of the Father. 'Grace and truth' summarize the ministry of our Lord as the fourth gospel describes it. Grace is apparent in the deeds that give life and light to those who believe; truth is apparent in the words by which Christ makes known what he has heard from the Father. Indeed, grace and truth are present in deeds and words alike. So complete is this revelation of God that the language of vision becomes in a sense admissible, for even now men and women can 'see' God. But this is not the fullest vision: there is a vision yet to come when the Son has been glorified with the glory that he had with the Father before the world began, and the disciples are led to the vision of this glory (John 17.5 and 24; cf 1 John 3.2): for the vision of God is the transfiguration of a person.

(GG 57–8 and 61–2)

The glory of Christ's self-giving love

In everything Jesus depends upon the Father. His complete self-giving to the Father is interwoven with the Father's giving of all things into his hands (John 3.34–5; 5.30; 6.57). It is in this mutual self-giving of the Father and the Son, expressed in the dependence and submission of the Son throughout his earthly mission, that the deepest meaning of the glory is found. Jesus realizes his own glory only as he makes himself as nothing in the quest of the glory of the Father. The contrast is therefore plain between glory in the pagan sense and glory as Jesus reveals it. People seek the glory of personal distinction through the praise and esteem of others: Jesus reveals the glory of self-giving love, which is the glory of the Father and of the Son (John 5.44; 7.18; 8.54). Such is the glory wherein the Father glorifies the Son and the Son glorifies the Father, alike in eternity and in history. Here we touch the heart of the Johannine theology. The glory seen in the works of Jesus is a glory whose secret the Passion ultimately discloses; and it is no accident that the ministry of the signs in this gospel leads on to the event of the Passion itself (John 8.28; 10.17–18). The paradox that the Passion and the glory are one will be learnt only in the practical obedience of discipleship, however. For the Servant, with no beauty that men should desire him (Isaiah 53.2) brings deliverance from sin. To the world, judgement, but to those who believe, glory: this is the paradox of Calvary.

(GG 65–8)

The feet-washing

Jesus is performing the action of a slave (John 13.1–5; cf Philippians 2.5–11), and he does this in the full consciousness that the Father has entrusted all things to him, and that he is returning to the Father from whom he came. By his servile act he is glorifying the Father, and the feet-washing, so far from being a veiling or an abandoning of glory, is a manifestation to the disciples of the nature of the glory of the eternal God. In utter contrast to the glory that people 'receive from one another' (John 5.44), the glory 'that comes from the only God' is mirrored in the figure of Jesus girded with a towel and pouring water into a basin. Humility is indeed the lesson, and the whole lesson of the event. It is the humility of the Son of God who knew that 'his hour had come'; and his action foreshadows the humility of the Passion: for the Passion as the supreme act of humility will be no less the supreme means of cleansing humanity. The feet-washing therefore prefigures it, both in humility and in cleansing: it is an act of truth and grace. For from the sovereignty of Christ there flows the sovereignty of the Church that represents him; but this sovereignty is grounded in the Lord's humility (John 13. 13–4, and 20.22). Although he will leave them in the midst of the world, he leaves them a bond: the new commandment to love one another even as he has loved them. He will show them that the command to love one another as Christ has loved them is inseparable from the entering into them of Christ's own love, the love of the Father and the Son revealed in the Passion (John 17.26).

(GG 69–70 and 72)

The gift of the Holy Spirit

The good things, which Jesus is predicting in his final discourse in this gospel, may be summed up as the glorifying of Christ by the Holy Spirit. This glorifying includes all that the Holy Spirit will do (John 14.17–18 and 26; 15.26–7; 16.8–11 and 13). In all this he will glorify Christ. He cannot add to Christ's unsearchable riches, but he will make them known and understood and in the end all-powerful in human history, as the splendour of Christ is more and more reflected in the lives of men and women. As the work of the Son in glorifying the Father has sprung from his utter submission to the Father, and from his constant receiving from the Father of all that the Father wills to give him, so also the work of the Spirit in glorifying the Son will spring from the Spirit's utter dependence upon the Father and the Son. The Son utters no message of his own, but only what he receives from the Father. Likewise the Spirit utters no message of his own, but what he too receives. While the things that the Spirit receives are from the Son, they are from the Son only because they are also from the Father (John 15.15; 16.13).

A Trinitarian doctrine of God is here inescapable. It is inescapable as touching the activity of God in history, for the glorifying of the Father by Jesus is perfected only in the glorifying of Jesus by the Spirit. It is inescapable as touching the being of God in Himself, for the sharing of the Son in all that the Father has is paralleled by the sharing of the Spirit in all that the Son has. The revelation of the glory of God to the disciples involves their coming to perceive that the Spirit is all that the Son is – namely God indeed.

(GG 74–5)

The suffering and self-consecration of Jesus

As the great discourse proceeds a tension is increasingly felt between the turbulence of the world, wherein Jesus is about to face death and the disciples persecution, and the peace, which Jesus possesses in himself and bids his apostles to share. This contrast stands out more plainly still in the prayer of Jesus in John 17. Jesus speaks to the Father as the Father's eternal Son, and yet he speaks from the midst of a historical crisis of human flesh and blood. The prayer thus belongs both to the timeless converse of the Father and the Son, and to the conflict within time, wherein the Son embraces the Father's will that he must die for the salvation of humanity. Yet the reader is conscious of no unreality or discontinuity in the words and the thought, for it is in the drama of time and history that the eternal glory is made known. If the tension between these two perspectives – the eternal and the temporal – makes the understanding of particular sentences difficult, it does not mar the unity of the prayer as a whole.

This prayer has sometimes been called the 'high priestly prayer', though this title does not seem to be earlier than the sixteenth century. If this title is used it must be remembered that nowhere in this prayer is there any explicit reference to the burden of human sin, or to the atmosphere of expiation connected with the day of atonement. Its tone is not that of *Kyrie eleison*: it is rather a prayer for victory uttered in the consciousness that the victory is already won. A better name for it, drawn from one of its own phrases, is 'the prayer of consecration'. Jesus consecrates himself on behalf of his disciples. It is unto death that he consecrates himself, and it is implicit in St John's teaching about sacrifice that Christ's death is for the expiation of sin. The prayer, however, dwells not upon the process of expiation, but upon the victory over the world that results from it. The true doctrine of atonement is the doctrine of *Christus Victor*: but it includes (what some of its exponents forget) expiation as the price and means of that victory.

(GG 75–6)

The glory of the Son's mission

Jesus prays in John 17 firstly that in the Passion that is now imminent the Father may give glory to the Son and enable the Son to give glory to the Father. This he will do by bringing the disciples eternal life in the knowledge of God. The godward act of glorifying the Father includes also the manward act of revealing him to men and women. As yet this revelation is only to a little company: but this little fragment of the human race represents a vaster potentiality, for 'all flesh' lies within the sphere of the authority that the Father has given him.

Secondly, Jesus, who has glorified the Father throughout his entire mission on earth, asks to be given a glory beyond the glory in the Passion, a glory that is no less than the eternal glory of God Himself. Nowhere does St John tell us that this glory was veiled or laid aside during the Son's incarnate life; but the Son took upon himself a truly human life in order to win by the road of human life and death a glory that was always his own. Now he asks that the human nature, in which he prays, may be exalted into union with God. Once more the godward act of glorifying includes the manward mission. For Jesus has glorified the Father by making the Father's name known to the apostles, and by leading them to learn that his mission was from the Father.

(GG 77)

'Sanctify them in the truth'

The connection between sanctification and truth is of the utmost consequence. The disciples in their mission in the world are required to be 'not of this world' in two ways. They are to be consecrated to God in opposition to the world's self-pleasing, and they are to represent the truth of God in opposition to the world's errors. The two requirements are inseparable, even as grace and truth are inseparable in the mission of Christ. Therefore Jesus prays 'sanctify them in the truth'

The Lord of Glory

(John 17.17). For there is no holiness apart from the theology that he reveals, and there is no imparting of that theology except by consecrated lives.

To this end Jesus sanctifies himself. 'It means that the Son of God consecrates his blameless life as an effective sacrifice on behalf of the disciples in order that they might be set forth in the world as the righteousness of God, dedicated to the service of God, even unto death for His glory. The consecration of the disciples therefore depends upon the consecration of the Son of God. But the similarity rests upon a great dissimilarity: they are consecrated, but he consecrated himself and his consecration must precede theirs' (Hoskyns). Amidst the stubborn and unbelieving world there is placed the Church of God. Its members know whence Jesus came; and he has declared to them the protection of the Father's name and will declare it to them again, that they may be overshadowed by the love with which the Father loves him.

(GG 78–90)

The glory of the Passion

The prayer in John 17 has ended: the Passion begins. Throughout the narrative of the Passion, St John shows that the prayer is being answered and that the Son is being glorified. In the garden the soldiers who came to arrest Jesus fall to the ground, awestruck at his majesty. In the judgement hall it is Jesus who is the judge and Pilate his craven prisoner. Before the people Jesus is shown forth as king, dressed in purple and with the crown of thorns. Master of his destiny, Jesus carries his own cross to Calvary, for he has the power to lay down his life and the power to take it again. On Calvary he reigns, ordering the future for his mother and disciples, and crying out 'it is accomplished', fulfilling the Scriptures and freely surrendering his spirit to the Father. So the hour came that the Son of man should be glorified, and the corn of wheat fell into the earth and died (John 12.23–4).

For Calvary is no disaster that needs the resurrection to reverse it, but a victory so complete that the resurrection follows quickly to seal it. St John thinks of the glorifying of Jesus as completed on Easter day. The glorifying completed, the Spirit can now be given (cf John 7.39). Coming to the apostles on the evening of that day, Jesus breathes on them and says: 'Receive the Holy Spirit.' By the breath of a new creation the Church is brought to birth and sent upon its mission: 'as the Father has sent me, even so I send you' (John 20.19–23). The mission of the Church makes the judgement and the glory of God known to human beings, and the world can take its choice.

(GG 81)

Glory and the Christian Faith

The Biblical concept of the glory of God can be traced in every part of the Old and New Testaments. The glory – *kabod* – of the Lord includes ideas of power, character, radiance and physical accessibility, which can be neither wholly disentangled nor set in a simple historical sequence of development. The Greek word in the Septuagint for glory – *doxa* – finds a new meaning to express the Biblical concept in its variety and unity, and to provide a pattern upon which the New Testament writers could work. Then came the revelation of the glory of God in the face of Jesus Christ. Still the ideas of power, character, radiance and physical accessibility are included, for if the physical suggestions of glory are now made utterly subordinate to its ethical and transcendental aspects, they never wholly disappear. To the end the human quest remains what it was in the days of Moses – the *seeing* of God. The Christian does not despise the ancient longing: 'Show me, I pray, your glory.'

Tracing the doctrine of the glory discloses the pattern of the faith of the Bible. The God of the Bible is manifested in His created works, and yet He transcends them all. He rules in history with the sovereignty of His righteous purpose: He showed His glory in delivering Israel to be His own people, and although His glory cannot be circumscribed in time or place He set it in the midst of them as His presence within the tabernacle. But again and again he judged them for ascribing glory not to Him but to themselves. In the fullness of time, God manifested His glory decisively in the birth, life, death and resurrection of His only Son. Once more he redeemed a people and set the glory of His presence in their midst, a glory that faith alone can discern. But again and again He has judged the Church for ascribing glory not to Him but to itself.

Meanwhile our present discerning of the glory of God by faith is not worthy to be compared to the vision of glory when we shall see Him as He is. In this glory not only redeemed humanity but all creation will share, even though it now groans in bondage and awaits its deliverance into the liberty of God's children (Romans 8.22–3). In His glory righteousness and power are inseparably one, in radiance bright so that men and women may receive real knowledge of the truth, yet so bright that the fullness of truth remains beyond their understanding. Thus the concept of glory illuminates every part of the Christian faith.

(GG 82–3)

God

The glory of God has been disclosed in His created works (Psalm 19.1; Romans 1.20). But although God is known in His creation, He transcends it utterly. Without Him it cannot be, but without it His being is perfect. It is not that the existence of creatures is necessary to His glory, but that His creating them is the utterance or the overflowing of a glory that eternally lacks nothing. The Biblical doctrine condemns the recurring human sin whereby men and women worship the creature in place of the Creator. It also denies two further errors: the neglect of the *testimonia gloriae* in nature, humanity and history, and the error of treating God and the created world as co-partners that are mutually necessary to each other. To glorify God is to rejoice in His works, and to own their absolute dependence upon their Creator.

It is perhaps surprising that the word 'glory' does not occur in the synoptic record of the teaching of Jesus about God. But in all that he taught about the providence, graciousness, fatherhood and judgement of God, Jesus was implicitly speaking of the divine glory. Above all, he brought into particular prominence the fatherhood of God: 'Father' became not just one title among many, but *the* title by which God is to be named. In the Lord's Prayer the 'name', the 'kingdom' and the 'will' of the Father comprise the Father's glory. Jesus reveals the Father not by expounding a doctrine of the universal fatherhood of God, but by completing his own mission as God's Son, by teaching men and women that God is *his* Father, and by leading them to learn of *his* sonship. Only when the mission of the Son has reached its climax in the Passion, and when the Spirit of the Son has been sent into their hearts, crying '*Abba* – Father' (Galatians 4.6), can they come to know the Father's glory.

It is in the revelation of the Son and the gift of the Spirit that the Father's glory is fully disclosed. It is disclosed in an inseparable union with the glory of the one God, Father, Son and Holy Spirit. The obedience of Jesus to the Father in his life and death, and the vindication of Jesus by the Father in the resurrection, are the disclosure within time of the glory of self-giving love, which belongs to God from all eternity. The worship finally evoked by the events of the gospel is neither a cult of Jesus, nor a reformed prophetic Judaism with God's fatherhood in a new prominence, but rather the adoration of the triune God.

(GG 83–4)

Incarnation

'The Word became flesh and dwelt among us; and we saw his glory' (John 1.14). But not all who saw Jesus saw the glory, but only those with faith to discern it. From the rest it was hidden, for if the rulers of the world had known it, 'they would not have crucified the Lord of glory' (1 Corinthians 2.8).

It was in humiliation that the divine glory was revealed on earth. There was the humiliation whereby the eternal Word took upon himself the particularity of historical existence, with all the limitations which that particularity involved. There was the humiliation involved in the 'messianic secret', which the synoptic gospel writers describe. There was the final humiliation whereby his mission was completed only by suffering and death. But if this threefold humiliation was, viewed from one angle, a concealment of glory, it was, viewed from another angle, only an aspect of that glory. That the Son of God could thus make his own the frustrations of human life and death was a striking manifestation of the glory of self-giving love. The mission of the Lord was at once the descent of someone who trod the road of frustration, ignorance, pain and death, and also the ascent of one who was realizing in humiliation the glory that had been his from all eternity.

This paradox of the Incarnation is apparent in the Johannine language. On the one hand the Son retains on earth the glory that he ever had with the Father, as in the words of the ancient hymn: 'the heavenly Word proceeding forth, yet leaving not the Father's side'. On the other hand the Son prays that the Father will bestow glory upon him in the Passion and in the exaltation that will follow. There has been no abandonment of glory: yet the Son prays for glory, and he awaits the day when he will receive it. It seems therefore that it is in his *human* nature that the Son receives glory from the Father; and he asks that through the Passion and resurrection his human nature may be exalted into the eternal glory of God. Yet the Son's abiding glory and his reception of glory through death and resurrection are but two facets of a single mystery. For it is by the humiliation of the Son's winning of glory in the toils of history that the eternal glory of the divine self-giving is most notably disclosed.

Such is the glory of the incarnate life. We read of it in the narratives of the ministry and the Passion. But behind it is the glory of the act of Incarnation itself: *Verbum caro factum*. It is not only in the story of the Incarnate Lord, but in the fact that he became incarnate that the glory is made known, evoking the worship of angels and human beings.

(GG 84–6)

Atonement

It might be thought that the concept of glory, linked as it is with the Incarnation, has less to do with the doctrine of Atonement. But closer study shows that the glory not only provides a pattern for the doctrine of Atonement, but illuminates the inner unity of some aspects of that doctrine that have too often been separated.

Primarily and obviously glory suggests that aspect of the Atonement, which is described in the phrase *Christus Victor*. The glory shown forth on Calvary was a kingly power mightier than the human and cosmic evil ranged against it. The prince of this world was defeated and judged, and the world was overcome. But the doctrine of *Christus Victor* does not stand on its own: in St John's gospel it includes the doctrine of the godward offering whereby sin is expiated. The Passion is a glorifying of the Father inasmuch as it is the laying down of the Son's life as a sacrificial offering (John 6.51; 10.18). The prayer for glory is also the prayer for Christ's self-consecration as a victim on behalf of the disciples (John 17.1, 19). Hence in the story of the Passion the imagery of the victorious king who reigns from the tree is blended with the imagery of the sacrificial victim who expiates sin, and brings communion between God and man, slain as he is at the Passover time, and slain as a peace offering without the breaking of a bone (John 19.14, 36).

The victory and the expiation are thus inseparable, and the word – *doxa* – expresses this. The glory is the utter self-giving of Christ to the Father which, released by his death and brought into touch with human lives by his Spirit, can become the new principle of self-giving within them, and can banish from them the old principle of self-centred selfishness. Just as in the letter to Hebrews the sacrifice of Christ, through the sprinkling of the blood of sacrificial self-giving upon the consciences of men and women, breaks the power of sin, so in St John the glory of Christ's self-giving breaks the power of human sinful self-glory. Christ's godward sacrifice for sin, Christ's victory over sin, Christ's sanctification of men and women by his Spirit: these aspects of Atonement are held together within the doctrine of the glory.

(GG 86–7)

Church

'The glory that you gave me, I have given to them: that they may be one, even as we are one' (John 17.22). Herein lies the meaning of the Church. It is the mystery of the participation of men and women in the glory that is Christ's. Baptized into his death and made sharers in his resurrection, they become members of Christ's Body and branches of the vine that is Christ himself. Here the Spirit glorifies Christ, taking the things that are Christ's and declaring them to men and women (John 16.14). Here the Father is glorified by the fruitfulness of the disciples (St John 15.8). Here too men and women are glorified, even as they are called and justified (Romans 8.30). Here they are being transformed into Christ's image from glory to glory as by the sovereign Spirit (2 Corinthians 3.18). But beneath every act in the Church whereby this many-sided work of glory is being accomplished, there is the truth about the Church's essential being, namely that the glory of Christ is there. The glory into which Christians are to grow, and to manifest by the practical response of Christian life, is a glory that is theirs already (cf 1 Peter 2.4–5; 1 Corinthians 3.16–17; 2 Corinthians 6.16; Ephesians 2. 21–2).

The knowledge that the glory dwells already in the Church may betray its members into the ancient sin whereby God's people ascribed glory to themselves, unless they remember two warning truths of apostolic teaching. The first is that the glory in the Church is an invisible glory. Although the Church is visible as an institution, the glory is not to be confused with earthly majesty and splendour, for it is a glory discernible without and realized within only through faith. It is hidden from the eyes of the unbelieving world and can never be displayed for the world's admiration. It is often hidden also from the members of the Church and can never be enjoyed by them in any worldly manner. Only at the Coming of Christ will the glory become visible.

The second truth is that the glory of the Church is but a foretaste of the glory that is to come, and therefore the Church's sense of possession is mingled with its sense of incompleteness. Here the powers of the age to come are already at work within the Church's humiliation: there the open vision of glory awaits the Church on the day when judgement will begin in the household of God. It follows that the Church's claims are ratified by its humility, and the Church's riches are indicated by its hunger for what is lacking. Torn from this eschatological context the doctrine of the Church becomes simply the doctrine of one institution among many other institutions in history. Set in this eschatological context, however, it is the doctrine of a Church filled already with glory, yet humbled by the command to await both a glory and a judgement to come.

(GG 87–9)

Eschatology

Throughout this investigation of 'glory' it has again and again been apparent that the 'last things' are not a far-off outwork of the structure of the Christian faith, but rather a determining factor within its structure. If there is already salvation, redemption, life, glory, it is only so because, through the work of the Holy Spirit, anticipation has been given to us of the salvation, redemption, life and glory that belong to the age to come. We have been allowed to taste of the powers of that age (Hebrews 6.5).

The idea of the 'last things' has often been presented in terms of the destiny of the individual: 'what happens to me when I die?' But the Christian doctrine sees the destiny of the individual as one part in the pattern of the divine design for humanity and for *all* creation. God, who created the world for His glory, will glorify His creatures and lead them to glorify Him. The goal is a new creation, forged out of the broken pieces of a fallen one, filled with glory and giving glory to its Maker.

The crown of God's creation is human nature, made in the Creator's own image and possessing an affinity to Him in virtue of which men and women may come to know Him, to obey Him, to love Him and in the end to see Him. The service of God in the reflection of God's holiness and love is subsumed in the worship of God: both worship and service are subsumed finally in the seeing of God as He is. The seeing of God amid the shadows of history in the incarnate life of the Son is far less than the seeing of God which will be 'face to face'

(1 Corinthians 13.12) and 'as He is' (1 John 3.2). This perfect seeing awaits the transforming of humanity into the image of Christ, and their being made 'like Him'.

Besides humanity's affinity to its Creator, in whose image men and women are made and to whose vision they strive to attain, human nature also has a special place in relation to the rest of creation. Human beings are set to rule over it as God's deputy, 'crowned with glory and honour', and with all things in subjection (Psalm 8.3–8). In the worship of God, the human person is the representative of all created things. The mystery of evil afflicts not only human beings but all creation too. Human suffering in the present time, the bondage of corruption in nature (Romans 8.18–21), and the fact that we do not yet see all things made subject to human rule (Hebrews 2.8) all indicate the frustration of the divine design by the fall of humanity. But by the Cross and resurrection of Christ the inauguration of a new creation has begun, and this new creation will include human beings brought to sonship and glory, and nature itself renewed in union with humanity in the worship and praise of God (Romans 8.21; Hebrews 2.10). The Christian hope is therefore far more than the salvaging of individual human souls into a spiritual salvation: it is nothing less than the re-creation of the world, through the power of the resurrection of Christ.

Thus the hope of the beatific vision is joined by the hope of the vindication of the divine design not only in human nature but also in all things. The hope of the resurrection of the body, when the body of our present low existence is transformed into the body of Christ's glory (Philippians 3.21), is the reminder of our kinship with the created world, which the God of glory will redeem in a new world wherein the old is not lost but fulfilled.

(GG 89–90)

The Gospel of the Transfiguration

The Transfiguration stands as a gateway to the saving events of the gospel, and is a mirror in which the Christian mystery may be seen in its unity. Here we perceive that the living and the dead are one in Christ, that the old covenant and the new are inseparable, that the Cross and the glory are one, that the age to come is already here, that our human nature has a destiny of glory, that in Christ the final Word is uttered, and in him alone the Father is well pleased. Here indeed the diverse elements in the theology of the New Testament meet.

Forgetfulness of the truths for which the Transfiguration stands has often led to distortions. The severance of the New Testament from the Old, the separation between God the Redeemer and God the Creator are obvious illustrations. It is possible, alike in Christology, in sacramental teaching and in the idea of the Christian life, to regard the supernatural as replacing the natural in such a way as to overthrow the nature of a sacrament. It is equally possible to regard the redemptive act of God in Christ in terms so transcendental that nature and history are not seen in real relation to it; or to identify the divine act with nature and history in such a way that the otherworldly tension of the gospel is forgotten. Against these distortions the Transfiguration casts its light in protest.

So great is the impact of theology upon language that the word 'transfigure', drawn from a biblical story to which scant attention has often been paid, has entered into the practical vocabulary of Christian life. To the Christian suffering is now transfigured; knowledge too is transfigured, for the knowledge of the world and its forces may be used for the service of human pride and destruction, or else for the unfolding of God's truth and the enlarging of God's worship. To the Christian the world appears transfigured: now liberated from its dominance, it is discovered afresh as the scene both of divine judgement and of divine renewal within the new creation of Christ. The measure in which a Christian accepts the judgement is the measure in which he or she discerns, in the face of every calamity, the divine renewal through the raising of the dead.

The transfiguring of pain, of knowledge and of the world is attested in centuries of Christian experience, embodied in the lives of the saints. It comes neither by an acceptance of things as they are, nor by a flight from them, but by that uniquely Christian attitude, which the story of the Transfiguration represents. It is an attitude rooted in detachment – for pain is hateful, knowledge is corrupted and the world lies in the grip of evil; but which so practises detachment as to return and perceive divine sovereignty in the very things from which detachment has had to be made. Thus the Christian life is a rhythm of coming and going; and the gospel narrative of the ascent of the mountain of Transfiguration and then the descent to a faithless and perverse generation is a symbol of the mission of the Church in its relation to the world.

Our contemporary distresses have not made the message of the holy mountain obsolete, for the Transfiguration meant the taking of the whole conflict of the Lord's mission, just as it was, into the glory which gave meaning to it all. Confronted with a universe more terrible than ever in the blindness of its processes and the destructiveness of its potentialities, men and women must be led to the Christian faith, not as a panacea of progress or as an otherworldly solution unrelated to history, but as a gospel of Transfiguration. Such a gospel transcends the world and yet speaks directly to the immediate here-and-now. He who is transfigured is the Son of Man; and as he discloses on the holy mountain another world, he reveals that no part of created things, and no moment of created time lies outside the power of the Spirit, who is the Lord, to change it from glory into glory.

(GG 144–7)

PRAYER

The life of prayer is the heart of Christianity, and it was certainly the secret of Michael Ramsey's spiritual ministry. His final book, Be Still and Know *sums up his own experience in an inimitable fashion, which affected the lives of many of its readers.*

He saw prayer as both personal and liturgical, and never apart. His own approach was biblical, devotional and contemplative: biblical in the sense that he regarded the language of the Bible as tongued with divine fire; devotional in the sense that his love of Jesus was immediate and deep; contemplative in that he believed profoundly in seeking the silence of God.

From this there flowed a steady stream of intercession, which he understood to mean 'being with God with people on your heart'. His vision of divine compassion permeated his whole approach to those who came within the orbit of his and his wife's pastoral care, hospitality or friendship. They knew and they cared deeply, and people at home and abroad sensed and valued this, and remembered them for it with gratitude.

The Lord's Prayer

Christians are bidden to pray and to worship. In order to learn what this means they must turn first of all to the prayer given as a pattern by our Lord to his disciples in Galilee. In the Lord's Prayer the whole meaning of prayer is summed up. The Lord's Prayer cannot, however, be understood apart from the whole ministry and teaching of Jesus. Its significance is unfolded as Jesus moves forward in his work among men and women; for in this work, and above all in his death and resurrection, there is revealed the meaning of the words around which the Lord's Prayer centres – the Father, the name, the kingdom, and the will of God. God's Fatherhood is shown forth in many acts and words of Jesus, which culminate in the '*Abba* – Father' of Gethsemane (Luke 22.42), and in the 'Father, forgive them' and 'Father, into your hands' of Calvary (Luke 23.34 and 46). The Father's name is glorified in the Passion (John 13.31), and the Father's will is expressed by the sacrifice of the will of Jesus (Hebrews 10.5–10).

Thus the key words of the Lord's Prayer set before us a picture of the whole work of Jesus Christ, and to pray the Lord's Prayer in his name we too must leave Galilee and go up to Jerusalem, where we see the Father's name and kingdom and will expressed in the Lord's Passion. Prayer in Christ's name means prayer through all that he is and all that he has done. A Christian who prays thus looks first at this divine action in Jesus: for it is there that prayer starts, and not with human needs and feelings; and it is into this divine action that the whole of life must, by thanksgiving, be brought. For God has drawn near to us through the tenderness of the Incarnation and the Cross; yet this very nearness brings a sense of awe before one whose love and wrath are past all comprehension.

(GC 86–90)

Christ in you

Like the word 'Body', the words 'name' and 'glory' speak both of a redemptive action and of an indwelling power. The implication of this for the meaning of worship is far reaching. Worship is not merely the act of Christians who gaze upon an action of God; it is rather the act of Christ himself within them. Christ in his Body glorifies the Father, and his members share in what he does. The Holy Spirit prays within Christians (cf Romans 8). It is as though a stream of love flows forth from God to human beings, and returns to God through Christ. Christians cast themselves into this stream; and while their own efforts are called forth in full measure, the stream, which is the essence of worship and prayer, is that of God Himself.

Christian prayer is therefore primarily liturgical. It is sharing in the one action of Christ as, through dying to self, Christians are joined in one Body with his death and resurrection. They set before them the Father's name and kingdom and will, with meditation and thanksgiving, and only after this do they pass on to petition. Two truths therefore should always be present in Christian worship.

Firstly the centre of worship should not primarily be the needs and feelings of men and women, but the redeeming acts of God, and the eternal truths that these acts reveal. The language and structure of worship must first point away from the changing and topical to the divine action in the death and resurrection of Jesus, and to the same action now present in heaven in the whole Church. The centre of Christian worship is the high-priestly action of Jesus Christ, in heaven and in history.

Secondly it follows that all Christian worship is the act of the one Body of Christ. The voice of the individual Christian is drawn into the voice of the Body, and represents that Body. Indeed two or three gathered together in Christ's name represent the Body in that particular place (cf Matthew 18.20). The most private and apparently spontaneous prayers are in fact a part of the one act of Christ in his Body, and of the prayer of the one Spirit, who cries within us, '*Abba* – Father' (Romans 8.15–6). Hence a Christian congregation assembles not just to offer its own worship to God, but also to join as a small fragment in the one act of Christ in his whole Church in heaven and on earth. Christians now share in the thanksgiving and self-offering of Jesus (cf Matthew 11.25); and in them the Spirit cries '*Abba* – Father', joining them with his prayer in Gethsemane, and with his final 'Father, into your hands' on the Cross.

The whole New Testament is in itself an act of worship, expressing the truths of God as Creator and redeemer, of the Body of Christ, and of the name and the glory of God. These truths demand their proper outward expression in the Church's acts of common worship, and by an outward structure which points beyond human needs and feelings to the divine sacrifice on the Cross and in heaven, and beyond the individual and the local fellowship to the continuous life of the universal Church. If the Eucharist sets forth the Lord's death and resurrection, and the eternal truths which this action reveals, and affirms the presence of this action within Christians as the one Body, then it will indeed sum up all that the New Testament teaches about worship: 'Do all in the Name of the Lord.'

(*GC* 93–7)

The nature of Christian prayer

We need to see Christian prayer, not as an isolated religious exercise, but as an aspect of a many-sided converse between human beings and their Creator. In Christian belief, God makes Himself known to men and women in many ways: through the beauty of nature, by stirrings of conscience, through inspired men and women and their writings, through events in history, and supremely through Jesus Christ. To these intimations of God the human response is no less varied: by gratitude, trust and love, by awe and wonder, by grief and contrition, by acts of practical service and the pursuit of a Christian way of life. In this response there is a movement of the heart, mind and will towards God, partly but not wholly expressed in words. A relationship of word and silence, passivity and action: such is the context of prayer in Christianity.

(BS 11–12)

Contemplation and intercession

It is not always realised, either by seekers of contemplation or by its critics, that contemplation is not only a quest for the inner peace of God, but an exposure to the love of God in intercession. The Church is called to be a community that speaks to the world in God's name, and speaks to God from the middle of the world's darkness and frustration. The prayer with beautiful buildings and lovely music must be prayer that also speaks from the places where men and women work, or lack work, and are sad and hungry, suffer and die. To be near to the love of God is to be near, as Jesus showed, to the darkness of the world: that is the 'place of prayer'. For Christians, Jesus is the teacher of prayer, and the one whose own prayer is the source of our prayer, and the power for its renewal. His prayer is a converse with the Father, which includes the obedience of his life and death; and while it belongs to another world, it is set within the darkness of the world we know.

(BS 13–14)

Prayer as relationship with God

The prayer of Jesus is part of his whole relation to the Father in the obedience of his mission, and so the prayer of the disciples is not just a verbal utterance or a movement of the heart separable from the quest of divine righteousness. The relationship of the children to the Father includes within itself the whole range of human attitudes and activities. The Beatitudes in the Sermon on the Mount (Matthew 5.1–11) describe the blessedness of those whose lives are linked with God in poverty of spirit, in hunger and thirst for righteousness, in purity of heart, in peace-making, and in the endurance of persecution. To love one's enemies is to be children of the Father, and to strive towards perfection is to be in converse with the Father who is perfect. The second great commandment therefore lies within the true practice of the first.

(BS 34)

Trinitarian prayer

We learn from St Paul's prayers how the great themes of the Lord's Prayer prevail in the prayer of the early Christians. As the apostolic age proceeds, a Trinitarian pattern of prayer becomes apparent. Prayer is to the Father, and Jesus is not only the one through whom Christians pray, but also the one who evokes a devotion that would be idolatrous if he were not indeed divine. It is the Holy Spirit who enables Christians to pray '*Abba* – Father' (Romans 8.15), and to acknowledge the lordship of Jesus. Experiencing a threefold relationship to God in their prayer, Christians encounter a threefold relationship within God Himself; and the discourses and prayer in St John's gospel begins to unveil this. It is within the Trinitarian character of Christian prayer that the theology of the Trinity grows.

(BS 42)

Being with God

From glimpses of Jesus praying on the hills of Galilee and in the Garden of Gethsemane we pass to a familiar sight, the Christian who prays today. It may help us to recall the word for intercession that the letter to Hebrews uses to describe the prayer of Jesus: it means 'to be with' or 'to encounter'. Jesus is ever with the Father with the world upon his heart. May we think of our own prayer as being for a while consciously with the Father, no more and no less than that? If we think of prayer thus, we may find that the many aspects of prayer are embraced within the act of being in God's presence.

When you have a great friend you may plan to spend time with him or her, and may be careful not to miss it. The use of time is unlikely to be planned, but within the time news may be shared, requests may be made, regrets or gratitude may be spoken, and minds be exchanged, sometimes by talking and listening, and sometimes with little word or gesture. The use of time is not organised, but the time itself may be protected with care and trouble. May not our prayer be rather like that? It is the keeping of a little time in the conscious awareness of one who is our friend as well as our Creator and redeemer. To be with God for a space: within this may be included every aspect of prayer.

To intercede is to bear others on our heart in God's presence. Intercession becomes not the bombardment of God with requests so much as the bringing of our desires within the stream of God's own compassion. For His compassion flows ceaselessly towards the world, but it seems to wait upon the co-operation of human wills. This occurs partly when God's creatures do the things that God desires to be done, and partly by prayers, which are also channels of God's compassion. In intercession therefore we dwell first upon the loving-kindness of God in recollection, praise and thankfulness. It is there that intercession begins, dwelling upon God's greatness and flowing from the act of worship.

(BS 73–4)

The Jesus Prayer

The little prayer known as 'the Jesus Prayer' is not just a remedy for distraction in prayer, but rather a glorious prayer in its own right: used and loved by Orthodox Christians for many years, it has recently become loved and used increasingly by many Christians in the West. This prayer is the repetition again and again of the words: 'Lord Jesus Christ, Son of the Living God: have mercy upon me, a sinner.' The thoughtful repetition, many times and many times, is found to quieten the distracting parts of our personalities, and to keep us wonderfully subdued and concentrated. As we repeat the words again and again we may also bring into our heart the many people and needs about whom we really want to pray. As the words proceed, the heart has the people on it one by one. To intercede need not mean to address phrases to God about this person or that, but to bear them upon the heart in God's presence.

(BS 76)

Praying for the world

Praying Christians draw inspiration from the world for which they pray constantly. Sometimes the beauty in the world will stir them to wonder and worship. Sometimes the presence of the divine word in human lives of goodness or wisdom will kindle gratitude and reverence; the presence of self-sacrifice in human lives will call to mind Calvary. More often perhaps the agony of the world will draw them afresh to the compassion of Jesus and stir the will to pray. They will know that by their worship and prayer Christians serve the world powerfully. To worship in this way is to recapture the truth expressed by St Irenaus: 'The glory of God is a living man, and the life of man is the vision of God.' The role of Christians in the world is strikingly described in the anonymous letter to Diognetus of the second century: 'As the soul is in the body, so are Christians in the world.' By their praying Christians are helping the world to recover the soul that it has lost.

(BS 79–80)

Mysticism

Mysticism is an intense realization of God within the self, and of the self being embraced within God in vivid nearness. It is a phenomenon known in a number of religions, and in those religions very similar language is used in describing the experience. There is deep darkness, the darkness of not knowing; and there is light, with flashes in which the self knows the unknowable God as terribly near, and itself as never before. Through the centuries, Christian teaching has emphasized that the significant thing is not just mystical experience in itself, but its place and its context within the whole of Christian life. God sometimes gives the experience to a person, who seeks Him in a life of humility and charity, and whose life is turned towards righteousness as well as the beauty of God. The effect of the experience of mystical union, sometimes described as 'passive contemplation', is not to cause a person to long to have the experience again and again, but rather to long to serve God and to do His will. Those who have had such a mystical experience will not want to tell everyone about it: they will instead have a longing to serve God in daily life, for in His will is our peace.

Mystical experience is given to some, but contemplation is for all

The Lord of Glory

Christians. Our own prayer means essentially being with God, putting ourselves in His presence, being hungry and thirsty towards Him, wanting Him, letting heart, mind and will move towards Him, with the needs of the world on our heart. It is a rhythmic movement of our whole personality into the eternity and peace of God, and no less into the turmoil of the world, for whose sake, as well as for ours, we are seeking God. If that is the heart of prayer, then the contemplative part of it will be large; and a Church that starves itself and its members of the contemplative life deserves whatever spiritual leanness it may experience.

(CTP 59–60)

Silence and meditation

The meditative element frequently appears in Christian prayer. Both in personal prayer and in the liturgy Christians should be thinking about God, however slightly, before they speak to Him: mind and heart should be drawn towards God in reflection before any formal prayers begin. The more space that is given to this aspect of prayer, the more will prayer come to have the character of listening as well as of talking, of converse rather than just a monologue. While liturgy is indeed itself meditative, it is, however, in silence that this aspect of prayer has its supreme opportunity.

Silence enables us to be aware of God, to let the mind and imagination dwell upon His truth, to let prayer be listening before it is talking, and to discover our own selves in a way that is not always possible when we are making or listening to noise. There comes sometimes an interior silence in which the soul discovers itself in a new dimension of energy and peace, a dimension that a restless life can easily miss. If the possibilities of silence were often hard in biblical times, they are infinitely harder in the world in which we live today. A world frightening in its speed and noise is a world where silence alone may enable true human freedom to be found.

Then people find that their wanting of God is a deep and real part of themselves that longs to be stronger. It is sad that there are many who at this point may abandon prayer, feeling it to be a failure; for it may be at this very point that prayer is finding a new nearness of God. It is by its passivity that prayer of this kind opens the way to a new pouring of the love and power of God into the soul, which has been stripped naked of all but the wanting of God. This prayer may indeed be as powerful as it is passive. So far from being remote from the needs of the world, this kind of prayer may indeed be serving the world as greatly as any prayer, by being a channel of God's outflowing love.

(BS 81–6)

Contemplation and the dark night of the soul

Contemplation as the mystics understand it is prayer in which brain and imagination, and the knowledge and enjoyment of God's creatures, fade away in a passivity in which the depth of the soul is disclosed and the love of God is poured into it. It is the prayer of wanting, receiving and loving. It is preceded by what is called 'the dark night of the soul'. This phrase does not necessarily mean external sufferings of mind or body, though the Cross will have its place in the course of any Christian life. Rather does it mean that within prayer itself there is darkness, for the reality of God is unlike all previous glimpses of Him. The self is stripped of all but the love that God will give, and the love that will respond. This darkness is indeed an aspect of God's own light, and a phrase used by one of the mystics tells of this 'ray of darkness'. Sometimes the descriptions of this night and of contemplation are very close together like two sides of one event.

The dark night is often described in two phases: the night of the senses, and the night of the spirit. The first means the stripping away which we have seen to be the prelude to contemplation. The second precedes the deepest kind of contemplation: it is the disappearing into darkness of that pattern of faith in God which the soul has believed and known; for such is the mystery of God, that when we say that God *is* this or that, the reality so transcends the language that it is as true to say what God *is not*. The first of these nights is the familiar prelude to all contemplation. The second night is described by those who have known the deepest contemplation of all.

It matters greatly for the renewal of the Christian Church that the contemplative vocation be more known and recovered. It matters for us all, whatever our own form of service, for we are all one family. Just as it helps us in our day-to-day struggles that there are martyrs who have given their lives for Christ, so it helps us in our feeble praying that there are those who know the dark night, and have God poured into their souls. For we are all one family and we share one life in Christ.

(BS 87–8 and 105)

Union in love

The Christian way, as known and expounded in the New Testament, is not to be defined in terms of mystical experience. It is a way of union with God in Christ through faith, issuing in love and hope. One of the anticipations of the Holy Spirit, given to some, is the mystical experience known as 'passive contemplation', when the soul knows itself to be possessed by God to the depth of its existence. That such experiences should happen is a source of encouragement and joy to those who receive them, and sometimes to other Christians. But it is not by such experiences that the Christian way is defined: for it is defined by that which is the privilege of *all* Christians, the response of faith and love in all the variety of its stages and gifts. Let it again be emphasised that the Christian mystic does not long for experiences: he or she longs to love and serve God, and the outcome of mystical experiences is not a desire for their repetition, but an enhanced desire to do the will of God.

For all is God's gift, whether the mystical experience of St John of the Cross, or that kind of contemplation of God that is accessible to all those who want God, however feeble their wanting may be. All is of God; and no one can be nearer to God than the person in the parable who said: 'God be merciful to me a sinner' (Luke 18.13), or the robber who cries from his cross on Calvary: 'Jesus, remember me when you come into your kingdom' (Luke 23.42).

('The Mysticism of Evelyn Underhill' 14)

The spirit of Christian worship

Christian prayer and life are properly inseparable. As the sonship of Jesus on earth was a relationship to the Father in words, wordless converse and in the obedience of life and death, so the adopted sonship of Christians has its facets of word and silence and act. The sonship of Jesus was to the Father's glory not his own, and in serving that glory he consecrated himself on the world's behalf. So too Christians know the worship of God to be first duty of all; but they know also that this worship is an idolatrous perversion unless it is reflected in compassion towards the world.

Within Christian worship are acts of wonder at the beauty of God in the created world and his transcending holiness beyond it; and also acts of gratitude for his costly redemption of humanity in Jesus. It is worship in which sometimes the mind and imagination dwell upon God's beauty and goodness, and sometimes they enter the darkness as the unimaginable love of God is poured into the soul. It is worship whereby the pain of the world is held upon the heart in God's presence, and the desires of men and women are turned towards the desire of God as we pray in the name of Jesus.

In the Eucharist, with the risen Jesus present as our food, we are worshipping with the saints and angels in heaven. But the risen Jesus, who is at the heart of heavenly worship, is also Jesus who was crucified: and we share in heaven's worship only by sharing also in Jesus who suffers in the world around us, reminding us to meet him there and to serve him in those who suffer.

(*BS* 120–2)

* * * * * *

4

The Body of Christ

THE UNITY OF THE CHURCH

Michael Ramsey saw himself very much as a priest of the Church of God serving within the Church of England and the Anglican Communion. This distinction between 'Church' and 'church' was fundamental and it appears quite clearly in his first book, The Gospel and the Catholic Church, *which is, among other things, one of the most important and prophetic works of Anglican ecclesiology in the twentieth century. The main lines of his argument there appear in this section.*

Coming from a Nonconformist background, Michael Ramsey had a healthy sense of detachment regarding the structures of the Church, but also a dread of religious individualism. No one can be a Christian in a vacuum, 'for what have you that you did not receive?' He believed instead that the Church is a divine gift, created by Christ and indeed his Body. It is the place of 'living through dying' where Christians, individually and together, are remade in the image and likeness of Christ, and through which divine life flows for the healing of the world. Institutional Church life should ever seek to conform itself to this hidden reality that alone can give life.

He believed that the unity of the Church is a fact and a reality to be discovered through prayer and repentance, rooted in the depths of the heart, and to be made manifest in the visible life of the Church. This was his guiding principle in ecumenical relationships, and again his first book proved prophetic of their development during the time when he was Archbishop of Canterbury. His grasp of history as well as of theology determined his understanding of the Anglican Church, of the Papacy and the role of bishops, and of the nature of Catholic belief in its relationship to the gospel. His sympathy with Orthodoxy emerges too, and to his friendships in this area as well as to Orthodox theology he owed a great deal. Indeed, on his own admission he was an Orthodox among Anglicans. He had no doubt that drawing closer to Christ in prayer enables the Holy Spirit to strengthen unity between

Christians: this is the secret of the Church's hidden life – nearer to Christ, nearer to each other.

Why the Church?

Now why the Church? Cannot someone be a Christian without the Church? Several points are relevant here. We only know about Jesus at all because the Church in its early days handed down records about him. We accept his deity because of his impact on the community of Christians who worshipped him as divine, and drew others into their experience and conviction. This community has carried the knowledge of Jesus down the ages to us. So a Christian is not in a vacuum, and never can be in a vacuum. However individualistic he or she may want to be, they are always in debt to the Christian community for their knowledge of Jesus. There is a further point: Jesus himself founded the Church, and promised to it the power of the Holy Spirit. Within the community of the Church we believe that men, women and children are in touch with this divine power, derived from the lordship of Jesus, which can make a difference to human lives, as it has made a difference to many lives between the first days of Christianity and today.

(Problems of Christian Belief 25)

The inner meaning of the Church

Whereas 1 Corinthians gives an external picture of the Church in its glory and its shame, 2 Corinthians discloses in agony and ecstasy its inner meaning. And the inner meaning is that, because the power whereby the Church is sustained is that of the resurrection, the members of the Church recapture this power only by being brought near to the Cross. When their tasks are beyond them, when they know their frailty and are ready to share Christ's sufferings, then life is present; and life presses on in the winning of souls and the building of the Church in unity.

(*FC* 25)

Living through dying

The meaning of the Christian Church becomes most clear when it is studied in terms of the death and resurrection of Jesus Christ. The study of the New Testament points to the death and resurrection of the Messiah as the central theme of the gospels and epistles, and shows that these events were intelligible only to those who shared in them by a more than metaphorical dying and rising again with Christ. In this dying and rising again the very meaning of the Church is found, and its outward order expresses its inward meaning, by representing the dependence of its members upon the one Body, in which they die to self. The doctrine of the Church is thus found to be included within the Christian's knowledge of Christ crucified. The structure of the Catholic Church has great significance within the gospel of God, and apostolic succession is therefore important on account of its fundamentally evangelical meaning. If the Church's meaning lies in its fulfilment of the sufferings of Christ (Colossians 1.24), then every part of its history is intelligible only in terms of the Passion of our Lord. The right interpretation of the Church's mission, in this as in every age, will begin with the biblical study of the death and resurrection of the Messiah, wherein the meaning of the Church is contained.

(GC – preface)

The relevance of the Church

The New Testament suggests that the relevance of the Church of the apostles consists not in the provision of outward peace for the nations, nor in the direct removal of social distress, nor yet in any outward beauty of the Church itself, but in pointing to the death of Jesus the Messiah, and to the deeper issues of sin and judgement: sin in which Christians share, judgement under which they stand together with the rest of humanity. In all this the Church is often scandalous and unintelligible to men and women, but by all this and by nothing else is it relevant to their deepest needs.

For the relevance of the Church can never be any easier than was the relevance of the Messiah. He provoked questions and doubts among many of the wisest and holiest of his race. He perplexed those who looked to him as a national leader, as a reformer, a prophet, a teacher and a healer, even as the Messiah. For he abandoned his useful and intelligible works in Galilee in order to bring in Gods' kingdom by dying on the Cross. So ended his earthly life, but in the manner of its end and in the 'why?' uttered on Calvary (Mark 15.34) there was present the power of God; for Jesus knew whence he came and whither he was going (John 13.1–3).

His Church on earth is also scandalous, with question marks set against it by bewildered men and women, and with the question mark of Calvary at the centre of its teaching. Yet precisely there is the power of God to be found, if only Christians know whence they come and whither they go. They are sent to be the place where the Passion of Jesus is known, and where witness is borne to the resurrection from the dead. Hence the philanthropist, the reformer, the broad-minded modern person can never understand, in terms of their own ideals, what the Church is or what it means. Of course it is scandalous, of course it is formed of sinners whose sinfulness is exposed by the light of the Cross, of course there is an awful question mark at its centre. These things must needs be, if it is indeed the Body of Christ crucified and risen from the dead.

The first need of a Christian, in face of the apathy and bewilderment about the Church, is to know and to be able to say plainly what the Church really is. This does not mean to know and say what the Church ought to be, for 'it does not yet appear what we shall be' (1 John 3.2). Before Christians can say things about what the Church ought to be, their first need is to say what the Church is, here and now amid its own failures and the questionings of the bewildered. Looking at it now, with its inconsistencies and its perversions and its want of perfection, we must ask what is the real meaning of it just as it is. As the eye gazes upon it, it sees the Passion of Jesus Christ; but the eye of faith sees further: it sees the power of Almighty God. Christians will not try to answer the philanthropist and the reformer by meeting them on their own terms or by hiding the scandal of the gospel. They will say plainly what the Church of God is, and to what it points. Philanthropists point to the conditions of human life; the Church points to the deeper problem of humanity itself.

Before ever the apostles realized the full doctrine of the Incarnation or thought of the Church in terms of it, they knew the Church through knowing the Lord's death and resurrection. Thus while it is true that the Church is founded upon the Word-made-flesh, it is true only because the Word was identified with humanity right down to the point of death, and so enabled men and women to find unity through a veritable dying to self. The doctrine of the Church, its order, ministry and sacraments, will be expounded not primarily in terms of an institution founded by Christ, but in terms of Christ's death and resurrection, of which the one Body, with its life and order, is the expression.

(GC 4–7)

Unity and disunity in the Church

The movement towards the reunion of Christendom is also compelled to see its problems in close connexion with the Passion of our Lord. Before passing on to schemes of reconciliation, Christians are compelled to pause and ask what the present fact of disunity means. Why is it? They will not simply say that it is wrong, and flee from it in the quest of new visions, ideals and policies: they will pause again and dwell upon the facts, just as they are. In them is the Passion of Jesus; and in them already is the power of God. Both divisions and unity remind us of the death and resurrection of Jesus. Division severs his Body; but unity means the reality of the one Body, in which every member and every local community dies to self in its utter dependence upon the whole. Thus the structure of the Body sets forth the dying and rising with Christ. If the problems about schism and reunion mean dying and rising with Christ, they will not be solved through easy humanistic ideas of fellowship and brotherhood, but by the hard road of the Cross.

Those who cherish the Catholic Church and its historic order need to expound its meaning, not in legalistic and institutional language, but in evangelical language, as the expression of the gospel of God. If the historic structure of the Church sets forth the gospel, it has a meaning, which any evangelical Christian will understand, and reunion without that structure may well impair the very gospel that the evangelical cherishes. The philanthropist is also confronted with the death of the Messiah. As he or she longs passionately for the mitigation of the economic sufferings of humanity, their longing is after the obedience of Christ, for he healed the sick and fed men and women, and commands his Church to do the same. But as Jesus, in the midst of his works of healing and feeding, was moving towards his death, so also is his Church. For the Church exists for something deeper than philanthropy and reform: it exists to teach men and women to die to self, and to trust in a resurrection to a new life. Because this life spans both this world and another world, it can never be wholly understood here, and must always puzzle the world's idealists. As the Body of Christ crucified and risen, the Church points men and women to a unity and a peace which they generally neither understand nor desire.

Thus the Church points beyond theology, beyond reunion schemes, beyond philanthropies, to the death of the Messiah. It leads the theologian, the churchstatesman, the philanthropist, and itself also, to the Cross. This dying is a stern reality, for the theologian, ecumenist, philanthropist each learns that their work and their ideal is, in itself and of itself, nothing. But all that is lost is found; and the Cross is the place where the theology of the Church finds its meaning, where the unity of the Church is a deep and present reality, and where the Church is already sharing the peace of God and the bread from heaven with the nations of humanity.

(GC 7–9)

Life in the Church

We do not know the whole fact of Christ incarnate unless we know his Church, and its life as a part of his own life. Yet the language in Ephesians (1.23 and 4.15) in which Christ is called the head over the Body warns us against a mere sense of divine immanence, and reminds us that to know the Church is not to know the inexhaustible truth of Christ, who has ever more to give to men and women. Nonetheless the Body is the fullness of Christ, and the history of the Church and the lives of the saints are acts in the biography of the Messiah.

Christianity therefore is never solitary. It is never true to say that separate persons are united to Christ, and then combine to form the Church. For to believe in Christ is to believe in one whose Body is a part of himself, and whose people are his own humanity; so to be joined to Christ is to be joined to Christ in his Body. The experience of St Paul shows us that the Christian is confronted by the one Body at conversion, in the experience of justification by faith, and at every stage in growing knowledge of Christ. Christians therefore never escape from the Church: it is a part of their own existence since it is a part of Christ himself. For without the Church a Christian does not grow, since Christ is fulfilled in the totality of all his members.

That Christ died and rose, and that Christians share in his death and resurrection and become members of his Body, are historical events which the New Testament records. But history cannot exhaust the meaning of these events, since in them the powers of another world are at work, and the beginnings of a new creation are present. The heavenly status of the Church can hardly be exaggerated, but it is a sovereignty of dying and risen life that is apprehended through faith in the Cross; its power is known in humiliation, and neither the resurrection of Christ nor the place of the Church in relation to him can be perceived by the mind of the world.

(GC 35–9)

The death of individualism

'Individualism' has no place in Christianity, and life in Christ truly means its extinction. Yet through the death of 'individualism' the individual person finds himself or herself. For through membership in the Body, the single Christian is discovered in new ways, and becomes aware that God loves him or her in all their singularity, as if God had no one else to love. Christians can speak of a conscious union between themselves and Christ: 'He loved me, and gave himself for me' (Galatians 2.20). Hence two kinds of language have always been legitimate for Christians: one that dwells upon the Body of Christ in which the individual is joined, and the other that speaks of the individual Christian in conscious union with Christ. But both kinds of language describe what is truly one reality: for the individual Christian exists only because the Body exists already. The self is known in its reality as a self when it ceases to be solitary and learns its utter dependence; thus the individuality of Christians, in all its rich variety, springs from their death and resurrection in the Body that is one. In the Body of Christ the self is found, and so within individual experience the Body is present. Thus the losing and the finding are equally real.

(GC 38)

Union with Christ

In showing us Christ, the New Testament takes us beyond his historical life and death into a region as hard to define, as it is real to Christian experience. This region is described by the writer to Hebrews, when he says: 'Jesus Christ is the same yesterday and today and forever' (Hebrews 13.8); or when St Paul says: 'Christ lives in me' (Galatians 2.20). The word 'mystical' immediately suggests itself, and it is a word that has often been used to describe the union of a Christian with the Lord in a relationship as real as that experienced by the first disciples. But here lurks a subtle danger, since in it is a temptation for a Christian to cling to the immediacy of their own experience of Christ, and so in the midst of the Body of Christ to become ensnared into another form of individualism and self-satisfaction, which belie the truth about the one Body. Against this danger the New Testament asserts two important safeguards: the importance of the historical events of the life and death of Jesus; and the importance to individuals or groups of realising that the one Body existed before their own conversion, and has one continuous historic life in which they are called to share.

In the light of these two safeguards Christians will forget themselves and instead bear witness to the redemption wrought once for all, and to the Church in which men and women die and rise. In later language the Church is called 'apostolic' because it is sent by the one Redeemer, and 'catholic' as living one universal life; and both these marks of the Church are essential to its existence as expressing the Lord's death and resurrection, wherein its 'holiness' consists. By their place in the Body, Christians find the gospel of death and resurrection active around and within them. To believe in 'one Holy, Catholic and Apostolic Church' is therefore to die to self. For the relationship between Christians and the one Church is a part of their relationship to Christ himself.

(GC 43–5)

The root of Christian unity

The Church's unity is connected with the truth about Christ himself. It is the unity of his own Body, springing from the unity of God, uttered in the Passion of Jesus, and expressed in the order and structure of the Church. The one race of men and women united to Christ exists first; it precedes the local church and is represented by it. The one universal Church is primary, and the local congregation expresses the life and unity of the whole Church. This unity is between men and women who, dying to themselves, give glory to Christ's one redemption in history and are drawn into the one Body. The Eucharist is a sharing in the body and blood of Christ, and the means whereby Christians become 'one bread one body' (1 Corinthians 10.16–17), because it brings them very near to his actual death in the flesh (1 Corinthians 11.26).

The New Testament leads us still more deeply into the meaning of unity. It takes us behind the one race and behind the historical events to the divine unity from which they spring: 'One Lord, one faith, one baptism, one God and Father of all' (Ephesians 4.5–6). The unity that comes to men and women through the Cross is the eternal unity of God Himself, a unity of love, which transcends human utterance and understanding (cf John 17.11, 20–2, 24). Before and behind the historical events there is the unity of the one God. Unity is God's alone, and in Him alone can anything on earth be said to be united.

(GC 47–50)

The order of the Church

In the life of the Church the inner and outward are inseparable, and the Church's inner meaning is expressed in the Church's outward shape and structure, wherein the parts depend upon the whole. Therefore the outward order of the Church is no indifferent matter; it is, on the contrary, of supreme importance since it relates to the Church's inner meaning, and to the gospel of God itself. For the good news that God has visited and redeemed His people includes the redeemed person's knowledge of death and resurrection through his or her place in the one visible society of the Church, and through that death to self, which every member and group has to die.

In telling of this one visible society, the Church's outward order tells indeed of the gospel. For every part of the Church's true order bears witness to the one universal family of God, and points to the historic events of the Word-made-flesh. Thus Baptism is into the death and resurrection of Christ, and into the one Body (Romans 6.3; 1 Corinthians 12.13). The Eucharist is likewise a sharing in Christ's death, and a joining of the individual within the life of the one Body (1 Corinthians 10.17 and 11.26). The apostles are both a link with the historical Jesus and also leaders of the one Church, upon which every local community depends. Hence the whole structure of the Church tells of the gospel: not only by its graces and virtues; but also by its very organic shape it proclaims the truth. Baptism, the Eucharist, the apostles (and their heirs), tell us of our death and resurrection, and of the Body that is one. The structure of Catholicism is therefore an utterance of the gospel.

Baptism, with the laying on of hands (Confirmation) as its normal completion, is the first significant event for a Christian. It declares that the beginning of a person's Christianity is not what he or she feels or experiences, but rather what God in Christ has done for them. Their feelings, experiences and virtues have meaning not in themselves, but as bearing witness to the one Body in which alone the individual can grow to their full humanity. For the life of Christians is a continual response to the fact of their baptism: they continually learn that they have died and risen with Christ, and that their life is a part of the life of the one Christian family.

(GC 50, 54 and 59–60)

Development and the Papacy

Developments within Christianity took place, but they were all tested. The tests of a true development are whether it bears witness to the gospel, whether it expresses the general consciousness of Christians, and whether it serves the organic unity of the Body in all its parts. These tests are summed up in the Scriptures, wherein the historical gospel and the experience of the redeemed and the nature of the one Body are described. Hence, while the canon of Scripture is in itself a development, it has a special authority to control and check the whole field of development in Church life and doctrine.

Judged by these tests, and by Scripture which sums them up, the marks of the Church – Baptism, Eucharist, apostolate, creeds – are abundantly vindicated, since they were the means whereby the gospel of God prevailed over one-sided theories and perversions of Christian life. The theologians of the second century who dwell most upon Church order, St Ignatius and St Irenaus, are precisely those whose whole theology is most controlled and pervaded by Scripture.

The question at once arises whether the Papacy is an equally legitimate development, growing out of a primacy given by our Lord to St Peter (cf Matthew 16.18–9), and symbolising the unity of the Church? The answer must be found in these same tests. A Papacy, which expresses the general mind of the Church in doctrine, and which focuses the organic unity of all the bishops and of the whole Church, might well claim to be a legitimate development in and through the gospel. But a Papacy, which claims to be a source of truth over and above the general mind of the Church, and which wields authority in a way that depresses the due working of the other functions of the one Body, fails to fulfil the main tests. That is where the issue lies; and the fuller discussion of the ministry, of the sacraments, and of authority must precede a fuller answer to the question of the Papacy in history. Meanwhile it must be insisted that neither the apostolic age nor that which immediately followed it, nor the period when the creeds, the canon of Scripture and the episcopate emerged knew the see of Rome as having any monarchical place in the one structure. The structure of the Church is the catholic fact. How far the Papacy expresses this main fact or distorts it is a subsequent historical question.

It may well be argued that a primacy of a certain kind is implied in early Church history, and is ultimately necessary to Christian unity. But there is all the difference between a primacy, which focuses the organic unity of all the parts of the one Body, and a primacy, which tends to crush the effective working of the other parts. For behind all subsequent schisms in the West there stands the great schism of the eleventh century, the parent of them all. A sundered Christendom can still integrate and make saints; but it can never make men and women whole in the inner and outer unity of the one Church.

These historical facts, however, cannot justify a complete refusal to consider the Petrine claims. It seems possible that in the reunited Church of the future there may be a special place for a *primus inter pares* as an organ of unity and authority. But it remains very difficult to define the functions and limits of such a primacy. For a primacy should depend upon and express the organic authority of the Body; and the discovery of its precise functions will come, not by discussion of the Petrine claims in isolation, but by the recovery elsewhere of the Body's organic life, with its bishops, priests and people. In this Body 'Peter' will find his due place, and ultimate reunion is hastened not by pursuit of 'the Papal controversy' but by the quiet growth of the organic life of every part of Christendom.

(GC 64–5, 163–5; Appendix 1 – 227–8)

Church and churches

The only appeal back to Jesus, which is logically and spiritually coherent, is an appeal to the gospel of God uttered in the one Body by its whole structure. However much the Church may have suffered distortion in history, this structure proclaims the gospel by pointing men and women beyond this or that experience, this or that achievement, this or that movement, revival or institution, to the universal society in which all these are made full. If we would draw near to the naked facts of Calvary and Easter, we can do so only within the one fellowship whose very meaning is death to self.

The Catholicism that sprang from the gospel of God is a faith in which the visible and ordered Church fills an important place. But this Church is understood less as an *institution* founded upon rules laid down by Christ and the apostles, than as an *organism* that grew inevitably through Christ's death and resurrection. The Church, therefore, is defined not in terms of itself, but in terms of Christ, whose gospel created it and whose life is its indwelling life.

The Church's order, however, does not imply that those Christians who possess it are always more godly than those who are without it.

For it does not bear witness to the perfection of those who share in it, but to the gospel of God by which alone, in the one universal family, human beings can be made perfect. It is not something Roman or Orthodox or Anglican; rather does it declare to men and women their utter dependence upon Christ, by setting forth the universal Church in which all that is Anglican, Roman or Orthodox, or partial or local in any way, must share by an agonizing death to its own pride.

Many fruits of the Spirit are found apart from the full Church order; yet these fruits and all others will only grow to perfection through the growth of the one Body, in which Christ is all, and in all fulfilled. It is this Church order that in every age bears witness to the existence of the one Body, of which every movement, experience, party and achievement, must know itself to be a fragmentary part. Baptism, Eucharist and episcopacy are part of the utterance of God's redemptive love, and they proclaim that human love is only made perfect by the building up of the one Body, in which alone by the due working of all its parts, the truth that is in Jesus is fully learnt.

(GC 66–7)

Episcopacy

Episcopacy is to be seen primarily as something closely related to the gospel and to the one Body. Grace is bestowed always by our Lord himself and through the action of his whole Church. Every act of grace is his act and also the act of the one Body that is his. So the succession of bishops is not an isolated channel of grace, since from the first, Christ has bestowed grace through every sacramental act of his Body. But certain actions in this work of grace are confined to the bishops, and thereby the truth is taught that every local group or church depends upon the one life of the one Body, and that the church of any particular generation shares in the one historic Church, which is not past and dead, but alive in the present.

Thus the Church's full and continuous life in grace does depend upon the succession of bishops, the apostolic succession, whose work, however, is not isolated but bound up with the whole Body. As guardians of teaching, performers of the apostles' own functions, and as channels within the one Body's continuous life of grace, the bishops set forth the gospel of God. Every act of grace is the action of the whole Church: bishops, priests and people all exercise their share in the one priesthood of Christ. But each order by its own function represents a part of the truth; and by learning its own dependence glorifies not itself but Christ, whose Body is one.

We are led therefore to affirm that the episcopate is of the essence of the Church; but we must beware of misrepresenting the issue. All who are baptized into Christ are members of his Church, and baptism is the first mark of being a Christian. Yet the growth of all Christians into the measure of the stature of the fullness of Christ (cf Ephesians 4.13) means their growth with all the saints in the unity of the one Body; and of this the episcopate is the expression. Episcopacy therefore speaks of the incompleteness of every section of a divided Church, whether of those who possess it, or of those who do not. Those who do possess it will never boast that it is 'theirs'. For it proclaims that there is the one family of God before and behind them all, and that all die daily in the Body of him who died and rose.

(GC 82–5)

The meaning of Catholic belief

The faith of the Bible leads straight to the Catholic Church, but this gets its meaning only from the gospel of God. Thus interpreted, catholic belief is not a burden upon the mind of the thoughtful Christian, but rather the means whereby he or she can indeed be free. For it frees a person from partial rationalisms that have sometimes identified Christianity with the Bible alone, or with some scholastic system, or with some transient humanist assumptions. Instead it delivers a person into orthodoxy that no individual or group can fully possess, since it belongs only to the building up of the one body of Christ in love. As a person receives the catholic sacrament and recites the catholic Creeds, he or she is learning that no single movement or partial Christian experience within Christendom can claim final obedience; and that a local church can claim loyalty only by leading men and women beyond itself to the universal Christian family that it represents. In this way, catholic belief and order is not a hierarchical tyranny, but the means of deliverance into the gospel of God and His timeless Church.

Far from foreclosing the activities of the human mind, the Catholicism of the gospel bids men and women to think as freely and as fearlessly as they can, and by saving them from human rationalisms, religious or otherwise, it enables them to use their reason to the full. For 'all things were made by Him' (cf John 1.1–5), and all honest endeavours in science, philosophy, art, and history, manifest the Spirit of God. But the ultimate key to these mysteries of nature and of human existence is the Word-made-flesh. To him alone shall the Church point, for in him alone shall men and women know the truth, and the truth shall make them free (John 8.32–6).

The true definition of Catholicism is found in the gospel, and its order has its deepest significance, not in terms of legal validity, but in terms of the Body and the Cross. Its Eucharist proclaims God as Creator and redeemer, and its confessional is the place where men and women see that in wounding Christ their sins wound His Body, and where by learning of the Body they learn of Christ. Its reverence for the saints is a part of its worship of the risen Lord, for the claim of Catholicism is that it shows to men and women the whole meaning of the death and resurrection of Jesus.

(GC 135 and 179–80)

The Church Fathers

The study of the New Testament leads on to the study of the Church of the Fathers, the Patristic period. But the importance of the age of the Fathers must not be misunderstood. It is important, not as a golden age nor as a model for imitation by Christians, but as an age when the whole gospel found expression in the life and liturgy of the one Body, with a balanced use of all the Church's structure, and with a depth, breadth and unity which contrast strikingly with every subsequent epoch. In these early centuries, the Syrian, Greek and Roman Christians were in one fellowship, with a Eucharistic worship exhibiting a balance of all the elements of thanksgiving, commemoration, fellowship, sacrifice and mystery. The Church was world renouncing, first with its martyrs and later with its hermits; it was also world redeeming, with its baptism of Greek culture and humanism into the Faith. Amid all these varieties of type and temper, the Body was still one; and the doctrine of the mystical Body retained its inner depth and breadth, since the doctrine of redemption still controlled it. The close relation between the doctrines of the Body and of redemption is apparent in all the important teaching about the Church from St Paul to St Augustine, even though from an early date there appear differences of emphasis between East and West.

(GC 140–1)

The significance of Eastern Orthodoxy

The reverence of saints in the Eastern Church is practised as a part of the life of the one Body. It does not mean the elevation of marked individuals to special places of influence and intercessory power, enthroned between God and human beings. It means rather giving glory to Christ in his one Body, whose family life, seen and unseen, is a manifestation of Christ's own life. Hence, in the East, there has never been the rigid distinction, apparent sometimes in the West, between praying to and praying for the saints and the departed. The sense of the one family prevents such rigid conceptions, and binds saints and sinners in one: for holiness belongs only to the one Body. In reverencing saints, people reverence the life of Christ in them, who is the life of them all. Hence also the Eastern cult of the Virgin Mary, the Mother of God, has meant the veneration, not of an isolated figure enthroned in heaven, but of one whose humanity is indwelt by God, herself the first-fruits of the Church, in whom is focused uniquely in history the truth about the whole Body of Christ.

The deepest initiation into Eastern Orthodoxy comes not from the texts of the Fathers but from sharing in the Divine Liturgy. For there the worshipper will find what the textbook can never make articulate, the sense (as prominent in the East as that of the Crucifixion is prominent in the West) of the triumph of Christ who has risen from the dead, and has shattered the gates of Hell, of the resurrection as the present reality about the Christians who are His Body, and of the heavenly host whose praises are shared by the family on earth.

The drawing together of East and West, including the movement of Anglicans and Orthodox towards unity, has an importance for every member of the entire Christian Church. For the schism between East and West was the parent of later schisms. The East has conserved elements of faith, life and worship, which the West sorely needs for realizing its own inner Catholicity: the mystery of worship, the communion of saints, of the Church as a family, the close relationship between doctrine and life expressed in the Eastern idea of 'orthodoxy', the resurrection as the centre of the Church's being.

The presence in the West of the dispersion of exiles from Russia, where faith has been sealed with martyrdom, has an importance as great as that of any of the central events in Christian history. The growing unity between East and West goes behind, and brings deliverance from, the failings of centuries of mutual isolation. It does not hinder but in fact it helps the healing of the divisions in the Western Church.

(GC 147–9 and 178–80)

Is Christ divided?

Is Christ divided? In so many ways Catholicism has appeared in broken fragments of what it is meant to be. It is severed into at least three main elements: Latin, Eastern Orthodox and Anglican. These divisions obscure its historic Church order, so that the place of the episcopate as the sign of the Church's universal life, and the meaning of the sacraments as acts of the one Body, are sometimes hidden from sight.

Yet, if the rent in the robe of Christ has been a part of his Passion, there has been in the midst of it the power whereby saints are made, and whereby civilizations have been moulded. Hence the broken history of the Catholic Church is not a mere parody of Catholicism, but a manifestation in flesh and blood of the Way, the Truth and the Life. Not only in the saints whose names the Church commemorates, but in men and women whose lives have been secret, a love and humility have been seen whose roots are in heaven. Such men and women, and countless others also, are less conscious of what the Church has failed to do than of what the Church has done and is doing within them, and its name spells only thankfulness and praise. For the quest of ideal Catholicism must not deny the actual.

The essence of Catholicism all through the ages has consisted not in partial systems that have been its servants and its dividers, but in the unbreakable life to which the sacraments, scriptures, creeds and ministry have never ceased to bear witness. Unity therefore exists already, not in what Christians say or think, but in what God is doing in the one race of men and women day by day. The outward recovery of unity comes not from improvised policies, but from faith in the treasure, which is in the Church already.

(GC 174–5)

The Anglican Church

The Church of England cannot be explained in terms of Tudor politics alone, although the English church did not always perceive the meaning of its own episcopal order in its deepest relation to the gospel and

The Body of Christ

the universal Church. But its existence declared the truth that the Church in England was not a new foundation, nor just a local realization of the invisible Church, but the expression on English soil of the one historical and continuously visible Church of God. Bishop Lancelot Andrewes expressed this in his *Preces Privatae* when he prayed 'for the whole Catholic Church, Eastern, Western, and our own'. In the later words of Newman: 'I kept ever before me that there was something greater than the Established church, and that was the Church, Catholic and Apostolic, set up from the beginning, of which she was the local presence and expression.'

If our reading of the New Testament, and especially of the Pauline epistles, is correct, the two approaches to Christian truth, evangelical and catholic, are ultimately one. To understand the Catholic Church and its life and order is to see it as the utterance of the gospel of God; and to understand the gospel of God is to share with all the saints in the building up of the one Body of Christ. Hence these two aspects, expressed in Anglicanism, cannot really be separated. Anglicanism possesses full catholicity only if it is faithful to the gospel of God, and it is fully evangelical insofar as it upholds the Church order by which an important aspect of the gospel is set forth. Hence 'catholicism' and 'evangelicalism' are not two separate things, which the Church of England must hold together by a great feat of compromise. Rightly understood, they are both realities that lie behind the Church of England, and as the New Testament shows, they are one reality; and any church's witness to the one Church of the ages is a part of its witness to the gospel of God.

The Anglican Church is committed, not to a vague position wherein the evangelical and catholic views are alternatives, but to the scriptural faith wherein both elements are one. It is her duty to train all her clergy in both these elements. Her bishops are called, to be not the judicious holders of a balance between two or three schools of thought, but without any consciousness of party to be the servants of the gospel of God and of the universal Church. The Anglican Church can lead the way in tackling the problems that confront it only if it digs down to its own foundations, which are the gospel of God, the sacramental life, and the soundest learning that its clergy and laity can possess.

Meanwhile the Anglican Church can help prepare the way for Christian reunion, not by indifference to the historic Church order, but by restoring a truer presentation of it in the context of the gospel and of the universal Church. It does this as it preaches that gospel, as it lives the life of Christ's Body, as it recovers the true place of bishops, priests and people in the liturgy of the Body's life; and as it points to a reunited Church, wherein the truths seen in every section of Christendom must be preserved in full measure. In that Church, the instrument of unity will be the one episcopate, never just because it is Anglican, but always because it belongs to the universal family of God.

While the Anglican Church is vindicated by its place in history, often with a strikingly balanced witness to the gospel, the Church and to sound learning, its greater vindication lies in pointing through its own history to something of which it is a fragment. Its credentials are its incompleteness, with tension and travail in its soul. It is clumsy and untidy; it baffles neatness and logic. For it is not sent to commend itself as 'the best type of Christianity', but by its very brokenness to point to the universal Church wherein all have died.

(GC 204–9 and 216, 219–20)

The quest for Christian unity

In the search for the unity of the Church, the theologian digs in the field of Christian origins and of the Church's history. The process reveals some plain lessons. From Christian origins it is clear that the visible Church and its order is an integral part of human knowledge of Christ crucified. From history it is clear that institutionalism fails unless it is mindful of the gospel, which gives it its meaning; and that the faith of the gospel can wither and fade unless it is mindful of the one historic Church. But the digging discloses not only lessons but also the reality of the divine foundation of the Church. For as the debris of old controversies and one-sided systems are cleared away, there appears the pattern of a structure, whose maker and builder is God.

The return of all Christians to this divine structure is not a movement backwards to something ancient and venerable, nor a submission by some to what especially belongs to others. It is the recognition by all of the truth about themselves as members of the one people of God, whose origin is the historical life of Jesus, and whose completeness will be known only in the building up of the one Body. For every part of Christendom this recognition means not only the recovery of the one Church order, but the experience of the Passion of Jesus, wherein that order has its meaning. For the unification of outer order can never move faster than the recovery of inward life. Meanwhile no Christian shall deny his or her Christian experience; but all

The Body of Christ

Christians shall grow more fully into the one experience of Christ in all its parts. The historic orders of ministry have indeed been obscured by disunity; however, all Christians need the restoration of the one episcopate so that all may share in the one Eucharist, which is, both inwardly and outwardly, the act of the one Church of God.

When, through the Passion, the outward unity of the Church is restored, then the world itself will know that the Father sent the Son. Meanwhile a broken Church is closer to the needs of men and women than they can ever know, for it is the Body of Christ, who died and rose again. Its order, worship, history, its problems of unity and disunity all signify the Passion of Christ. For the Messiah chose to die: and as he went to die, he embodied in his own flesh the whole meaning of the Church of God. For its Baptism, Eucharist, order, the truth that it teaches to men and women, and the unity it offers to them, all simply mean: 'You died, and your life is hidden with Christ in God' (Colossians 3.3).

(GC 221–4)

Spirituality and unity

It is on the plane of spirituality that we can with great profit search for Christian unity, less in the thoughts and formulations of the mind than in the depths of the soul, and those actions that are controlled from it. I think of Roman Catholics praying, 'Christ before the eyes, Christ in the heart, Christ in the hands.' I think of Eastern Orthodox Christians praying the prayer that came from Mount Sinai called 'the Jesus Prayer', drinking the name of Jesus into the soul along with the rhythms of human breath. I think also of Anglican Christians coming to the Eucharist, now celebrated daily in many of our cathedrals and parish churches, and commemorating the sacrifice of Calvary, and feeding upon the Body and Blood of our Lord together with the divine Word in the scriptures. Here indeed is a unity found in the depths of the soul. But it is more. It includes the use of sacred scriptures as *lectio divina*, and the concept of the liturgy as *mysterium Christi*. Furthermore this unity in the depths of the soul is possible only because of the Holy Spirit, by whom alone Christians can pray '*Abba* – Father'. This is baptismal unity, a unity – however unconsummated, however incomplete – which is real in virtue of the fact of holy Baptism.

Wherever there is Christian spirituality there is already a link between souls on earth and the very life of heaven, and there is already a recovery of the inner soul of Christendom. Already, even in a tiny way, there is fulfilment of the old Gelasian prayer, 'that things which were cast down may be raised up, that things which had grown old may be made new, and that all things may return unto unity through Him by whom all things were made'.

The Church of God must therefore go out to learn and to use whatever divine wisdom discloses in the modern world, and to meet the agonies that are in the world. It can do this with conviction, because it knows the truth about the world and the truth about itself. The world is the place where Christ, by his death and resurrection, has won a cosmic victory: it is in his hands already, and all unseen his power draws it into unity; that is the orthodox faith of Christ victorious, as the fathers and the liturgy attest. The Church is his Body where, amidst its many sinful and fallible members, Christ is present as the Church's inward life; for the portion of the Church on earth is ever one with the Church in paradise and in heaven.

(CEA 30–1 and 73)

MINISTRY

The best-loved of Michael Ramsey's books is probably The Christian Priest Today: *addressed to those he ordained to the Christian ministry within the Church of England, it comes close to the heart of his own understanding of the priesthood and of the spirit of Christian service. It is also a vivid record of his inimitable style of speaking that could induce compunction in those who listened to him.*

For him priesthood and ministry was essentially a ministry of prayer; without that it is nothing. Its focus is the Eucharist, and its heart is contemplative intercession. He believed unashamedly that regular confession is vital for the spiritual renewal and vigour of any Christian ministry, and he frequently lamented its decline in the Church of England. He used to say that the failure to confess is in line with the failure to pray.

The purpose of the ordained ministry is to focus the unity of the Church among a particular group of people in a specific place. It is not an end in itself, and the duty of the priest is to make God real to others in an unselfconscious way. This can only happen if those ordained draw close to God himself in loving obedience to Jesus, and open themselves daily to the outpouring of his Spirit.

The last piece in this section is drawn from Michael Ramsey's enthronement sermon in Canterbury Cathedral as the new arch-

bishop. It captures very well the way in which he was able to impart encouragement and vision to those who shared with him in the ministry of Christ.

The priest at prayer

The priest, in the Church and for the Church, is a person of prayer: in a special way this is the role of a priest, and because it is so the Church's prayer will be stronger. As a teacher of theology a priest must pray, for theology that is alive includes not only the study of books, but also the authentic knowledge of God, which comes through prayer alone. As a minister of reconciliation a priest must also pray, for the priest must be one with those who are sinful, in the bitter estrangement of their sin and in the hopeful grief of their repentance. At the same time the priest is one with Christ in his sorrow for sinners and his joy at sin's conquest. As absolver and pastor no less than as theologian and teacher, the priest has a prayer that focuses the Church's prayer: in the priest the Church's prayer is expressed in strength and so becomes stronger.

    The priest is also a person of the Eucharist. As celebrant the priest is more than the people's representative. In taking, breaking, and consecrating the priest acts in Christ's name, and in the name not only of a particular congregation, but also of the holy Catholic Church down the ages. The office of the celebrant symbolises the focusing of the Eucharist in the givenness of the historic gospel and in the continuing life of the Church that is rooted in that gospel. The priest finds that at the altar he is drawn terribly and wonderfully near not only to the benefits of Christ's redemption but also to the redemptive act itself.

(CP 9–10)

Contemplative intercession

Jesus prayed on earth: he goes on praying still. The nights of prayer, his prayers a great while before day, the prayer in the garden, are somehow not of the past alone. When we say 'he lives to make intercession' (Hebrews 7.25), we note that the verb 'intercede' means to meet, to encounter, to be with someone on behalf of or in relation to others. Jesus is with the Father: with Him in the intimate response of perfect humanity; with Him in the power of Calvary and Easter; with Him as one who bears us all upon his heart, our Son of Man, our friend, our priest; with Him as our own. That is the continuing intercession of Jesus the high priest. Now we can begin to see what is our own role as people of prayer, as priestly intercessors. We are called to be near Jesus, with Jesus and in Jesus: to be with God with the people on our hearts. You too must promise to be daily with God with the people on your heart. Your prayer then will be a rhythmic movement of all your powers, moving into the divine presence in contemplation, and moving into the needs of people in intercession. In contemplation you will reach into the peace and stillness of God's eternity; in intercession you will reach into the rough and tumble of the world of time and change.

It means putting yourself near God, with God, in a time of quietness every day. You put yourself with Him just as you are, in the feebleness of your concentration, in your lack of warmth and desire, not trying to manufacture pious thoughts or phrases. You put yourself with God, empty perhaps, but hungry and thirsty for Him; and if in sincerity you cannot say you want God, you can perhaps tell Him that you want to want Him. You can be very near Him in your naked sincerity, and He will do the rest, drawing out from you longings deeper than you ever knew were there, and pouring into you trust and love, like that of the psalmist whose words may soon come to your lips.

Being with God with the people on your heart is the meaning of the daily office, of the Eucharist and of every part of your prayer and service of people. In the daily office we are lifted beyond the contemporary; and let us be sure that we will serve the contemporary scene effectively only if we are sometimes lifted beyond it, praying with the Church across the ages and with the communion of God's saints. The Eucharist is the supreme way in which the people of Christ are, through our great high priest, with God with the world on their hearts. The priest will show them that they are being brought near to the awful reality of the death of our Lord on Calvary as well as to his heavenly glory, for Christ upon whom they feed is one with the pains of humanity around them. As Christ's own minister in the words and acts of consecration, a priest is drawn closer to Christ's own priesthood than words can ever tell. Meanwhile, anywhere, everywhere, God is to be found: you can be on the Godward side of every human situation, for the Godward side is a part of every human situation. Think of your prayer simply as 'God, myself, and other people': being with God for them, and with them for Him.

(CP 13–18)

Confession and repentance

The motives that lead people to make their confession are powerful indeed. There is the feeling that thoroughness is called for in our confession, and the sacramental way certainly ensures this. There is the feeling that some painful and costly act on our part is not amiss in the confession of sins that wound the heart of our Lord. There is also the feeling that the corporate nature of the Church makes appropriate an acknowledgement of our sins to the family of which the priest is representative. Finally, the word of absolution has a salutary decisiveness, blending word and act in a truly evangelical way.

The Anglican tradition of spiritual direction seeks to hint and suggest ways of advance rather than to dominate or control, and sees the priest's role more as that of a doctor than that of a judge. The practice of confession can bring a Christian vividly near to Christ crucified. Experience shows that we need to confess not only those grievous lapses that worry our conscience, but also our whole condition of failure in all its symptoms, so that all may be disclosed and cleansed in the divine light. The light of absolution will then penetrate the entire self. Too often the failure to confess is in line with the failure to pray. Meanwhile let an enhanced awareness of the sins of society lead an individual to see not less but more clearly in the light of Christ that his or her sin is their own. I would plead for a deep and wide recovery of *repentance* in its biblical meaning.

To repent – *metanoia* – is to turn and to have a change of mind. This turning and change of mind are God's gift, and they are a turning and a change of mind towards God. We begin with a glimpse of the vision of God in His power, wonder, beauty and goodness. But a central point within this vision is the Cross of Calvary where Christ died for us. In turning towards him and changing our minds towards him there comes the realization of our littleness and insignificance as his creatures, of the absurdity of our pride, selfishness and fear, and the shame of our ingratitude. We see ourselves in his light, exposing every corner of our being to him. We grieve bitterly, but we rejoice in the truth. For we are sinners, and we cannot climb up again by our own act: impotent, undeserving, we await his act, his word – 'I absolve you.'

Many find that the significance of sacramental confession for them may change through the passing of time. A first confession may be an occasion of vivid realization of the Cross, and a decisive turning-point in spiritual depth. Subsequent confessions in the early years can have a similar vividness. Then a time may come when the vividness fades and confession seems to have the staleness of a humdrum discipline. So there comes the tendency to say, 'why bother?' and amidst the intense busyness and tiredness of life and work to let both self-examination and confession slip. It is, however, when going to confession requires a sheer discipline of the will that a new and creative aspect of it may begin to emerge. For the act of the will in confessing may enable you to escape vagueness and drift, and to regain a true picture of yourself. Then you may find in new ways how the loving kindness of God can hide, as it were, beneath the recesses of your failure, and you are humbled by discovering how God can use you in spite of yourself. Your humility and your grateful trust in Him are renewed, and your joy in the priesthood revives for the good of your work and of your people.

(CP 46–53)

Making God real

The message of the gospel is that if human beings have lost the capacity to humble themselves before their Creator, then the Creator will humble Himself towards His creatures. So the divine humility breaks upon the scene of human pride: Bethlehem, Calvary, the feet-washing at the Last Supper, all say that 'he who humbles himself will be exalted' (Luke 18.14): for divine humility is the power that comes to make the human race different (cf Philippians 2).

Your humility therefore will be the condition of your ministry and witness, which represent our Lord and make him known and loved, and enable people to have an awareness of God. For there is only one kind of person who makes God known and realized by other people, and that is the person who is humble because they know God, and knows God because they are humble. There is no substitute for this. It is only the humble person who is authoritatively a man or woman of God, a person who makes God real to others.

Through the years people will thank God for you. Let the reason for their thankfulness be not just that you were a person whom they liked or loved, but because you made God real to them. Put yourselves into God's hands in joy and thankfulness, and in the words of St Peter, 'Humble yourselves under the mighty hand of God, that He may exalt you in due time, casting all your care upon Him, for He cares for you' (1 Peter 5.6–7).

(CP 77–8 and 81)

Disappointment

'Fret not thyself because of the ungodly' (Psalm 37.1). There is certainly much to fret about: not only the world but also the Church as an institution can make you fret. There will also be fretting of a more personal kind always round the corner. The world is in God's hands; but His sovereignty is one of self-giving love, of the Cross and resurrection, of life through death: it is the sovereignty of suffering transfigured. There our fretting has its supreme answer, and you will see the truth of the Cross and resurrection in the men and women whom you try to love and serve. Remember also that the Church is both divine and human, and that it is God who judges the Church in its human element, and after judging can raise up a faithful remnant.

Whenever fretting threatens to get you down, turn to our Lord: he is grieving. Think of his sorrow, and the sting of self-pity will be drawn from yours. Every Christian and ordained person must come near to the grief of Jesus, seeing with his eyes, feeling with his heart. We come to learn that any disappointment, setback, or personal sorrow, or any wound to our pride can be made different if we are near to the grief of Jesus. You may then be able to say with the psalmist, 'It is good for me that I have been in trouble' (Psalm 119.71).

Many lives will be healed and made strong by your teaching, your care, and by your love for them. Our Lord will be there, with the words, 'Peace be unto you, as the Father has sent me, even so I send you' (John 20.21). But with the words, 'Peace be unto you' go always the wounds in his hands and his side. In the years to come you will know the wounds more than in the past, and you will also know the peace more than you know it now. Then one day many will thank God for all that you will have done to make the wounds and the peace of Christ known to them.

(CP 84–7)

Whose hearts God has touched

Today, someone enters his task as the chief shepherd of a great portion of the Christian Church: it is a task beyond all human strength, and many in this country are not so much hostile as indifferent and aloof. But he sets out not alone; there goes with him the great band of those whose hearts God has touched with the faith of Christ.

Today is an enthronement, but what does that mean? It is the putting of a man into the seat of a ruler, for in Christ's name he will rule in the Church of God, not indeed as lording over it, but as serving it, for, under Christ, authority and humility must go together. It is also the putting of a man into the chair of a teacher, for a bishop is the shepherd of the people by being also the teacher of God's truth, proclaiming the truth of God's majesty, God's compassion, God's claim upon all men and women, and God's wonderful gift of Himself to them in Christ. To shepherd and to teach, in the service of Christ, himself the Good Shepherd and himself the Truth: to this there is called one more man, the hundredth in this place, with all the frailties of human flesh and blood.

All the time there is, for all of us whose hearts God has touched, the supreme task ourselves to bring home to people God himself, in His majesty, His compassion, His claim upon men and women, His astounding gift of His very self in Jesus, the Word-made-flesh. We cannot fulfil the task for this country unless we are also striving to fulfil it towards the whole of the world. It therefore demands the service of men and women who will go anywhere in the world in Christ's obedience, who will witness to Christ's love in the insistence that all races, black and white, are brothers and sisters of equal worth. Here at home our mission means for the Church a constant involvement in the community, which we must approach as learners as well as teachers. We need to be learning not only many new techniques, but also what God is saying to us through the new and exciting circumstances of our time. Yet, because it is God to whom we witness, we need no less a constant detachment, a will to go apart and wait upon God in quiet, in silence; lest by our very busyness we should rob ourselves and rob others of the realization of God's presence: 'Be *still*, and know that I am God.' Would that everyone whose heart God has once touched would guard times of quietness amid our noisy, bustling life, to let God touch our heart again. Is there a more urgent need than this for every layperson, priest, bishop or archbishop in our Church?

So this is my own prayer today: 'Lord, take my heart from me, for I cannot give it to thee. Keep it for thyself, for I cannot keep it for thee; and save me in spite of myself' (St Augustine). Will you, as you come with me, make it your prayer, for me and for yourself? We must help one another, and serve one another, both in our family of the Church of England, and in Christendom near and far. Help one another, serve one another, for the times are urgent and the days are evil. Help one another, serve one another, as from this hundredth ceremony at the throne of St Augustine of Canterbury there goes forth a band of those whose hearts God has touched.

(CEA 165–8)

SAINTS

Michael Ramsey believed strongly in the communion of saints, and his belief was reinforced and guided by his keen sense of history. Worship with the saints means entering into a living past that can guide and deepen the living present of Christian experience and prayer. In this section we see some of those whom he most valued: Benedict, Gregory the Great, Anselm, Julian of Norwich and the other medieval English mystics. Different aspects of their teaching and personalities appealed to him and sustained him in his own prayer and ministry.

He believed also in the tradition of Anglican spirituality, running from Lancelot Andrewes and the Caroline divines to the early Tractarian movement, with which he closely identified. Its expression in the lives of Charles Gore and William Temple was important to him and formative too. His appreciation of Friedrich von Hügel and Evelyn Underhill in reviving contemplative prayer in the Church of England in his youth was profound.

He encouraged those called to the monastic life, and had a special sympathy with those called to contemplative intercession and spiritual conflict, to which he was particularly alert. His testimony to Father Benson, the founder of the Cowley Fathers, was matched by his being visitor of Mirfield and an active friend to the Benedictines at West Malling and to the Sisters of the Love of God in Oxford. He used to describe them as 'spiritual bolsters', the hidden resource underpinning the Church's unity and witness. His own reading of St John of the Cross was vital to him and profound, even to the very end of his life.

He loved the cathedrals and historic churches of England, and spoke lovingly of them as visible signs of the invisible stream of sanctity and Christian witness throughout so many generations. He believed that the deep renewal of the sense of the communion of saints would restore unity to the Church on earth, as it already exists in heaven.

St Benedict

It was the work of St Benedict and the monks of Monte Cassino to recover, in a corporate monastic life in the sixth century, the true concepts of Christian asceticism. To St Benedict nature was good, and worship meant not a flight from God's good works but the praise of God for them, and the offering of them back to Him. His community was devoted to the praise of God, not as a collection of individuals seeking perfection but as a *familia* – family. The self was to be forgotten in the brotherhood of a common life; and with the worship of God there went the daily work – *opus Dei* – wherein God claimed the common life as His own. Characteristic too of the Benedictines was the concept of *stablilitas loci*: instead of the restless roaming from place to place to escape from the world and themselves, Benedictines emphasised staying where you are called to be and consecrating life *there* to God's honour and presence. Benedictinism is an ascetic life, of poverty and chastity, with a particular emphasis on obedience; but it is asceticism reaching near to humanism. It is significant as an epitome of the principles of Christian life, applicable to different forms of Christian vocation.

(SS 21)

St Gregory the Great

How are contemplation and action to be blended together, for the life of the Christian community is a kind of rhythm of coming and going between the two? Probably none is greater than Pope Gregory the Great as an exponent of the blending of the contemplative and active. To St Gregory the contemplation of 'divine brightness coming scantily to the blinking eyes of the mind' was the supreme thing in his life, and he taught that the best kind of life on earth was the contemplative one, because it anticipated heaven and the vision of God Himself. Yet few in this world are called wholly and precisely to that because contemplation requires in life the love, righteousness and selflessness that are the secret of heaven itself. Not for a moment therefore is there any lessening of the ethical emphasis that runs through all of Christian life, but rather a constant rhythm between the active and contemplative life.

(SS 42–3)

St Anselm

How many are the aspects of St Anselm that come to our minds. We think of him first as a man of learning and philosophy. But he grew

The Body of Christ

from the love of letters as a scholar to the love of God as a monk, and he devoted his incomparable powers of thought to the deepest questions about God and the world. One great theme was constantly in his mind, the consistency of Christian doctrine with human reason. Reason indeed cannot create truth, reason alone cannot discover it: the order must always be *fides quaerens intellectum* – faith seeking understanding. But because reason is a God-given faculty, theology must be capable of commendation to reason. All those who through the centuries have understood the role of reason in theology can hail St Anselm as a guide and a spiritual father.

We think also of St Anselm as a monk, priest and pastor. Love towards God and humility in God's presence was the root of his own tenderness, sympathy and gentleness towards those in his spiritual care. A spirit of single-minded devotion to God was with St Anselm till the day of his death. With it there went his loving care of people. As a great teacher he cared for his pupils as much as for the truth, and the method of dialogue in his writings is a symbol of the interplay of mind with mind, of person with person. The love and sympathy that he showed towards his pupils and his fellow-monks was shown no less to both friends and enemies in the tumultuous years of his archiepiscopate. Reluctantly, unwillingly, this scholar saint found himself embroiled in politics, and contending for the rights of the Church against the Norman kings who wanted to override those rights. By constancy and integrity he won battles, however, without the weapons of worldly subtlety or strength.

(CTP 87–90)

Julian of Norwich

We recall Lady Julian of Norwich. Living in a time of catastrophe in England, the Black Death, she saw in and through a vision of the Passion of Jesus a glimpse of the unity of creation, sin and pain, transfiguring grace, the goal of heaven, tied all together in the love of God, which the Passion showed her. 'She sees in the Passion of Christ, in which she participates, all the suffering there ever was; the whole drama of humanity is summed up in one point' (Donald Allchin).

Julian's understanding of the oneness of the Christian pattern is rooted in her vivid vision of the Passion, when she desired like St Paul to know only Jesus Christ and him crucified. She said: 'I conceived a mighty desire to receive these wounds in my life: the wound of true contrition, the wound of kind compassion, and the wound of steadfast longing towards God.' In the Passion she saw the black horror of sin; and in the same moment the horror of sin is pierced by the love of the blessed Trinity, the love perfectly attained in the self-giving of Christ, which caused him to suffer. In that love creation is held fast, and all existence is seen as a tiny hazelnut in the hands of its Creator; and 'it lasts and ever shall last for God loves it'. So, not apart from life's calamities but in the midst of them, there comes flooding in the vision of heaven whose essence is Christ himself, and the certainty that 'all shall be well and all manner of things shall be well'.

No writer in the apostolic age describes this sort of experience of glimpsing the unity of truth in a single point: 'I saw God in a point.' But in several passages in the New Testament there are flashes of insight into a hidden divine pattern with the Passion of Jesus as the key: such flashes occur in Romans 8, in Hebrews 2, and in the Apocalypse. Julian is one of a number of mystics (including St Benedict and St Columba), who in different periods of history have grasped in the vision of a single moment what is really the pattern of the apostolic faith: the good Creator, the sinful human creature, sin and pain suffused by divine love, and Christ as himself the divine self-giving and himself the goal for human life. The point of coherence is Christ himself, whom to know is to be sure of the depth of human misery, the joy of God's heaven, and the hands of a faithful Creator.

(CTP 22–3)

Anglican spirituality

There is an Anglican sensitivity to the significance of spirituality, the life of prayer and theology. We see this often from Lancelot Andrewes to William Temple. In the twentieth century the growing interest in the study of religious experience, of the psychology of religion and of mystical phenomena seen in that context might have led many into subjectivism and shallowness, had not Anglican thought drawn upon the deep stream of Christian spirituality coming from past centuries. During that era there came a revival of interest in the great masters of the spiritual life. It meant much that many Anglicans were learning from the writings of Friedrich von Hügel a new sense of the human adoration of the Creator. Nor can the more popular influence of Evelyn Underhill, herself a disciple of von Hügel, be easily set aside. The width and depth of K.E. Kirk's study of many centuries of spirituality in the *Vision of God* shows how Anglicanism can draw upon something larger than itself, to correct or deepen passing tendencies that might otherwise become trivial and shallow. This unity of theology and spirituality owed much to the revival of the monastic life and vocation. I mention only R.M. Benson, the founder of the Cowley Fathers, whose profound grasp of the Creed was in the context of the life of prayer, and J.N. Figgis of the Community of the Resurrection at Mirfield, whose writings exposed the inner disease of Edwardian culture with the power of one who was a monk as well as a scholar and prophet.

(GT 164–5)

William Temple

William Temple's interest in particular doctrines was for the sake of their bearing upon theology proper, upon God Himself. Thus the kenotic question about Christ's self-emptying interested him less for what it suggests about the mode of the Incarnation, than for what it suggests about the nature of divine omnipotence and love. Atonement interested him not only for the sake of human beings and their salvation, but also for what he believed it to tell us about sacrifice in the heart of the eternal God. Miracle, at which he had at one time stumbled, came to matter to him for his belief that God is personal. The visible Church was significant as a sacrament of eternity in the midst of time. For him everything was related to God, and to be cherished and studied in that relation. Both as a thinker and as a person, Temple had a vast circumference of human interests and an unchanging centre: for all his interests were united serenely in his faith. Religious experience was for him the experience of anything and everything. He was thus, if ever a person was, a theologian by temperament and intuition.

(GT 146–7)

Father Benson

The mission of the Church is a work partly visible on earth and partly wrought in heaven. As the Church dies to the world in pain and patience souls are won; and Christ knows, as we do not know, whether he will save by many or by few, whether he will save rapidly or slowly.

So, for example, Father Benson believed that church buildings can often spring up to be in the end the sepulchre rather than the home of the living Church, while those called to the contemplative life must gaze rather towards God and do battle with Satan, which is the essential characteristic of all Christian life.

In the task of putting the Church's life into the context of secular human existence, this can only happen in an authentically Christian way and with joy, if there is deep within us the awareness of the conflict between Christ and the world as the New Testament sees it. Christian identification with the world entails a real death to the world, unless we are to be apostates from the scandal and the power of the Cross. When we look for the renewal of the Church, we must not confuse Christ's criteria of success and failure with our own criteria of success or failure. So when Father Benson speaks of 'evangelising with the cross of many a wearing year without results, and yet feeling that our labour in the Lord is not in vain', he is a good deal nearer to the spirit of the gospels than is the modern idea that if we toil in a place for a few years with no very visible results everything must be wrong and hopeless.

No part of Father Benson's message, however, is more important for us than what he says again and again about joy, and its place in the Christian and in the life of the Church: for to be without joy may be as big an apostasy as to be without love. The secret of joy lies in death to self, and in the joy of Christ, alike in success or failure; and without that joy the world will not be won.

(CTP 69–73)

Victory over evil

Some may wonder why, in the light of Father Benson's teaching on the divine victory, his sense of hostility to the world continues so strongly, for to him the world is still the enemy to be died to. On the other hand the transfiguring of persons and of suffering is a recurring theme of his teaching and meditation. The world has been deprived by Christ of its ultimate power as the organism of sinful humanity hostile to God; and by dying to it we can live in freedom from it. But the world still remains as a snare until the Lord returns and his kingdom will be all in all. Sin is indeed monstrous and tyrannical in its grip upon the human race, and deliverance from it can only be at terrible cost. The good news of Christianity is that the cost has been borne by God Himself in such a way that to believe and to share in what God has done in Christ is to know a powerful and contagious freedom.

('Bruising the Serpent's Head: Father Benson and the Atonement', in M. Smith (ed.), *Benson of Cowley*, 59–60)

The Church

Every Christian church was built because there exists the other hidden Church of which St Peter speaks: 'Come to Jesus, to that living stone, rejected by men, but in God's sight chosen and precious; like living stones be yourselves built into a spiritual house' (1 Peter 2.4–5). That is what the word *Church* meant to the early Christians: not stone or brick or wood, but the Christian people themselves. Jesus rejected by men and done to death on Calvary, but precious in God's sight and now raised from the dead, is its corner stone. When men and women are converted and baptized they are united to him, and so there grows, stone by stone, a spiritual house, Christ's home, Christ's temple, through whom Christ is now made known to the world. It is of this house of God that a cathedral such as this at Lincoln, or any church building is a symbol; and of all its glories the greatest is that it is a symbol of the house made of human lives. Through the centuries this other Church has stood: human lives united to Jesus, receiving his presence, and showing his goodness, his love, his sacrifice, his humility and his compassion. Living stones – what a mingling of metaphors! It tells of firm, solid, unmovable loyalty, and of persons alive in joy, in freedom, in creativity, in influence. This is the Church that Jesus Christ founded, the Church of which he said that the gates of death would never prevail against it.

(CTP 83)

Unity in Christ

'Called to be saints with all those who in every place call on the name of our Lord Jesus Christ' (1 Corinthians 1.2). What words those are! How they lift us out of our limitations into the supreme reality: we are one in Christ not because of our own ability to grasp things or any virtues we may be supposed to have, but because Christ has called us and we accept his call. When we say that Christ has called us we are at once in his hands, we are held by him, for him to do with us what he intends to do: for we are called *to be saints*. We are called to resemble

Jesus, called to be moulded into the likeness of Christ crucified. That is what Christianity is about: 'called to be saints', says St Paul; 'we shall be like him, for we shall see him as he is' (1 John 3.2), says St John. If that is what Christianity is about, it is no less what Christian unity is about: called to be saints, *with all who in every place* call upon the name of Jesus. Here indeed is a unity not made by us, not chosen by us, but created by Christ, from whose call we cannot escape. He is stronger than us, and he has prevailed. We therefore pray for that nearness to Jesus in the working out within each of us of the calling to be saints. May he who humbled himself in the stable in Bethlehem and on the wood of Calvary so humble us that something of his likeness may begin to be ours. To this he has called us, and has made us one with all in every place who have received the same call and dare not look back.

(CTP 94–8)

Unity and renewal

The message of Pope John XXIII was that unity is inseparable from renewal. The drawing together of churches can happen only through their being renewed both in inward spirituality and in vigorous service towards men and women. The credibility of the Christian faith in Europe of the future turns upon there being Christians who show by the Christ-likeness of their lives that Christ is living and true. While spiritual renewal is indeed happening within the institutional churches, it is also seen in movements that are impatient with the institutional churches and that seek Christian fellowship and social action in groups outside the visible churches. In many ways, both within and without the institutions, the Spirit of God is blowing powerfully today. But true Christianity will hold together the faithful of today with the saints of past ages only as the Church witnesses to truth that is timeless, and to those things that are not shaken. The saints of Europe now in heaven are near to us, and their prayers help us in our conflict. In them may be seen the Spirit by whom Christianity conquered once, and the Spirit by whom Christianity will conquer still.

(CTP 119)

The communion of saints

The prayer of a Christian is prayer with all the saints, and the phrase in the creed 'communion of saints' tells of this. These words have a richness and simplicity that are often missed, for the original Latin *communio sanctorum* can mean both the fellowship of holy people and participation in holy things. These two understandings indeed interpenetrate, for when Christians share in the Body and Blood of Christ they share as members of one another.

The word *koinonia* – *communio* means participation, and according to the New Testament writers, believers participate in the Father and the Son, and also in the Holy Spirit; they participate in the Body and Blood of Christ, in the sufferings of Christ, and in the lives of one another. Inevitably therefore the themes of holiness and participation interpenetrate, for the Holy Spirit, in making believers holy, lifts them out of their individual isolation, so that to share in the Spirit is to share in one another. The phrase, which we translate as 'the fellowship of the Holy Spirit', tells of this two-fold participation.

Deep renewal is needed today if the communion of saints is to be realised in its ancient meaning and power. The role of Mary is apparent: her role has been a great one in bringing the communion of saints into existence, for it was by divine grace and human response, divine command and human obedience, that the Incarnation happened and God's new creation began. As 'God-bearer' Mary has helped in the creation of the communion of saints. As a creature with ourselves, she gives glory to her Creator and ours, to her saviour and ours: more glorious than the cherubim and higher than the seraphim, she leads our praises to God.

It is within the reflection of Christ's glory that the prayers of all the saints continue. Within the family of saints we may ask the prayers of those who are near to the vision of God, and we may pray for all in earth or paradise or heaven. But we do not forget that the family includes those who are weak and struggling like ourselves, and those whose saintliness is very faint because the world has been reclaiming them. Our prayer looks towards the weak, as well as towards the strong; and if we are faithful it will reach both ways, since the glory of Christ is always one with the agony of his compassion. Such is the meaning of the words: 'I believe in the communion of saints.'

(*BS* 112–19)

Worship with the saints

The adoration of God is the first privilege and the final goal of us as His creatures and children. The claim that worship comes first rests upon the basic fact that God created us in His own image and after His likeness, and longs that we shall have with Him the closest relationship possible in love and in converse: a love and converse intimate and yet filled with awe and dependence upon Him as our Maker as well as our Father. He has made us for Himself, and our hearts are restless until they find their rest in Him (St Augustine).

In worship, our own generation of Christians belongs to the communion of saints reaching across the generations. Time seems to disappear as we find our family union with saints and martyrs of old, with the apostles, with the Mother of our Lord. Let us realize more vividly the communion of the saints in the bond of prayer and the Eucharist; and let us be sure that to do so is not to be merely looking backwards in history, but rather to be looking onwards and upwards towards the vision of God in heaven as, in fellowship with the saints who are nearer to that vision, we say: 'O God, thou art my God, early will I seek thee' (Psalm 63.1).

(CEA 74–6)

The living past

The deepest significance of the past is that it contains reflections of what is eternal. Saintly men and women of any age belong to more than their own era: they transcend it. Therefore openness to heaven is necessary for a Christian. Heaven is the final meaning of human beings created in God's own image for lasting fellowship with Him. Openness to heaven is realized in the communion of saints in deliberate acts of prayer and worship. But it is realized no less in every act of selflessness, humility or compassion: for such acts are already anticipations of heaven in the here and now.

(GW 115)

HEAVEN

Michael Ramsey had a lively sense of the reality of heaven, and used frequently to speak of it as the vital ingredient of Christian life, and

The Body of Christ

with great emphasis as his own life drew to its close. Prayer is the gateway to heaven; so too is the Eucharist. Humility is the sign that heaven has impinged on a human life, and every act of genuine compassion brings it very near.

Sensitivity to heaven kindles vision and hope, and this is vital for the life of the Church. Without it doubt and uncertainty can get the upper hand. Michael Ramsey believed in resting in God and submitting to a creative passivity through which God Himself could act. His sense of heaven was the wellspring of his joy and kindness, which was always life-giving in its warmth and hope.

The goal of human life

God is the friend of men and women; but because of human creatureliness it is a friendship mingled with awe and dependence. The biblical words 'glory' and 'glorify' express this relationship. When a person glorifies God, he or she reflects His love and righteousness like a mirror, and the more this happens the more that person humbles themselves in God's presence, ascribing all to Him who is the author of all good. Men and women whom we call saints have been marked by a growing reflection of the divine character, mingled with awe, penitence and humility.

Since men and women are made in the divine image, and the love of God for each and every member of the human race is infinite, the goal is heaven, which is the perfect fellowship of God's human creatures with Him in glory. In heaven God's creatures perfectly reflect His goodness in their selfless service of Him and of one another; and they enjoy the vision of Him, and the inexhaustible adventure of knowing, serving and seeing one whose goodness and beauty are perfect. Heaven is eternal, for God is eternal; and it is the fulfilment of the meaning of human life as created in the divine image, and of God's infinite love for each and for all. Thus heaven gives perspective to the present existence of men and women, and human life in this world is but a brief prelude to the goal for which they were created.

(SS 3)

Resting and seeing

How may we think of heaven? Let us recall some words of St Augustine: 'We shall rest and we shall see, we shall see and we shall love, we shall love and we shall praise, in the end that is no end' (*City of God* XXII.30). Resting, seeing, loving, and praising: these words describe not only the goal of heaven but also the message of Christianity in the world. For the world has lost the way of resting, seeing, loving, praising. Swept along in ceaseless activity, the world does not pause to consider. With no resting and no considering the power to see is lost: to see where we are going, to see the larger perspectives, to see beyond the group, nation or race, to see human beings as they really are with the image of God within them. Where seeing is dim, love becomes faint; and praise is lost, for we praise only when first we have seen and loved. Human beings lose the praise of their Creator, which is the goal of their existence and the source of their resting, seeing and loving.

If the words, rest, see, love, praise, tell of heaven and of the true life of human beings on earth, they tell no less of the Church's renewal at this or at any time. It has been all too possible in the life of the Church for 'rest' to mean a complacently tranquil piety; for 'seeing' to be the seeing within tradition without contemporary awareness, or the seeing of some contemporary enthusiasms without the perspective of history; for 'loving' to be within the circle of the likeable, and for 'praising' to be a kind of aesthetic enjoyment. The renewal of the Church will mean, and indeed there are signs that it does already mean, a rest that is exposed to the darkness and light of contemplation, a seeing of both the heavenly perspective and the distresses of the world, a loving which passes into costly service, and a praising which is from the depth of the soul.

(*BS* 123)

The joy of heaven

To have joy in God means knowing that God is our country, our environment, and the very air that we breathe: 'God is the country of the soul,' said St Augustine. Living in that country, we do not turn away from the griefs of our present environment; indeed we may expect a greater sensitivity to these. But we are in the perspective of God, of heaven, of eternity. I believe that much of the present obsession of our Church with doubts, uncertainties, negativities, loss of nerve, is due to our failure as a Church to live with God as the country of the soul. In that country we face problems with integrity, but we also share in the joy of the saints.

Christ draws us to watch with him, and to watch will mean to bear and to grieve. As the cloud of God's presence in the tabernacle in the Old Testament was pierced from within by a burning light, so the sorrow of Jesus is the place of reconciling love pouring itself into the world, and his joy there is radiant. 'Ask and you shall receive so that your joy may be full' (John 16.24): for 'your joy no one can take from you' (John 16.22). 'As sorrowful yet always rejoicing' (2 Corinthians 6.10): it is to this that you are committing yourself to the Lord Jesus Christ, saying:

Lord, take my heart and break it: break it not in the way I would like, but in the way you know to be best; and because it is you who break it, I will not be afraid, for in your hands all is safe, and I am safe.

Lord, take my heart and give it your joy: not in the ways I like, but in the ways you know are best, that your joy may be fulfilled in me.

(CP 91–3)

* * * * * *

Part Two
Reflecting on Michael Ramsey

Michael Ramsey: Man of God

JOHN HABGOOD

I first met Michael Ramsey some fifty years ago in a basement flat in Kensington, London. At the time, he was a fairly new Bishop of Durham, and I was the newest curate, one of six, at the parish church, St Mary Abbots. The flat belonged to my landlady, a certain Mrs Owen, who lived there with her daughter, Faith. I had found the lodgings quite by chance, through an advertisement in the local newspaper (curates had to do that in those days, as well as paying the rent), and until I was living there I had no idea who Mrs Owen was, or what her history had been. In fact she was a bishop's widow. Her husband, Leslie Owen, had been Warden of Lincoln Theological College in the early thirties, had then moved to Durham, first as Archdeacon and then as Bishop of Jarrow, and in 1944 had been made the first Bishop of the Forces. In the final stages of the war, he was in the sanctuary of the Guards Chapel in London when it was hit by a flying bomb during a service. There was a massive loss of life, and he was one of the very few survivors. On being translated to Lincoln in 1946, he died almost immediately after his enthronement, probably as a result of all the dust in his lungs after the bombing.

Why did Michael Ramsey visit Mrs Owen in her basement flat? Because early in his ministry he had been her husband's close friend and colleague. From 1930 to 1936 he was Leslie Owen's Sub-Warden at Lincoln, having first served a two-year curacy in Liverpool. Mrs Owen used to describe him as a very odd young man, at times near mental breakdown. There were episodes when she would find him lying on his bed, seemingly incapable of doing anything. But it was at Lincoln that he wrote his theological masterpiece, *The Gospel and the Catholic Church*, which made his theological reputation, and eventually won him a Canon Professorship at Durham. There he once again found himself living and working alongside Leslie Owen, who by this time was Bishop of Jarrow. In 1942 Michael married Leslie's secretary, the remarkable Joan Hamilton, who was to transform his life. Joan had also served as Bishop Owen's chauffeur, which must have been a test of faith on his part as it is said that she learnt to drive by trial and error. We got to know Joan well in later life. She was enormously likeable and competent, but I would not wish to have been driven by her. Michael never learnt to drive at all. He was physically clumsy, apt to go into trances, and would have been a disaster on the roads. Joan civilized him, and was a tremendous influence for good in all the practical business of living. It was completely characteristic of her that she should choose as her bridesmaid Faith Owen, Leslie's only daughter, who had been damaged at birth and was what we would nowadays call 'somewhat mentally disadvantaged'. All of which explains why Michael Ramsey used to appear from time to time in a basement flat in Kensington, as did many others.

Leslie Owen must have been an extraordinarily inspiring man. He gathered around himself a group of clergy who were to become renowned as spiritual directors. Eric Abbott, who succeeded him at Lincoln Theological College and later became Dean of Westminster, was one of them. At Michael's wedding, he was best man, and he too was a frequent visitor to Kensington. Reginald Somerset-Ward, perhaps the best known of all the spiritual directors in the Church of England at that time, had been another member of the group, as had Kenneth Carey, Principal of Westcott House, who later stole me from Kensington to become his Vice-Principal. Earlier in their ministries, he and Leslie had together largely created the present system of assessing candidates for ordination.

It is said that Leslie Owen used to describe his aim in training clergy as being to teach them to 'pray theologically'. Both words were important. There is no way of knowing God, or communicating anything worthwhile about him, except by prayer. But it has to be informed prayer – prayer rooted in deep reflection on what is actually given to us in the Christian faith. Much of the inspiration for this emphasis on prayer came originally from an earlier Kensington resident, Evelyn Underhill, an Anglican laywoman who revived the study of mysticism in the Church of England, wrote a ground-breaking book on worship, and was a much sought-after retreat conductor. She herself had developed spiritually under the guidance of Baron von Hügel, a Roman Catholic lay theologian and philosopher, who also had lived in Kensington at the turn of the century, and had himself written a classic study of mysticism.

Evelyn Underhill was deeply endebted to von Hügel, and it shows in her writings. Mrs Owen gave me as a leaving present Leslie's marked copy of one of her earliest books of retreat addresses. Typical of marked passages are a quotation from Walter Hilton: 'the city of the love of God was built "by the perfection of a man's work, and a little touch of contemplation."' And another from Mother Janet Stuart: 'Think glorious thoughts of God and serve him with a quiet mind!' And here is Evelyn Underhill's assessment of the current state of religion in 1926:

> A shallow religiousness, the tendency to be content with a bright ethical piety wrongly called practical Christianity, a nice, brightly-varnished this-world faith, seems to me to be one of the ruling defects of institutional religion at the present time. We are drifting towards a religion which consciously or unconsciously keeps its eye on humanity rather than on deity – which lays all the stress on service, and hardly any of the stress on awe; and that is a type of religion, which in practice does not wear well.

It was all summed up for me by a large framed picture on Mrs Owen's bedroom wall, which contained the single illuminated word – ETERNITY.

These, then, were some of the influences that impinged on Michael Ramsey early in his ministry. Some quotations may help to give a flavour of them. Von Hügel placed tremendous emphasis on religious experience, but he was also touchingly realistic about it. Hence this characteristic piece of advice in a letter to his niece.

> Religion is dim – in the religious temper there should be a great simplicity, and certain contentment in dimness. It is a great gift of God to have this temper. God does not make our lives all shipshape, clear and comfortable. Never try to get things too clear. In this mixed-up life there is always an element of unclearness. I believe God wills it so.

Here is another entirely characteristic remark: 'To sanctify is the biggest thing out.'

How far this close contact with the Owens and their group helped to shape Michael Ramsey's spirituality is difficult to say. The centrality of prayer in his life was obvious, as was a broad, unfussy catholic understanding of the Church, and a concern for the inner life as the primary focus of spirituality. But he was also very much his own man and, as a New Testament scholar, much more biblically orientated than those I have been quoting. He had come by his own route to a biblically-based Catholic Anglicanism. This avoided the pitfalls of what used to be known as 'spikiness', and was centred on a deep sense of the mystery of God in the Church at worship.

It was a route that by-passed the family tradition. Although his mother was an Anglican, the dominant ethos at home was set by his father, a prominent Congregationalist and a distinguished Cambridge mathematician, whose religion was clearly not very appealing to Michael or to his brother. Michael first became interested in religion through Eric Milner-White, later Dean of York, who was then chaplain of King's College Choir School where Michael began his formal education. He broke with the family tradition by being prepared for confirmation at Repton by its headmaster, Geoffrey Fisher, who was later to be his predecessor at Canterbury, and still played the headmaster when Michael himself was at Canterbury. As a boy he used to cycle round the countryside looking at Anglo-Catholic churches, and was particularly struck by St Giles's Church in Cambridge, near his home in Magdalene College. As he said later, he found there:

> a sense of mystery and awe and of another world at once far and near, a sense that we are at once in the presence of the Passion of Jesus and also vividly near to heaven, to which that Passion mysteriously belonged, so as to be brought from the past into the present.

That sense of awe and of the centrality of the Eucharist in worship were to remain with him for the rest of his life.

There was a very different kind of influence from his elder brother Frank, a mathematician and philosopher, who was even cleverer than Michael, and who from the age of 17 had been an atheist. This presented a double challenge to Michael, first, because it constituted a direct threat to his own faith, and second because when Frank, whom he loved and admired, died at the tragically early age of 26, Michael was faced with acutely worrying questions about the fate of unbelievers.

It is important to realize just how brilliant Frank must have been. As an 18-year-old undergraduate, and later as a Fellow of King's, Cambridge, he became a close friend of the philosopher Wittgenstein, for whom he had translated his virtually unreadable, but ground-

Michael Ramsey: Man of God

breaking, book *Tractatus Logico-Philosophicus*, from German into English. It was a book that was soon to change the direction of British philosophy. Frank was at first one of the very few people who understood it, better in fact that Bertrand Russell who wrote the Preface to it. Frank also wrote a brilliant review of it for the philosophical journal *Mind*. Later he co-operated with Wittgenstein in preparing a detailed revision of the book, and Wittgenstein subsequently wrote of him,

> I was helped to realise (my) mistakes – to a degree which I myself am hardly able to estimate – by the criticism which my ideas encountered from Frank Ramsey with whom I discussed them in innumerable conversations during the last two years of his life.

It cannot have been easy for Michael to have that kind of brother.

As a mathematician Frank believed with Bertrand Russell that it ought to be possible to reduce mathematics ultimately to logic, and Russell himself spent years of his life trying to do just that. It is the sort of claim which fits comfortably with philosophical atheism, the belief that, in studying any system or phenomenon, reason and logic by themselves can take us all the way. But, as Russell was later to discover, they can't. In 1931, the year after Frank's death, there was a formal logical proof of why they can't, and why logic always needs some starting point outside itself. The proof was the mathematical equivalent of demonstrating why it is impossible to pull yourself up by your own bootstraps. Whether we are talking about mathematics, or philosophy, or science, there are always insights and assumptions outside these systems which are needed to get the whole process of logical analysis started. Frank instinctively seemed to know this, and acknowledged the emptiness of logic on its own. Unlike Michael, though, he felt that outside strict logic there was nothing except personal feelings and opinions. The larger questions about life, the universe and everything else, he described as nonsensical. Michael, in contrast, had already learnt that there is more to life than can be contained within the bounds of reason and logic – things that affect the happiness and well-being of people; and these are not nonsensical. Perhaps this is one reason why he was first drawn to politics, encouraged by the debating skills he had acquired in the Cambridge Union.

Like Frank, Michael too was clever, and one aspect of his cleverness was a photographic memory. I had vivid illustrations of this when for a time during his retirement, and when he was in his eighties, he and

Joan lived in a flat we made for them in Bishopthorpe. He used to love meeting clergy when they came to the Palace, and would almost always remember who they were, though it was a long time since he had left York. Most striking of all, though, were our conversations after morning chapel when I would tell him about people I had met on my travels the day before. At any mention of a priest he had known, in almost any part of the country (and he seemed to know most of them), he could tell me his life history in considerable detail. No doubt he prayed for them all, and perhaps followed their careers in Crockford. But I felt put to shame by his knowledge of, and concern for, people whom he had probably not seen, or been in contact with, for a great many years.

I want to speculate about another aspect of his mind that I think indirectly revealed the difference between him and his brother. The occasion that provided the clue was the farewell dinner the bishops gave him in New College, Oxford, just before his retirement from Canterbury. Our meetings in those days used to take place in Cuddesdon. It was then vilely uncomfortable, but he loved the place, and rather unwisely went to live in Cuddesdon village for a time after his retirement. We moved our meetings to Salisbury when Donald Coggan succeeded him, but that was not much of an improvement. The meetings themselves were curious affairs. Michael's way of chairing a meeting was to say nothing, and appear to be asleep. Then when he thought we had all said enough, he would open his eyes and pronounce, usually very sensibly, on what needed to be done. By contrast Donald Coggan's invariable response to any problem was to appoint three wise men. Robert Runcie had a disconcerting habit of telling us what he thought we ought to do, before we had actually discussed anything. But I digress. I was merely accounting for the fact that Michael's farewell dinner was held in Oxford. At it he made a speech that few of us who were there will ever forget. There cannot be many of us left, and unfortunately there is no written record of what he said apart from a few remembered fragments.

He told us how he had dreamt that he was at a sherry party in heaven given by former Archbishops of Canterbury. One by one they had come up to him to convey their greetings and say something in character. He went through a long list of them without referring to a single note – another example of his extraordinary memory. Cranmer, for instance, came up to him saying, 'Ramsey, I don't think much of Series 3.' Fisher fussed around organizing everybody else, all too characteristic, I am afraid, given the degree to which he blighted Michael's ministry at Canterbury by constant interference. But Michael's greatest joy in his dream was meeting Anselm:

> at the end a little man came up whom I immediately recognized as Anselm. When we met we embraced each other because here I felt was a man who was primarily a don, who tried to say his prayers, and who cared nothing for the pomp and glory of his position.

Owen Chadwick, who somewhere found this snatch from the speech, comments that the bishops saw in this portrait of Anselm, Michael's own ideal for himself, an enthusiasm he shared with Pope Paul VI.

Why Anselm, and who was he? Archbishop of Canterbury from 1093 to 1109, a monk from the great monastery at Bec in Normandy, a leader who, like most medieval archbishops, was much involved in conflicts with the Norman kings, a philosopher and theologian who wrote important books on the Incarnation and Atonement, and, as we have seen, a humble, unpretentious man who said his prayers, and was declared to be a saint. He was also, I suspect significantly for Michael, an original thinker who saw faith as a precondition for the right use of reason. His formula, *credo ut intelligam*, 'I believe in order to understand', has been of profound significance to Christian philosophers for some 900 years. I am speculating, but I wonder whether this insight was part of Anselm's attraction for Michael in his intellectual struggle with Frank. He certainly picked on this as one of Anselm's great contributions to theology when in 1967 he went to commemorate him at the Abbey of Bec. On that occasion he also quoted the opening words of one of Anselm's books:

> Come now, little man, put aside your business for a while, take refuge for a little from your tumultuous thoughts; cast off your cares, and let your burdensome distractions wait. Take some leisure for God; rest awhile in him. Enter into the chamber of your mind; put out everything except God and whatever helps you to seek him; close the door and seek him. Say now to God with all your heart: 'I seek thy face O Lord, thy face I seek.'

They are words Michael must often have applied to himself. For Anselm they were the essential preparation and starting point for theologizing about God. They bring us back to the relation between reason and faith. Given the insufficiency of reason by itself, are there insights, assumptions, beliefs, experiences, sufficient to provide a valid starting point? This is one of the questions at the heart of many of our intellectual divisions today, and my guess is that it is the one which ultimately divided Michael and Frank. 'I believe in order to understand.' Do I have to?

Apart from his famous formula, Anselm is probably best known nowadays for his extraordinarily teasing argument for the existence of God, the so-called ontological argument, and I want to use this to elaborate briefly the role of insight. We can best approach the argument as a sort of meditation on the first verse of Psalm 14: 'The fool hath said in his heart, There is no God.' But, asks Anselm, what does the fool mean by God? He must mean what everyone else means, namely, 'something than which nothing greater can be conceived'. But, Anselm went on to argue, if this concept of God is only an idea in the fool's mind, then the fool is involved in a contradiction, for there is something greater than this idea, namely, that which is not just an idea, but which really *is* greater than anything which can be conceived. Therefore God must be more than just an idea.

You may not find this very convincing, and you would be in good company. The proof has been endlessly discussed as a logical conundrum, and constantly dismissed. In fact none of the formal proofs of the existence of God have convinced philosophers of religion because, if they worked as intended, they could only prove that God is part of the world of existing things – just as we are. But God does not exist in that sense. God is not one among a lot of other existing things, but is the ground and source of all existence. The notion of existence as applied to God is of a different order altogether. God may be perceived through what he has brought into being, and in that sense the formal proofs that begin from human experience of the world can help us to glimpse some of his attributes, as creator, fountainhead of order and purpose, source of all true values, and so on. And that is the level on which Anselm's proof also works. He gives us a concept of God – that than which nothing greater can be conceived – and points to its inevitability. What it does is to light up our awareness of the infinite, of that which utterly transcends us. It is a way of giving some content to what it is that the idea of God is pointing towards, a content that can open our minds, and enlarge our imaginations, touch our hearts, and stimulate our worship. The so-called proof is an invitation to think with all our powers about the God who surpasses knowledge, but who, in some profound sense, we already know. 'Faith seeking understanding.' Here we have a basic principle of all knowledge, even scientific knowledge, which relies ultimately on the belief that the world of nature exhibits a fundamental unity, and is thus open to rational understanding. The readiness to 'believe in order to understand' represents, as I see it, the essential difference between Michael and Frank.

Frank could be content with nothing less than precise definitions and formal logic. The same is true today of those who claim that the whole reality of life can be brought within, say, the compass of the exact sciences without any remainder. In the end, though, this too is a belief, which sidesteps the enormous questions about how we can know anything at all. Michael began with experience, with what he had discovered through worship, through the impact made on him by his study of the New Testament and his encounter with Jesus, and through the moral and social issues that stirred him to political action. And it was this experience that his theology could then begin to make sense of. There are hints that Frank too, when he knew that he was dying, yearned for a similar kind of experience, like many others before him. On his deathbed he asked Michael about religion, and in particular about the experience of the mystics. Michael felt that his mind was moving. Only a little. But it moved.

Michael said afterwards that his brother's death was one of only two occasions when he doubted God. He never doubted God's existence, but he did on these two occasions have doubts about what God *does*. The other occasion was his mother's death in a car accident just as he was beginning his training for ordination at Cuddesdon. But in the end nothing could shake his awareness of the presence of God, and this is something that those who knew him could immediately sense. Here was a man for whom God was the great reality of his life, and for whom there was no better way to live than by helping others to know and love God. It is no accident that the word 'glory' was constantly on his lips, and is perhaps why, after his great book on the Gospel and the Church, his next two books were on the Resurrection and the Transfiguration. At a tea party with some undergraduates someone once asked him what was the purpose of life. 'Why – to be changed from glory into glory,' was his reply. He then explained that 'Glory' isn't our human achievement or self-enhancement, making for rivalry. That is vainglory. True glory is losing life to save it, humbling, self-emptying. For Jesus to be glorified is to be lifted up on his Cross. Yet this exaltation brings him, and us with him, if we will, into true freedom. He made the same point in his little book on prayer, published towards the end of his life. 'For myself', he wrote, 'I am conscious that through the years "glory" has been central for my own thinking about the problem of Christian doctrine, the nature of Christian spirituality and the work of Christian evangelism.'

So what *is* glory? It is not a 'thing' or a state of mind. It is impossible to express all that it means without being enraptured by it. C.S. Lewis in a famous sermon described it as surpassing splendour and weight. I find the concept of weight interesting. It implies not only significance but also a sense of being burdened, of carrying responsibilities. Michael Ramsey made the same point. He loved to quote St Augustine's, 'We shall rest and we shall see, we shall love and we shall praise, in the end which is no end', but he was also aware of the dangers of introversion. Contemplative prayer, basking as it were in the glory of God's presence, has practical consequences. Jesus' going to the Father is also a journey deeper and deeper into humanity with its sin, its sorrow and its death. It is a journey both towards heaven, and towards the world's darkness. Worship itself can become an idolatrous perversion unless it is reflected in compassion towards the world. As Michael himself put it: 'To be near to the love of God is to be near, as Jesus showed, to the darkness of the world. That is the place of prayer,'

I have referred earlier to Michael's exposure to the mystical tradition in such writers as Evelyn Underhill. He certainly valued it, but in prayer, as in everything else, his main source of inspiration was the New Testament. This had convinced him that prayer is not primarily an individual exercise. It is primarily corporate and liturgical. We pray as part of the Body of Christ, and that is why the Church is not an afterthought, but central to the message of Jesus. This was the theme of his first and greatest book, *The Gospel and the Catholic Church*, but it also surfaces in his book on *The Glory of God and the Transfiguration of Christ*. He rejects an explanation of the Transfiguration as some kind of mystical phenomenon, experienced by the three disciples who were with Jesus as he prayed. He is insistent that the New Testament describes it as an experience of Jesus himself, a taking on board, as it were, of the work of his precursors, Moses and Elijah. The point he is making is that in this moment of visible glory Jesus was not alone, but was at one with the history of his people. And just as he was transfigured, so the Church has to be, and it too has to be willing to receive its inheritance in being changed from glory to glory.

Michael's commitment to what, in the mid-twentieth century, was called Biblical Theology was consistent with Anselm's 'believe in order to understand'. We have to take seriously what the Bible actually says before trying to assess it rationally. This was the exact opposite of what had been the main critical approach to the Bible since the mid-nineteenth century, particularly in Germany. There the tendency had been to whittle down the contents of the Bible to what nineteenth-century theological professors felt was credible. The revolt against this approach had been initiated immediately after the First World War by Karl Barth, and Michael had been inspired by his teacher, the only lecturer in the Cambridge Theology Faculty who took Barth seriously – Sir Edwyn Hoskyns. This was not fundamentalism, a distortion of biblical seriousness into a crass kind of literalism, which Michael never accepted. On the whole he was distrustful of evangelicals, particularly conservative evangelicals, in whom he observed a tendency to oversimplify what is actually subtle and complex. But the Bible was his lifeblood, which is why he was thrown off balance in the early 1960s by a new wave of criticism of Biblical Theology, which revealed its limitations. I must confess to having had a very minor role in this revolt, as one of a group of Cambridge theologians responsible for a volume of critical essays called *Soundings*. John Robinson had been excluded from the group, as being too conservative, and then immediately upstaged us by writing *Honest to God*. Michael subsequently regretted his overreaction to this book, because the questions all of us were raising were real ones. True, the Bible is our starting point for knowing what Christianity is, but we cannot actually use that knowledge without a proper understanding of the kind of world in which it is to be believed and applied. In a volume of essays written ten years later he acknowledged the problems and wrote:

> The lessons of the crisis of faith may have helped us and may help us still to know the glory of the Triune God, the Creator, the Judge and the Saviour of Man, and to proclaim it with more humility, more love, and more understanding of those who find faith hard ... it is through the facing of dark nights, whether in the mystery of God or in the agonies of the world, that the deepening of faith is realised.

He said once in a retreat address, 'There are *people* who make God near. That is the most marvellous thing that one human being can do to another.' It was true supremely of himself, but he was too humble to recognize it. This is the note on which I want to end. He and Joan were lovely people to know. There was much about Michael that seemed too unworldly to be really human – not least his total lack of small talk. But Joan made up for this. Despite the famous silences, there was a very warm human side to Michael that my wife and I were lucky enough to be able to experience. Shortly after we moved into Auckland Castle in 1973 he and Joan invited themselves to stay. We were somewhat alarmed to have the Archbishop of Canterbury descending on us quite so quickly after our arrival in Durham, but we need not have worried. All he wanted to do was to play croquet on the lawn with our children – that and passing on to me the Ramsey Rule – 'one in four . . . yes, yes, one in four . . .' – by which he meant 'block out one Sunday in four in your diary and allow no engagements'. It was wise advice, and I have tried to pass it on to those I have consecrated. I had further glimpses of his almost childlike humanity when I was lucky enough to have my portrait painted by the artist who had painted him three times, in Durham, York and Canterbury. The artist, George Bruce, dearly loved him, and used to travel with him on visits to parishes. He described Michael's amazement and delight on his move to York at being provided with a car which had a glass partition between himself and the chauffeur (a standard issue for archbishops in those days). It also had electric windows, and much of their journey time was spent by Michael gleefully pressing the buttons to watch the windows go up and down.

When after his retirement he and Joan had discovered the disadvantages of living in Cuddesdon and had decided to move to Durham, he humbly asked my permission as Bishop to do so. He didn't want to be in the way. In fact he was marvellous to have around, and I remember happy times sitting at his feet while he talked to students. When the house in Durham became too much for them, and we invited them to Bishopthorpe, they came as friends of the family, interested in all that was going on. And when even a ground-floor flat became too much for them, and they decided to move into a convent in Oxford, this great, holy and immensely learned man and his wife found a new friend and companion, who loved them and served them both for the remainder of their lives. He was a local hairdresser – Dennis Pratley – who had known them since 1974, when they had started their retirement in Cuddesdon. Now 13 years later, he moved them into their rooms, arranged their belongings for them, drove them wherever they wanted to go, and was always ready to abandon his own business to serve their needs. He went on doing this for Joan long after Michael's death. It is not everyone who can inspire such devotion. But then they were very special people.

Given at York.

Living through Dying: Suffering and Sanctification in the Spiritual Theology of Michael Ramsey

DOUGLAS DALES

In very truth I tell you, unless a grain of wheat falls into the ground and dies, it remains that and nothing more; but if it dies it bears a rich harvest.

(John 12.24)

Michael Ramsey stands in the distinguished and saintly lineage of those who went before him as pastors of the English Church – William Temple, Charles Gore, Edward King, John Keble, Lancelot Andrewes, Richard Hooker, St Anselm, St Dunstan, St Bede and St Gregory the Great, the Apostle of the English. His sanctity arose from his hidden life of prayer and was forged in the crucible of suffering and compassion. For so many people who knew or met him, Michael Ramsey embodied the truth that he proclaimed – Christ crucified and risen, and present by his Spirit. For those who were privileged to know him personally he was a person who made God real. His was a faith that proved in the end unshaken because it had sometimes been shaken. For as he said in his first book, *The Gospel and the Catholic Church*: 'the life bestowed by the Spirit is a life of which crucifixion is a quality, a life of living through dying'.[1]

* * * * * *

Michael Ramsey was a person who combined high intelligence with high sensitivity. In his education he had had to struggle with learning difficulties, and feeling overshadowed by a brilliant elder brother who later died in tragic circumstances. His preparation for the Christian ministry was marred by the loss of his mother in a car accident. As a result, his seminary, Cuddesdon outside Oxford, became for him a hill of vision darkened by suffering and the shadow of death. He was also a very shy person who appeared to some as eccentric. Nor did his approach to theology altogether fit with the prevailing fashions in Cambridge and elsewhere before and after the Second World War. He did not always feel as much at home in his own Church as might be thought, and he knew at times the pain of ostracism and misunderstanding from other clergy. His many travels as Archbishop of Canterbury opened his eyes and his heart to the suffering and darkness in the lives of so many men and women across the world. For him the problem of evil and pain never diminished, and the frustrations and disappointments of the Church's life sometimes weighed heavily upon him. As he once said: 'Christian faith has been for me a constant process of wrestling, of losing and finding, of alternating night and day. A sense of peace and serenity is a costly peace, a peace in the heart of conflict.'[2]

Michael Ramsey was a very private person whose inner spiritual experience remains largely inaccessible. But careful examination of his biography by Owen Chadwick and reflection on things embedded in his writings reveal a coherent pattern of experience from which he was able to speak with a moving eloquence, that could induce compunction in those who heard or read him. The trauma that befell him while he was an ordinand at Cuddesdon brought him face to face with the shocking reality of death, and with a sense of the fundamental vulnerability and fragility of human existence. He was familiar with the depression induced by the sense of futility and shock brought about by sudden bereavement. Preaching many years later at Cuddesdon, when he had become Archbishop of York, he said: 'It was here that we faced the truth about ourselves before the Cross of Christ, and with the painful shattering of our pride discovered that we have no sufficiency of ourselves to think anything of ourselves.'[3] It seems that in the darkness of that time he had a profound encounter with Christ crucified and risen, and careful reading of *The Gospel and the Catholic Church* reveals that this his first book encapsulates the spiritual vision that was born in him then, and by which he lived and taught through all his days. This realization of human weakness, coupled with his sensitive temperament, lay at the root of his own pastoral sympathy and personal humility.

Michael Ramsey was always acutely aware of human sinfulness, in himself and in relationships between people. As a student at Cambridge he had been drawn into the worshipping life of Catholic Anglicanism as much by its penitential demands as by the mystery to which its worship pointed. He inherited too from his Nonconformist and Evangelical background a strong moral sense and a deep conviction that Christ had died for him and for each individual person. He set great store by regular confession, practising it himself, and offering it to others with a gentle tact and wisdom. He came to the view that the modern Church too often skates over the grim realities of personal sin. He never doubted, however, the connection between individual sin and the sinfulness of human society, but he was adamant that repentance had to begin from within, and be taken up as a personal sacrifice and self-offering. He once said: 'The failure to confess is in line with the failure to pray.'[4] He also believed that this penitential discipline was vital for the spiritual life and moral integrity of the Church as a whole and for its ordained ministry: he once said: 'The Church shows the message of divine judgement to the world as she sees the judgement upon herself and begins to mend her ways.'[5] His view of the nature of divine judgement was guided by the teaching of St John's Gospel about Christ coming as light into the world and presenting a fateful choice to each person. For him this encounter with Jesus was profoundly personal:

> It must be in the figure of Jesus crucified and risen that we present the divine judgement and mercy. I see no other way of bringing the themes of sovereignty, power, compassion and judgement home to our contemporaries, except in terms of Jesus in whom these divine actions are focused.[6]

Repentance and prayer entail suffering, and inner spiritual change is never without cost. It means entering with Christ into the darkness of the world and sometimes of the Church too, the darkness found also within the human heart, and to glimpse the glory that descends and that lies hidden within each human person who responds to the call of Christ. In these numinous words, Michael Ramsey surely spoke from his own experience:

> The door into his sorrow is also the door into his joy. As the cloud of the presence in the tabernacle was pierced from within by a burning light, so the sorrow of Jesus is the place of reconciling love pouring itself into the world, and his joy there is radiant.[7]

His guide through this 'dark night of the soul' was St John of the Cross, whose writings remained close at hand until the end of his life.

The result of this going into the darkness with Christ is an enlarging of the heart and a deepening of vision, for it is often only in the darkness that the light of Christ may be glimpsed in its purity and wonder. 'Living through dying' results in a new sensitivity towards the presence of God in the midst of pain and frustration. It is an acceptance of the birth pangs of a new life within, that is being created by the wounded hands of Him who said, 'Behold I am making all things new.'[8]

For Michael Ramsey, sympathy and compassion were two sides of the same divine currency of love. Central to his teaching about prayer was the role of intercession, which he used to describe as bearing people in our hearts before God. Its foundation lay in the hidden contemplation of God in the depths of the heart. He described it in this way:

> It means putting yourself near God, with God, in a time of quietness every day. You put yourself with God just as you are, empty perhaps, but hungry and thirsty for Him. You can be very near to Him in your naked sincerity; and He will do the rest, drawing out from you longings deeper than you ever knew were there, and pouring into you trust and love.[9]

The Christian is called to follow the example of Jesus the merciful High Priest, described in the letter to the Hebrews, to which Bishop Michael often referred. 'Being with God with the people on your heart' lay at the root of his view of ministry and its role in leading the worship of the Church and the pastoral care of people. For 'anywhere, everywhere, God is to be found. You can be on the God ward side of every human situation; for the God ward side is a part of every human situation.'[10] Christians are called to engage actively through their prayers in the stream of compassion flowing out of the heart of God, confident that, in the words of St Gregory the Great, 'your good deeds shine where you are, and your prayers reach where you cannot be'. As Michael Ramsey himself said: 'In contemplation you will reach into the peace and stillness of God's eternity, in intercession you will reach into the rough and tumble of the world of time and change.'[11]

There is a cost to such prayer, however, and sometimes Michael Ramsey hinted at its nature, when for example he described the prayer of a religious community in words derived from Father Benson, the founder of the Cowley Fathers: 'the contemplative gazing to God, and doing battle with Satan, which is an essential characteristic of all

Christian life'.[12] He believed that the heart must engage with the world's darkness and suffering: 'the apartness must be real and costly, the nearness must be real and costly too'.[13] Contemplative intercession is the heartbeat of the Church's life, the conduit through which the self-giving love of God flows out through those united to Christ in His Body. St Augustine once said: 'Let God love Himself through you'. For to pray in this sacrificial and compassionate way is to be drawn within the communion that is at the heart of God, Father, Son and Holy Spirit. It is to be the place where love can be put in where love is not, and where all time, all chance, all circumstance may be held to and within Love's embrace.

* * * * * *

Michael Ramsey's vision of the heart of the Church's life and purpose was set forth week-by-week in the celebration of the Eucharist. Here the hidden spiritual rhythm of 'living through dying' comes to its sharpest focus: in the words of Jesus, 'Can you drink the cup that I shall drink, or be baptised with the baptism that I am baptised with?'[14] For in the words of St Augustine, 'Christians see set forth upon the altar that which they are called to become.' Regular participation in the celebration of Holy Communion was fundamental to Michael Ramsey's spiritual theology and ministry, formed as he was within the Tractarian tradition of careful preparation for and devotion to the Eucharist, but also anchored within the Evangelical tradition of personal surrender and dedication to Christ. The influence of Orthodox liturgy, to which he was exposed in the early part of his ministry and which he always valued, meant that he sensed that the earthly celebration of the Eucharist participates in something bigger than itself – the eternal and heavenly celebration of Redemption through the divine self-emptying revealed in the Incarnation and Crucifixion of Christ. He often pointed to the letter to the Hebrews and to the prayer of Jesus in John 17 as intimating the dynamic of divine love hidden within the communion that forms the life and identity of the Church.

By participating in the Eucharist, Christians come to see their own prayer and suffering as at the heart of their response to God's call to holiness, and also in the light of the Church's mysterious existence throughout the world and throughout the ages. As the Body of Christ, the Church shares in the suffering and redeeming love of God revealed in Jesus and made real by the Holy Spirit. The Eucharist expresses the intercession of Christ: in Michael Ramsey's own words:

Jesus is with the Father: with Him in the intimate response of perfect humanity; with Him in the power of Calvary and Easter; with Him as one who bears us all upon his heart, our Son of Man, our friend, and our priest; with Him as our own. That is the continuing intercession of Jesus the high priest.[15]

The Eucharist therefore is the key to the relationship between Christ crucified and the one Body. The suffering of repentance and love is the sign of the divine life within human nature as it is being remade in the image and likeness of Christ. 'By eating the bread and drinking the cup Christians will be brought within the death. In an unutterable way they partake of it; it is no longer an event outside them. His dying is become their food.'[16]

'Living through dying' means entering into the experience described for the first time by St Paul. For the secret of Christianity is 'Christ within you – the hope of glory to come.' To be a Christian means 'bearing in our body the dying of the Lord Jesus that the life of Jesus may be made manifest in our mortal flesh'.[17] Michael Ramsey spoke eloquently and movingly about the spiritual experience of St Paul as it is revealed in 2 Corinthians and also in his letter to the Philippians:

> Paul is ever near to the Cross in his own conflict with sin; in his bearing of sorrow, pain and humiliation when they come to him; in his bearing of the pains of others; in his increasing knowledge of what Calvary meant and means. But in all this he is discovering that the risen life of Jesus belongs to him, and with it great rejoicing.[18]

The language of the Eucharist therefore points beyond itself to this mystery, and by the power of the Spirit it enables Christians to participate in that of which it speaks, interpreting to them the meaning of their own growth through suffering into holiness. This is not just an individual vocation, however, for all are called to share in the communion of the self-giving love within God, Father, Son and Holy Spirit. Prayerful sympathy between Christians, often experienced as compassionate and sometimes heart-breaking suffering, is the decisive hallmark of the Church's true life and hidden unity:

> This unity in pain is very significant – it is the unity of the one single organism in joy and in sorrow. Suffering in one Christian may generate life and comfort in Christians elsewhere. 'So then death works in us, but life in you.' Thus the sorrows of a Christian in one place may be all-powerful for Christians elsewhere.[19]

This truth has certainly been borne out during the recent century of worldwide Christian martyrdom.

Whether conflict and travail in the life of the Church or in the lives of Christians will bring life or death depends on the willingness of churches and individuals to die in order to live. Addressing bishops in one of the last chapters of *The Christian Priest Today*, Michael Ramsey uttered these prophetic words:

> It may be the will of God that our Church should have its heart broken; and if that were to happen it would not mean that we were heading for the world's misery, but quite likely pointing the way to the deepest joy.[20]

Jesus said to his followers: 'You are salt to the world. But if salt becomes tasteless, how is its saltiness to be restored?'[21] He answered his own question by the blood, sweat and tears of Gethsemane and Calvary: for only from his broken heart flows out the living, life-giving water. It flows into the life of the Church through lives joined in sometimes painful union with Him, who is the head of the Church, which is his Body. To encounter Christ crucified in the Eucharist is therefore to embrace his life poured out in the mystery of the Resurrection. For as he himself promised: 'If anyone thirsts let him come to me, and whoever believes in me let him drink: for as scripture says – out of his heart will flow rivers of living water.'[22] The shape and content of the Eucharist retraces the suffering footsteps of Christ as he mounts the throne of his glory, which is the Cross. The whole drama of Incarnation and Redemption is set forth for adoration and participation. This is the mystery that lies at the heart of the Church's existence, by which God's judgement and glory in the face of Jesus Christ are made known. The celebration of the Eucharist therefore constitutes the Church's hidden unity and life, drawing with the voice of divine love those who come to Christ. As Michael Ramsey himself once said:

> Christ's presence in heaven is as a sacrifice, and in the Eucharist His presence cannot be otherwise. He is there as the one who gave Himself on the Cross, and who there and then unites His people to His own self-giving to the Father in heaven. Christ's unique act in history is the source of what Christians do.[23]

* * * * * *

Christ's unique act in history is also the source of what Christians become, for they are called to live life in all its fullness. As St Bernard once said: 'Life is given that we may learn how to love; time is given that we may find God.' How did Michael Ramsey perceive the joy and holiness of a life filled by the Spirit of Christ? How did he sense the reality of eternity peeping through the lattice of the Church's visible life? How did he relate to those who have gone before along the path of 'living through dying': the saints whose life lies hidden with Christ in God, men and women of every race and age, who have been transfigured by the fire of the Spirit within them? Some of these, for example, St Anselm, St John of the Cross and St Gregory the Great, clearly exerted a profound and lifelong influence upon him, so that he could speak of Christianity as the experience of 'a living past informing a living present'. For him holiness was a summons and a reality, and it was his charisma to be able to communicate it in this way to others.

Holiness may perhaps be defined as sensing God, being with God and becoming like God; and for Christians, in the words of William Temple that Michael Ramsey so often used to quote, 'God is Christlike, and in Him is nothing un-Christ-like at all.' Michael Ramsey taught many people how they might sense God and draw close to Him. One of his last books, *Be Still and Know*, exerted great influence by distilling the essence of his experience and approach. His classic collection of ordination charges to his clergy, *The Christian Priest Today*, continues to inspire and assist many priests and others called to Christian leadership and ministry. It is still possible in reading this book to catch the cadences of his unique way of teaching and preaching, and to sense the compunction that his own sensitivity to language, rooted in prayer, could induce. For him, holiness meant that, through a person's whole life and character, God could be sensed and be made real.

He once described being a saint in these words, which catch as in a mirror much that was so true of himself:

> The saint is one who has a strange nearness to God and makes God real and near to other people. His virtues do not make him proud, for he is reaching out towards a perfection far beyond them and is humbled by this quest. His sins and failings, which may be many and bitter, do not cast him down, for the divine forgiveness humbles him and humbles him again. He shares and bears the griefs of his fellows, and he feels the world's pain with a heightened

sensitivity; but with that sensitivity he has an inner serenity of an unearthly kind, which brings peace and healing to other people. This strange blending of humility, sorrow and joy is the mark of a saint; and through him God is real and near.[24]

Like St Gregory the Great, to whose teaching he often referred, he believed deeply in the 'perfection in imperfection' that lies at the heart of each human person, made in the image and likeness of God. To this hidden potential for perfection he tried to reach out in his own pastoral approach to people and in the spiritual guidance he gave them as a confessor and friend. The work of the Holy Spirit in each person is to burnish that image and restore that likeness so that the glory of the only God might be caught in the unique personality of each of his children.

'Humility, sorrow and joy' – these are the hallmarks of sanctity, and there are perhaps three key words that unlock Michael Ramsey's understanding of holiness and of the experience of joy that it brings. For his own joyfulness was at times contagious and memorable, bubbling out of him amid the silences of his shyness and thoughtful sensitivity. The first key word is 'compunction': the sense that nearness to God pierces the heart with an awareness of sin as a failure to love in response to God's love. He communicated a strong sense of God as a loving but demanding Father, from whom no secrets could be hid. He was himself such a spiritual father, embodying the high standard of God's holiness but at the same time making it accessible because of the humility of his love. It is an interesting fact that his writing can still induce a sense of compunction, composed at it is with great clarity and emotional charge from the depths of his own experience of God. He knew that divine love flows into human lives at great cost – to God and also to those receiving or mediating it. His joy was tinged by the experience of sorrow and penitence, and that is why he placed such emphasis on regular confession as the threshold of spiritual life in Christ.

The second key word is 'kenosis' – the Greek word used by St Paul in Philippians 2 that means 'self-emptying'. Here Michael Ramsey was very much a disciple of Charles Gore and William Temple in his theological understanding of how in Jesus God poured himself out in love for the world, so that the Incarnation reveals the inner dynamic of God's own existence. Jesus emptied himself in service and self-sacrifice, and by this self-emptying enabled the life of the invisible God to flow through him into the lives of all that would empty themselves to receive him. This is experienced through the Orthodox prayer of the heart that Michael Ramsey used, as a person stands penitent and empty but loving, open to the hidden presence of Christ within, praying: 'Lord Jesus Christ, Son of the living God, have mercy upon me, a sinner.' This is also the great mystery at the heart of Christian worship, symbolized by the empty chalice that stands on the altar, clean and stable and open to heaven, in order to receive the fire of the Spirit that descends, becoming the means of God's self-giving in Christ.

The third key word is one that has taken on a wide meaning in spiritual and ecumenical life: '*koinonia*' – or 'communion' – the transformation of human relationships by life in the Holy Spirit, and the sense that the Church is a single fellowship of friendship in Christ. Michael Ramsey had a lively sense of the reality of the Holy Spirit, both in the study of the Bible and in the life of prayer. The book that he published just after his retirement called *The Holy Spirit* represents the way in which he was able to hold theology and prayer together in a dynamic unity. He believed strongly that through the inspired words of Scripture God does communicate with human beings in a life-transforming way. But the understanding of Scripture relies on the partnership between prayer and theological study, as the Spirit of God illuminates the mind and stirs the heart. For him this came together in the Eucharist, and was encapsulated in the words of Christ in John 17: 'Consecrate them by the Truth.' The gospel of the Cross reveals the truth that human sanctification rests upon Christ's own consecration of himself for them, and the Eucharist mediates this sanctification. What is this sanctification if it is not to become drawn into the communion of the Father, the Son and the Holy Spirit? It is only as human persons are held within the love of God that they are healed, transformed and fulfilled, for we truly have no power of ourselves to help ourselves. Yet in His will is our peace, and Christ expresses that will and the Spirit brings that peace.

* * * * * *

Perhaps these words of St Isaac the Syrian, written in Iraq in the eighth century, the time of Bede, sum up the call of God hidden in the teaching and memory of Michael Ramsey:

> His path has been trodden from the ages and from all generations by the Cross and by death. But how is it with you that the afflictions

on the path seem to you to be off the path? Do you not wish to follow the steps of the saints? Or have you plans for devising some new way of your own, and of journeying there without suffering? The path of God is a daily Cross: no one has ascended into heaven by means of ease: in truth without afflictions, there is no life.

In the Galilee Chapel of Durham Cathedral, where Michael and Joan were married, these words are placed above where the Venerable Bede lies buried: 'Christ is the morning star, who, when the night of this world is past, brings to his saints the promised light of life and opens to them eternal day.' The witness of Michael Ramsey is this: that only as the 'night of this world' is endured, and repudiated, in the lives of individual Christians, and in the life of the Church, will the holiness of God be sensed and seen in those to whom Christ brings the light of his risen life. The call of 'living through dying' comes every time Christians draw together to share in the Eucharist, when through willing union with the divine sacrifice, by compunction and self-emptying, they find themselves enfolded within the communion of the love of the Father, the Son and the Holy Spirit, whose glory rests in His saints. It is for this that we pray, in the words: 'Come, Holy Spirit, fill now the hearts of your faithful people; and kindle within us the fire of your love. Amen.'

Given at Canterbury.

Notes

1. GC, p. 30.
2. *Problems of Christian Belief* – a BBC broadcast and publication, 1966.
3. CEA, pp.159–60.
4. CP, p. 48.
5. Ibid., p. 23.
6. Ibid., p. 25.
7. Ibid., p. 93.
8. Revelation 21.5.
9. CP, pp. 14–15.
10. Ibid., p. 17.
11. Ibid., p. 14.
12. CTP, p. 72.
13. Ibid., p. 67.
14. Mark 10.38.
15. CP, p. 14.
16. GC, p. 101.
17. Colossians 1.27 and 2 Corinthians 4.10–12.

18 *RC*, p. 95.
19 *GC*, p. 46.
20 *CP*, p. 99.
21 Matthew 5.13.
22 John 7.37–8.
23 *GC*, p. 116.
24 *CTP*, p. 53.

The Christian Priest Today

ROWAN WILLIAMS

Some years ago, the board that selected candidates for the Anglican ministry embarked on a study designed to clarify the question, 'What ordained ministry does the Church of England require?' in the hope of assisting colleges and courses to focus on appropriate priorities. As these exercises go, it was fairly successful, and made theological educators do a bit more theology about their own teaching of theology and its goals; but the very phrasing of the question reveals a rather typically Anglican quirk, the tendency to approach theological issues by description. Another tradition might well say that you ought to begin by asking what ordained ministry *God* requires (let alone what the Anglican God requires), and sorting out all your theological priorities from first principles.

But we should hesitate a little before assuming that this question shows us only a rather faded pragmatism. It is quite possible to come back and say, 'But it may be precisely in working out what the Church of England requires that we find out what God requires'; that is, we discover God's will for ordained ministry in the process of discovering what the Church needs in order to be itself, what the Church needs for its integrity, its mission, its intelligibility to itself. And this is just the process we see at work in the book commemorated in the title of this essay, Michael Ramsey's *The Christian Priest Today* – that book rightly described by Douglas Dales as 'the most treasured book that Bishop Michael ever wrote'. At the end of his immensely rich second chapter, he writes: 'In describing the priest's office . . . I have followed an empirical approach, beginning with the Church's practical experience and working back from this to an understanding of the ministry.' But he goes on to say that 'it is far from true that while the Church is our Lord's creation the ministry is only a device whereby the Church can be effective' (2nd edn 1987, p. 10). Looking at what in fact is needed ought to open up the whole question of what God requires – but also of what God has *given*: and any reflection on the

Christian priest today has to be a reflection not just on what we find helpful but on what has been provided for the Church. This is Michael Ramsey's method, and it crucially reminds us that we are in trouble if we start thinking that ordained ministry is an idea developed by us to make things run more smoothly.

This isn't about going back into the deadlocked debates over whether Christ explicitly established one form of ministry to be valid for ever; even in the sixteenth century, Hooker was critical of those who claimed absolute certainty about this. But it is about getting away from a view of the Church that is very seductive and very damaging – and very popular. This is the view that the Church is essentially a lot of people who have something in common called Christian faith and get together to share it with each other and communicate it to other people 'outside'. It looks a harmless enough view at first, but it is a good way from what the New Testament encourages us to think about the Church – which is that the Church is first of all a kind of space cleared by God through Jesus in which people may become what God made them to be (God's sons and daughters), and that what we have to do about the Church is not first to organize it as a society but to inhabit it as a climate or a landscape. It is a place where we can see properly – God, God's creation, ourselves. It is a place or dimension in the universe that is in some way growing towards being the universe itself in restored relation to God. It is a place we are invited to enter, the place occupied by Christ, who is himself the climate and atmosphere of a renewed universe.

Forget this, and you're stuck with a faith that depends heavily on what individuals decide and on what goes on inside your head. But if the Church really is larger and more mysterious than this, if the Church is *Christ's place*, it is a reality shaped – not in the remote past, but daily, here and now – by Christ's action. And that action is most deeply the unbroken movement of self-forgetful love towards the one he calls Abba, Father: all Jesus is on earth is an expression of this – his forgiving, his healing, his parables, his shared meals, his death and his Resurrection. In eternity and in time, Christ makes himself a gift; and in the turbulence and violence of human history, that gift is a gift that makes peace between humanity and God. It is a sacrifice, not in the sense of a bribe to persuade a hostile deity to overlook our failings, but in the sense of something given up, handed over, so that a mutual relationship may be both affirmed and recreated.

Being in the Church is being in the middle of this sacrificial action, the act of Christ's giving; it is being in the climate, the landscape, of priesthood. This is what is given to us as Christians, what we are rather incompetently trying to find words and structural forms for in our daily life as a human institution. The point is that the energy for this searching for words and forms is created by the fact of God's gift, not by any attempt to make a human community run better; it is an energy devoted to what will *show* the inner and prior fact. And this is where we turn again to the New Testament. When Christ calls, he calls, we are told, into a community with diverse roles and tasks, not into a mass of individuals vaguely looking for things to do; and one of those roles, from the beginning, is that of apostle. The apostle is given the task of witness, above all; the apostle has to point in word and action to the basic facts of the action of Christ, to witness to time spent in the company of Jesus, before and after his Resurrection (Acts 1.21–2, 4.13). The apostle is the one to whom *responsibility* is given for connecting this or that context, this or that community, with the fact of Jesus – and so of connecting communities with each other also.

Thus when Christ calls human beings into the community where the new creation begins, he calls some, from the very beginning, to be simply witnesses of that community's character. Initially, they are those whose words connect the hearers with Christ; they make Christ contemporary with all who hear the good news. And as the immediate personal link fades with the passage of time, the Church makes it clear that the task of witnessing to the contemporaneity of Christ is still essential to the Church's integrity in a twofold way – by the recognition of a fixed canon of Scripture as God's gift in the Spirit to the Church, a gift that is an act of divine speaking as it is read and received in the community; and by the recognition of apostolic ministry as a continuing element in the Church's constitution. The personal focus of worship and proclamation in the community is one who has publicly and demonstrably received, by a network and sequence of specific relationships, the word and power of the first witnesses.

The Church is therefore always a body that has built into its very structure a twofold measure of its honesty and fidelity, a twofold means of self-questioning and self-criticism, Bible and public ministry. The Church is never left to reimagine itself or reshape itself according to its own priorities of the moment; for it to be itself, it has received those gifts that express and determine its essential self as a place where the eternal self-giving of Christ is happening in such a way as to heal and change lives. The Bible and the ministry constitute the Church as literally a 'responsible' community, *answering* to what is there before it. And as the understanding of ordained ministry has developed, what this has come to mean is that this ministry is one of the things that renders every local community in its witness and worship responsible to the creative source of the Church's life.

What does this begin to mean for the priest today? If this account of the inextricable involvement of apostolic ministry with the very identity of the Church is right, the person exercising that ministry has one fundamental task which breaks down into a number of different responsibilities. The fundamental task is that of announcing in word and action in the middle of the community what the community is and *where* it is; it is telling the Church that it is the created universe insofar as that universe has been taken up into the activity of the eternal Word and transfigured by this fact, and that it is in consequence the place where Christ's self-offering continues to be most freely real and effective. The priest is therefore in the business of – as we could put it – immersing in Christ's action the gifts and prayers and love of human beings. These things, of themselves, are too weak and compromised to make peace, to sustain the loving relation of God with creation; so they are borne along by the one action that truly and eternally makes peace, the self-giving of the Word. In all this, we can perhaps see why and how the Eucharist is the central identifying act of the Church, simply because it is where our action towards God is taken up in God's action towards God; where the making our own of Christ's prayer at his table opens us up to receive Christ's life so that our own self-offering may be anchored afresh in his. 'Although we be unworthy . . . to offer unto thee any sacrifice, yet we beseech thee to accept this our bounden duty and service.'

For this to happen in the ministerial life, there must be skill and willingness and space for at least three things. The priest has to be free to be a *lookout*, an *interpreter* and what I can best call a *weaver*.

The priest must first of all be free to see. The language of the Hebrew Scriptures about the prophet as watchman (as in Habakkuk and Ezekiel) comes into its own here. The minister who has to tell the Church what and where it is must be free to see what and where it is. The entire point of being on watch is that you have the chance of seeing what others don't – not as a visionary privilege, but as a weighty and sometimes intensely painful responsibility undertaken for the sake of the whole community. 'Be aware', wrote Michael Ramsey, 'of the new and powerful trends in the world which bear upon the Church and its mission' (*CP*, p. 40). The priest has to have the opportunity of not being so swamped with 'duties' that he or she can't maintain a sense of the whole landscape. And this works both negatively and positively. Negatively, it has to do (as in Ezekiel) with seeing the unwelcome relations of cause and effect over time, seeing what behaviours and habits erode the integrity of God's people. The priest has to be beyond cliché, challenging the obvious and consoling stories people may tell so as to see the real faultlines. 'The Church is declining', say some people, 'because of too much accommodation to the modern world'; 'no', say others, 'the Church is declining because of too little accommodation to the modern world'. The good priest will want to say no to both these bromides and turn to other kinds of reasoning. What if the weakness of the Church is to do with a range of neutral and irreversible social factors, or to do with a climate of anxiety and joylessness? Less obvious slogans, needing a lot of careful following through; but this requires some patient seeing of the long-term history we're part of, *and* of the obscure inner rhythms and seasons of the Christian psyche. Those who have preached most effectively in this and other eras are, it seems to me, those who have known how to read the surface and the depths, but have had no great interest in the shallows. The effective and faithful priest is a witness to how Christ's offering takes up what is ours to make it a gift to God; if 'what is ours' is not the focus of patient and truthful attention, if the human complexity of what Christ came to share is not grasped, how can it be brought fully into the landscape of his sacrifice so that it can be transfigured?

This 'seeing', then, has to involve a fair bit of literacy about the world we're in – literacy about our culture (cultures, rather), about how our contemporary emotions and myths work, about the human heart. The priest's obligation to maintain such literacy is not just to do with the need to speak to people in the language they understand, in a missionary context; it is grounded in the need to show believers the world they live in and help them to respond not instantly or shallowly but with truthfulness and discernment. There has to be in every priest just a bit of the poet and artist – enough to keep alive a distaste for nonsense, cheapness of words and ideas, stale and predictable reactions. And this is a crucial part of being visibly a sign of what and where the Church is, the Church which is called to live 'in' the truth. So for the priest there is, as I've said, an urgent practical responsibility not to be so driven by what present themselves as duties and tasks that there is no time for this sort of education of seeing and listening, maintaining literacy in human reality. Along with whatever training to lead and manage that may be given in preparation for priestly ministry, along with instruction in theology and ethics, there must be active encouragement to nourish this seeing and listening, the novel and the newspaper and the soap opera and the casual conversation – even (especially?) when it looks like wasting time from some points of view. Otherwise, what threatens is what Christianity's greatest critics (Nietzsche above all) have homed in upon – a Christian discourse that is essentially about unreal persons with unreal desires and fears.

And this leads into the second kind of responsibility, that of being an interpreter – by which I mean not primarily someone who interprets culture to and for the Church or interprets the Church's teaching to the world outside, but someone who has the gift of helping people make sense to and of each other. Communities, in spite of the sentimental way we sometimes think of them, don't just happen. They need nurture, they need to be *woven* into unity (more of that in a moment). If the unity of the Church is not that of a mass of individuals with a few convictions in common but that of a differentiated organism where the distinctiveness of each is always already in play, then for the Church to be consciously itself it needs people to see and show how diversity works together. Sometimes this is a role of active co-ordination, drawing out gifts and deploying them, sometimes it is helping some people see that what others do is bound up with what they themselves do. It is articulating why different styles of mission and service serve each other – and sometimes articulating why different styles are harming or subverting each other. Interpretation can be involved with discipline and warning as well as harmonization.

Put more theologically, it is about helping believers to see Christ in one another. The interpretative work of the priest looks first at how to uncover for one person or group the hidden gift in another – especially when the first impression is one of alienness and threat. The priest is the instrument by which God's generosity is laid bare, and thus by which generosity becomes possible for believers. Of course, it can turn into a sort of sentimentality, an optimistic 'I am right and you are right and all is right as right can be' blandness. But the task of actually showing *Christ* is harder – showing not a generalized acceptability in another person and producing a generalized tolerance, but showing the specific challenges and graces of the real Jesus, and producing a specific gratitude. So the priest has to ask, Where in this life and witness is the healing and absolving of Jesus, where is the summons of Jesus to penitence, where is the bearing of the Cross, where is the Resurrection? In the context of conflict within the Church, local or global, the priest as a human participant charged, like it or not, with making particular decisions, may have to take sides at some points;

but before and beyond that, the priest has to remind everyone involved of what and where they are, and so of the expectation that, if the Church is what it claims, Christ will be visible on both sides in certain ways.

This can also involve showing people the suffering Christ in each other. One of the painful things priests (not to say bishops and archbishops . . .) have to hear is two parties expressing with equal anger and grief the sense that the other is always the favoured one, that they are powerless victims. The liberal and the traditionalist will give an uncanny echo to each other as each insists that their pain and anxiety are ignored by the powerful opposition who control everything. So that before further battle is joined, there is a role for the priest in enjoining a pause to ask, 'Can I see not only my suffering but the other's? Can I see the Cross not in my experience but in theirs?' Put it boldly: the priest sometimes has to speak not only as parent to the prodigal son, but as parent to the elder brother who can only see his brother's forgiveness as his own humiliation and loss.

And it is in interpreting people, especially believing people, to each other at this level that the priest has to act as the 'weaver' of communal life. The Church is, as we've noted, a variegated body, not a chaotic mass trying to apportion jobs; but it still needs a kind of orchestrating in order to show the activity of the one Christ in the diverse roles and functions and gifts being exercised. This is what the priest's leadership in public worship and sacramental life makes visible: the Romanian theologian, Dumitru Staniloae, wrote that the priest's role was to 'assemble and concentrate' the Christian people at prayer. When the priest gives voice to the praying identity of Christians at the celebration of the Eucharist, our prayers are located where they need to be located, assembled and concentrated in the act of Christ. So much of the debate about 'lay presidency' misses the point here: when Christians pray together in a way that places them in and with Christ, publicly and ritually, the one who animates and co-ordinates this is giving expression to the priestly essence of the Church; the very least we can say is that it is a coherent and intelligible sign of this fact if the president is, routinely, precisely the person who is charged with telling the Church where and what it is, in his or her daily and lifelong service.

But the weaving, the building into differentiated unity that the priest is committed to, does not stop with the celebration of the Eucharist – though everything else done will take its energy and urgency from that. The priestly task is a making of connections at many levels. Paul tells us in 2 Corinthians that Christ's is a ministry of reconciliation, and that we have to realize in our relations with each other that peace which Christ has made for us with God. The priest may simply be connecting persons – bringing the alienated to meet each other, peacemaking in the individual or the collective context, addressing racial and social conflict, listening to the tensions over justice between men and women, struggling with how we find ways of speaking from the wealthy 'post-Christian' world of the North Atlantic into the anguish and frustration of the developing world and the Muslim nations. The priest may be connecting visions and ideas – building bridges between the gospel and human concerns (those concerns that he or she strives to keep alive as a lookout and a truth-teller), working as an apologist who seeks to make faith humanly compelling. The priest may be brokering plans and aspirations in a local community through an Employment Forum, a community partnership.

It is a task that is necessarily profoundly co-operative, yet one in which there is an irreducible element of personal investment; which is why this aspect of priestliness can be so particularly draining and frustrating. To be yourself a place where lines of force intersect, where diverse interests and passions converge is one of the hardest aspects of that dimension of priestly life which is about living in the fantasies and expectations of others. It is unavoidably something to do with the heart of your personal being – and it is also something that can threaten your sense of yourself, your very integrity.

Is being a Christian priest today significantly different from what it was when Michael Ramsey wrote, or indeed when George Herbert or John Chrysostom wrote? Not really; but what I've been saying so far will already have hinted at some of what makes the role distinctively hard today (*don't* imagine it's harder than it's ever been; it's just that this is the particular way it's hard now). The role of lookout is complex when our culture is simply so diverse, and when we are constantly struggling with a climate of pervasive mild cynicism, where the corruption of a lot of our communication leaves you feeling very much at sea in trying to find words of transparent truthfulness. The interpreter's job is a nightmare when Christians are sometimes positively eager to conclude that they have nothing to say to each other. The weaver may feel his or her integrity disappearing in the effort to create a living web of generous relationship, because we are all these days so much more self-aware, in sometimes less than helpful ways, aware of how we are seen and 'read' by others, and of the muddle of our own motivation.

All the more reason to ask the hard questions about what resources we need for such a work. And again, some of what I've already said may point to a few directions here.

To be a lookout, telling unwelcome truths, you have to ask what sort of things make a trustworthy person. And one possible answer is that *faithfulness* is something that renders a man or woman trustworthy, the willingness to be consistent and patient. It can be the willingness to stick with a situation of dis-ease and conflict, and not look for a quick and false solution. It can be the readiness to put thoughts of short-term success on hold. It isn't realistic any longer (because communities themselves are so much less stable) to imply that the priest who spends thirty years in one parish is the pastoral ideal; yet there really are settings where a reluctance to spend significant time reinforces a community's perception that they're not worth much. And it's worth saying that self-supporting local ministries (why do we like that negative term 'NSM' so much?) can be a very powerful affirmation in this context.

But faithfulness applies, even more importantly, to the formation of personal discipline – an unfashionable and faintly embarrassing word. Does our personal rhythm of prayer and study show the marks of patience, persistence, healthy scepticism about hasty expectations? Does it move on deep tides, able to hold still in periods of frustrated or numb feeling, unafraid of silence? This may be – should be – the most secret aspect of the ordained life in many ways; but somehow, mysteriously, I think that believing people get a sense of whether a priest's life of prayer is or isn't characterized by this sort of steadiness, the long breaths for the long haul. The looking, the watching, on behalf of the community also requires that human hinterland I referred to earlier – a certain familiarity with just how human experience can be difficult and tragic. What plausibility is there in the words of someone who seems to see *less* in the world than others, whose understanding of the murkiness of human motivation and the frequency of human failure is smaller than that of the average believer? Here, surely, we stray in the direction of Nietzsche again, with his furious accusations that Christians create unreal emotions about unreal objects.

It is this familiarity with the face of humanity and this fidelity in prayer that equips us for the most demanding aspect of the interpreter's task. We can't uncover the face of Christ in people unless we have the habit of real attention to human faces in all their diversity – but also the habit of familiarity with the face of Christ. How do we recognize him, let alone help others to do so, if we are not spending time with that face, in the study of Scripture and in adoration and silence? Faithful and persistent looking into the face of Jesus is the essential condition for connecting people with each other; without that, all we can offer is human goodwill, human shrinking from the cost of conflict, our own limited skills of sympathy and listening. But if we try to remain familiar with Jesus, we believe that our listening and meditating has a sacramental dimension, mostly imperceptible to us, but real and energizing. We are allowing some fuller reality into the situation, the reality in whose climate we live: the priestly mediation of Christ.

Weaving the community together, then, while it draws out all our psychological and personal skills, is finally the work of Christ and the Spirit. To know that is to be grateful; and it is gratitude that sustains us in the tension of our own holding and plaiting together of the strands of human and Christian variety. If our ministerial priesthood is a making visible of what the Church is, it must be always referring itself to the action that makes and keeps it; if we know what that action really is, we shall be thankful. Gratitude and theology belong together (surprisingly?) Theology is supposed to let us know the depth and dimension of what has been done, the scale of the landscape we inhabit, so that we are less likely to see the Church as just a human association dependent upon skill, agreement and goodwill. Priests need *detachment* – not from human suffering or human delight, but from dependence on human achievement; and good theology offers training in such detachment, prompting us to keep our eyes on the landscape in its full scale, not our inept and uneven cultivation of it. To be a point where lines of force converge and are knitted together, there must be a level of stillness in us that allows this to happen, or at least allows us to see beyond the complicated efforts and political stratagems that we are tempted to invest in the process.

So the priest today needs a faithful and patient commitment in prayer and in work; a sense of the depth of the human heart, in good and ill, a certain three-dimensionality in understanding humanity; a patience with human diversity that is expressed by the willingness to keep looking at the human face; a familiarity with the face of Jesus that enables him or her to recognize it even when it is hidden; a habit of gratitude and a level of detachment. But all of this relates in one way or another to having a theology worth talking about, a picture of the universe within God's purpose and of Christ as both the agent and the environment of the new creation. Within and beyond all the debates about the detail of theological education and ministerial formation these days, the largest question still remains too often unanswered: what is the shape and unity of the Christian view of creation itself? What is the comprehensive story we tell? This is not a question about having more 'doctrine' in a course, but about how the whole process of ministerial education makes us natives in the landscape into which Jesus has invited us, and gives us some of the tools for celebrating how God has acted to introduce us into this place. We are not called on to give a bit more room to one module among others here, but to see this actual and present world joyfully and consistently in the light of God's being and doing, in the light of the trinitarian life and the incarnation of the Word.

When the vision of God's being and doing has become weak, theology becomes defensive – and so do Christians in general and priests in particular. One of the numerous things that have made Michael Ramsey's writings so liberating for many is the degree to which they are free from defensiveness. 'The God of the Bible is majestic enough', he writes, 'not to require such protection' (*CP*, p. 25) – the protection, in this instance, of an anxious urgency to maintain the literal sense of every inch of scriptural narrative. But he goes on, in words that have a good deal of resonance today, to be equally critical of 'defensive Catholicism' unwilling to take any risks for the sake of unity (p. 26): a poignant plea, if you think of his own disappointment over the failure of the Anglican-Methodist negotiations of that era. But somehow or other, we all have to undergo a fairly fundamental conversion from seeing revealed truth as a possession to be guarded to seeing it as a place to inhabit; not one bit of territory that needs protection, but the whole world renewed. We shall not proclaim Christ effectively if we are constantly reverting to what makes us anxious rather than what makes us grateful.

All I have said so far implies that the priest's task is centrally and essentially to proclaim that world renewed – in personal care, in public teaching, in sacramental action. And the point of such proclamation is to tell the assembly of believers who they are in God's presence, what it is to be involved with and in the priestly act of Jesus Christ and what that means in the daily interactions of human life in terms of reconciliation, judgement, risk and gift. So far, I haven't used the word 'mission' – partly because I think that sometimes we need to clarify the content before we use the actual word. But I hope that what has been said will have some obvious resonance with the challenges that currently stand before the Church in Britain, and that it is a picture that will make sense in the new styles of church life towards which we are undoubtedly moving. An ordained ministry that reminds the Church what it is in terms of its invitation into Christ's place will be an essential aspect of that necessary renewal which takes us beyond the identification of 'Church' with the way we have historically run things. Ironically in the eyes of some, a theology for 'emerging Church' ought to underline the rationale for ordained ministry, Catholic ministry, not to obscure it; because an emerging Church without the recognizable signs and relations embodied in Catholic ministry is in serious danger of lapsing into the mode of a human assembly of those who agree and sympathize with each other. But how Catholic ministry is deployed and resourced becomes an invitingly large question, to which institutions like this one will have a huge amount to contribute.

Pre-eminent among the contributions it should be making is, I believe, an insistence upon the two things that have reappeared consistently throughout these reflections – the human hinterland of priesthood, the enriching of an awareness of complex and diverse experience; and the sense of a landscape, of inhabiting a world that is in all sorts of ways strange and still to be explored but is unmistakably real, including, pervading, the concrete world around. This means – as for all training institutions, residential above all, but not exclusively so – a stewardship of time that refuses to be pushed into patterns that are dominantly functional, that assumes training to be about growth at least as much as skills and covering a syllabus. For the problems of ordained ministry today have a great deal to do with whether or not the priest can hold together the reality of this world with the reality of Christ's renewing act; and for this we need above all a theology that is alert to the full scope of what the Catholic creeds announce, the mystery of God's threefold life, the ungraspably radical fact of the Word becoming flesh, the fidelity of the Spirit praying Christ in us and into us, and sanctifying what we offer in our powerlessness and unworthiness.

'Today the ordained priest is called to reflect the priesthood of Christ and to serve the priesthood of the people of God, and to be one of the means of grace whereby God enables the Church to be the Church' (*CP*, p. 111). That is hard to improve on as a summary of what the Church asks of its priests – and it takes us instantly to that deeper question of what God asks of the Church. In this place, the Church has asked and not been disappointed; in this place, God's asking has been heard and learned, and from here so many have gone to relay that divine challenge and invitation to the Church. May the years ahead see the same resource and courage go into the formation of our lookouts, our interpreters, our weavers; may the same truthfulness be absorbed and the same landscape become visible as our Church – please God – learns how to be itself afresh, and is set free to speak for Christ.

Given at Cuddesdon.

Theology in the Face of Christ

ROWAN WILLIAMS

For God ... made his light to shine in our hearts to give us the light of the knowledge of the glory of God in the face of Christ
(2 Corinthians 4.6)

It is a text that could plausibly stand as a summary of everything Michael Ramsey believed mattered most in Christian life and theology. The best work to be written on his theology to date has the simple title *Glory: The Spiritual Theology of Michael Ramsey*, and anyone at all familiar with his writing will know the omnipresence of this theme. But Ramsey's theology was not just a celebration of the divine radiance or beauty; or rather it was a celebration of divine beauty which assumed that 'the knowledge of glory' was more than merely a metaphor for the enjoyment of that beauty. Ramsey spelled out in several places the sense in which the Pauline phrase was a quite specific prescription for doing theology. And in this, as in many other ways, he stood close to perhaps the greatest theological mind in twentieth-century Roman Catholicism, the Swiss Hans Urs von Balthasar, whose first major multi-volume work on theological method was entitled *Herrlichkeit*, 'Glory'. Indeed, as we shall see, the connection was more than a matter of parallels: Balthasar uses Ramsey's work in some key sections of his discussion of the New Testament, and helps us see where the Archbishop's fundamental theological insights might lead if developed more systematically.

The implication of Paul's words is that the face of Christ – not just the narrative of Christ or the words of Christ or even the work of Christ – is a source of knowledge because it is the bearer of glory. And early in his work on *The Glory of God and the Transfiguration of Christ*, Ramsey undertakes a careful study of the basic meanings of 'glory' in Jewish Scripture that begins to make sense of this in a way that takes it beyond a simply aesthetic response to revealed beauty. Like Balthasar again, he is concerned – though he would not have expressed it in these terms – to create a theological aesthetic, a doctrine of beauty anchored in consideration of God's own nature. 'Glory' is a word that expresses the internal solidity of some reality – it may be wealth or power or reputation, as in various passages from the Psalter and Isaiah, but it may also be the internal life of a person, as in Psalms 16 and 108, and Genesis 49.6. The root *kbd* expresses weight or magnitude; the verb *kabed* means to be heavy, to be many, to possess honour (just as we call someone a weighty person) – though also, by a quite understandable paradox, it can mean being dull or sad.

God's glory is thus, in this context, not only God's radiance, the visible form of God's power; it is inextricably linked with some idea of God's character, God's life. As Ramsey points out in these early pages of his book, the promise in the prophets that God will in the last days or in the new age manifest his glory is connected with the manifesting of God's justice: what is revealed is who God is. 'In the kabod of Yahveh,' he writes, 'radiance, power and righteous character are inextricably blended.' It is as if the word described the inner 'resource' of God, that which grounds and informs God's substantial, objective presence, a presence that is fleetingly uncovered in theophanies in the Hebrew Scriptures but whose full manifestation in the world awaits the last days. In the meantime, however, there is one setting in which we can say that the glory of God is regularly present and effective in ancient Israel – the Temple, upon which glory descends at its consecration (2 Chronicles 5.13–14), in which Isaiah encounters the glory that confers on him his prophetic vocation (Isaiah 6), from which glory departs in Ezekiel's vision (Ezekiel 11.22–3). In the Priestly writings, this is first associated with the tabernacle in the wilderness and then with the Jerusalem Temple – a perceptible presence, whose virtually physical quality is vividly expressed in the statement in 2 Chronicles that the priests could not stand to perform their duties when the cloud of God's presence descended. Although this manifestation seems less to do with character than some others, as Ramsey points out, it is worth noting that it functions in the texts referred to as a sort of intermittently visible sign of divine fidelity to Israel, so that it is not exactly neutral in respect of God's character.

Against this background, it is clear that the conception of glory in the face of Christ immediately speaks of Christ as revealing the divine character, the inner integrity of God, as we might put it, in the promised last days. If we say that we have seen glory in him, we recognize that the messianic age has come. Ramsey shows how both Paul and John work with this idea. Paul declares that Jesus already fully inhabits and diffuses glory, so that believers are promised both the vision of that glory and a share in its light: they too will be radiantly transfigured presences. Already we reflect glory when our faces are turned to Jesus; in the age to come we shall do so completely in our whole (renewed) material identity. For John, Jesus' journey towards the Cross is the record of a gradual unveiling of glory, moving in exact step with the outward closing in of Jesus' mortal fate: the Cross is in this sense the eschatological moment, the new age breaking in as its *kairos* arrives, and the followers of Jesus who have seen his glory gathering throughout the ministry have been made ready to receive the outpouring of the Spirit on the day of resurrection. They begin thereby to enter the state of glory promised them in Jesus' prayer in John 17; the mission that was Jesus' now becomes theirs by the gift of the Spirit, and if Jesus is glorified by the performance of his mission from the Father, so believers, working and witnessing in the Spirit, are equipped to share the same glory.

What is new in John, and decisive for Ramsey's theology here and elsewhere, is the focus upon John's association of glory in its fullness with the Cross. The glory of Jesus in the Fourth Gospel is always related to what might be called the 'other-directedness' of Jesus' vision: he receives glory from the Father because he does what he sees the Father doing, he accepts his identity, his destiny, from the Father's hand, so that his glory is always that of a Son whose being is derived from the Father's (John 1.14). Since the Cross is the climax of Jesus' obedience to the Father's will, it is the moment in which he is most entirely receptive to the glory given by the Father. On the Cross, he has nothing of his own: he 'hands over his spirit' (19.30) and becomes wholly transparent to the divine presence and action in that moment of self-dispossession. Already in *The Gospel and the Catholic Church*, Ramsey had emphasized that in the New Testament the distinctive sense of 'glory' was given by its association with 'self-giving' (p. 92), with a self having 'its centre in Another' (p. 25), so that the disciples are summoned to share in the divine unity by sharing in the divine 'self-negation'. And while this may be disputable as a general judgement on the New Testament's vocabulary, it is obvious that Ramsey sees the Fourth Gospel as providing the ultimate integrative principle for the rest of that vocabulary. It is perhaps also worth noting that he will have known the passing comment of his teacher, E.C. Hoskyns, on John 1.14, that two texts in Leviticus (9.6 and 9.23) associate the manifestation of God's glory in the Tabernacle with the hour of sacrifice (Hoskyns, *The Fourth Gospel*, p. 148). Given that, as Hoskyns also noted, the incarnate Word in the Fourth Gospel is understood as one 'whose Body is the numinous Temple of God' (p. 149), the connection of thought is very plain.

This is already a rich vein of exegetical reflection, and it was to be steadily mined in various ways by Ramsey in practically everything he wrote in the rest of his career. My question is how these themes can now help us 'plot' the locus and path of theology in a time when the biblical theology of Ramsey's era is largely forgotten or rejected. Ramsey's method of exploring and aggregating the meanings of key words in Scripture has long been overtaken by new techniques of textual analysis and historical research; as John Court observes in a critical essay on Ramsey as exegete, the theological dictionary is the typical deposit of this style of theology, with its assumptions that 'biblical' concepts in general are naturally distinctive and that they have a sort of intrinsic directedness towards a full and normative explication in the pages of the New Testament. The effect is to obscure the real distinctiveness of specific texts and traditions from each other and to flirt with a supersessionist attitude to Jewish words and meanings (Gill and Kendall, p. 97). While there may be some debate about how just this assessment is overall, it is certainly true that Ramsey's approach seems to reflect a 'dictionary' method. I want to ask how seriously this affects the essence of what he is arguing, before going on to see what further development of his basic ideas may be possible.

First of all, it is indisputable that, for example, *kabod* in Hebrew has precisely the physical connotations that are important to Ramsey and that we understand something of the word's use when we grasp this; and Paul's passing use of the phrase 'the weight of glory' suggests that he is not unaware of this background. Equally, it is clear that many of the texts of Christian Scripture under discussion are consciously reflecting on the complex of uses and meanings in Hebrew Scripture. Indeed, the truth is that, for the writers of the New Testament, the theme of God's glory is already a literary and theological datum; as Ramsey notes, it is something discussed in Jewish literature of the period. For the early Christians, it is, so to speak, already a 'dictionary' issue – that is, it has become one aspect of the literary unity that is 'Scripture' for Paul and his contemporaries. They are doing biblical theology: they are treating the texts of Hebrew Scripture as a synchronic reality, something that can be engaged with as a coherent whole. Of course there are differences between Hebrew usages and between different New Testament responses to them. But there is more of a continuum than a critic might at first allow. And one of the interesting features of some recent New Testament scholarship is, ironically, the recovery of certain lost or obscured themes that draw diverse material together: the significance of the ritual and myth of the Temple for the entire period, to take a pertinent example, has been identified more decisively than ever.

So it would be a mistake to conclude that Ramsey's method is as artificial as Court seems to suggest. Undoubtedly, scholarship has moved on; but its movement has not nullified the idea of searching for thematic connections. Reference to the Temple in recent exegesis points up very clearly the significance for first-century Jewish people of the building and the sacrificial system as concrete embodiments of divine presence. That Temple-related language is so widely spread in the New Testament writings implies that it was indeed debates over the location of divine *kabod* that fuelled much of the earliest Christological reflection. Certainly for Johannine thought, the actual material presence of Jesus is in the strongest possible sense the habitation of *kabod*; and it is not fanciful to see in the falling-back of the soldiers confronted with Jesus in Gethsemane a serious echo of Old Testament imagery such as that in 2 Chronicles: here too glory has a presence as powerful and exclusive as that of a material other, it impinges on those in its field of force. We are not dealing with a simple manifestation of divine radiance, but with something apprehended as both more continuous and more active. Granted the reservations that may be entered against certain versions of 'dictionary theology', the fact is that John's Gospel in particular is a complex single text reflecting on a complex scriptural heritage that is seen as a unified whole. It is not an arbitrary exercise to trace theological continuities and implications in such a setting.

John's Gospel famously lacks a transfiguration narrative: when those around Jesus see or are invited to see his glory, it is not an exceptional visual phenomenon that they are directed to. They see (or fail to see) in the context of Jesus' human activity – and ultimately in the context of his human suffering. In other words, to see glory in the Johannine world is to be given a possibility that is not just inherent in ordinary human capacity. The believer sees that God's solid, resistant objectivity, God's activity that 'pushes' at our own boundaries, is wholly identified with the physical presence of Jesus: not with particular works of power, though these may trigger recognition, nor with words of wisdom or prophetic insight, though these may be seen to be fitting to the underlying reality, but with the entirety of Jesus' identity, and most particularly his unequivocally human and finite moment, his death. And such a vision depends upon some modification in the believer's capacity, depends, in fact, upon the believer's 'death': John's Gospel ends with the enigmatic recommissioning of Peter for a future in which he will be bound and delivered up like his master. As we have seen, Ramsey insists, in *The Gospel and the Catholic Church*, on the Johannine linkage between unity and death: the trinitarian communion into which believers are introduced is a life in which all believers have relinquished their own centre in themselves so as to be centred in Christ and in the human other (pp. 24–7). Thus the truthful vision of Jesus that is given to the believer is a vision from somewhere other than the natural centre of the ego: it is the truth given by the Paraclete.

I have already mentioned von Balthasar's citations of Ramsey; and it is specially in the context of these themes that Balthasar most suggestively refers to him. Balthasar's discussion of the way in which God's life is present in the entirety of Jesus' humanity (*Herrlichkeit* III.2.ii, pp. 300–6) notes Ramsey's stress on the 'quasi-physical' character of glory in respect of Jesus' human story in making the point that the *Hoheit*, the exalted splendour, of Jesus is not something that can be separated, even by the most sensitive surgical tools of research, from the facts of his life. It is not a literary device or a matter of psychological reaction. It is the sense of divine freedom permeating Jesus' human identity; and it is recognizable only by gift, the gift of what Balthasar calls a *Sensorium*, a transformed sensibility, or, in scholastic language, a *connaturalitas*, a community of nature and instinct that allows us to see God's freedom in the light of or in virtue of a freedom granted to us. A little later (p. 328), Balthasar again refers to Ramsey to bear out his argument that Luke's Jesus is in fact set before us in a narrative in which it is just as clear as in John that his entire existence is to be seen as manifesting glory. Interestingly, Balthasar also refers to Kierkegaard's great meditation in the *Philosophical Fragments* on the anonymity of God in Jesus; though he (rightly, I think) identifies what is missing in Kierkegaard's reflections as the trinitarian dimension, which alone gives its full (and positive) sense to the Johannine narrative. The hidden glory is not simply an arbitrary paradox or simply a consequence of the impossibility of God appearing as God in the created order: it is the outworking in finite form of the eternal self-yielding, self-hiding we might almost say, of the Son before the Father, the Son who does not will to be 'visible' except as the living act of the Father – which takes us back to Ramsey's repeated emphasis on the eternal and inner-trinitarian ground of the Johannine sense of glory.

In the light of Balthasar's elaborations of the same basic motif, we can perhaps see more clearly how and why the glory of God is, for Ramsey, a reality that is about knowledge – as the Pauline text with which we began implies. The relinquishing of a centre in the self, the drawing out of love and faith towards Christ actually makes possible the understanding of who God is in Jesus – of the trinitarian life and the incarnational sacrifice. As the believer begins to be free of self-absorption, s/he begins to see a little of what might be thinkable about a God wholly free of self-interest. Such a God is, on the one hand, free to be present without self-protection or reserve in any place, including the places most remote from 'heaven': he can be in the hell of suffering and abandonment without loss of self, since the divine self is utterly invested in the other; and, on the other hand, such a God cannot be conceived as an eternal individual self, but as a life lived eternally in that 'investment' in the other. Thus the believer perceives what I have called the interiority and integrity of God, the resource and solidity of divine life: what is indestructibly solid in God is this life-in-the-other. To see the freedom of God to be in the Cross is to see glory, because it is to see how God's utterly non-negotiable presence and action can be real in the physical body of the tortured and dying Jesus.

The Jesuit theologian Edward Oakes, writing about von Balthasar, quotes a French Catholic philosopher as saying that, in the life of faith, 'Perception of credibility and belief in truth are identically the same act' (p. 141). Oakes explains why this is not in fact a wholly adequate formula, but there is a point here that illuminates Ramsey's thinking once again. Seeing why Christian belief is credible is inseparable from that transformation of the self and its habitual ways of working that is prompted by grace; when you see that the gospel is believable, you do so because you have in the same moment believed, that is, trusted yourself to the presence that decentres and dispossesses the self. The judgement that the gospel is believable is an act of self-commitment. Oakes's reservation is that this initial act is a sort of submission before it is really vision; *fides ex auditu*, 'faith comes from hearing', because there is a sense in which we hear before we see, we are addressed, affected, acted on, in a way that the language of 'seeing' doesn't quite capture. I think, though, that this is in fact some of the force of speaking about 'glory' and beauty in the way that Balthasar and Ramsey do, and the force of their stress upon the physical resonance of such words. Precisely because glory is not something that is capable of being mastered and because beauty is not something that can be domesticated into the self's agenda, encounter with glory and beauty might be said to be more like hearing than some kinds of seeing. Ramsey would have referred us to the proximity in 2 Chronicles of 5.13–14 and 6.1: the glory of the Lord is perceptible as a cloud, and God is one who 'dwells in thick darkness'. Similarly, Balthasar's theology of aesthetics turns on the fact that the crucified Jesus has no 'form' that is attractive to our expectations. The seeing of glory in the Cross and the crucified is not a panoptic sweep of the landscape, but a synoptic moment of grasping together unreserved love and unqualified pain and abandonment – seeing the Cross as an event whose 'centre' is an eternal and infinite stripping of self. It is the sole finally convincing demonstration of freedom, the vision of God's liberty to be not only for but in the other; as such it is the vision of glory, the inner resource, the inner logic, of God's life.

And the way in which Ramsey and Balthasar alike reach for the apparently crude and mythological imagery of the oppressive material cloud in the sanctuary is not only that it secures the notion of an otherness as starkly 'in the way' as any bodily presence, but that it also evokes that aspect of physical encounter which tells us that sheer material contact does not and cannot offer us a finished conceptual picture, an object or thought, but primarily an occasion for thought, the beginning of a process that will not ever supplant the encounter itself. Thought begins only when we have first been interrupted by encounter with the non-negotiable. This is true of all intellectual activity worth the name; but it is clear that where theology is concerned it is true in a very particular way which asserts that the 'object' of theology continues always to have this character of interrupting and resisting any possible attempt at conceptual finality. The bare thereness of Jesus as part of the material history of the world tells us that in no way can God be less resistant to our minds and agendas than the rest of the material order. Yet the unbreakable association of the infinite God with the material Jesus underlines, paradoxically, that God is never part of the system of the universe because he is absolutely and unreservedly free in his love to be, to live, in the place of death and hell. Seeing God in Jesus is at once to see that there is no way around or even 'through' the concreteness of the Incarnation, and that it is this very fact that establishes as nothing else could the complete liberty of God, and thus his radical difference from all finite reality, caught up in the balances of action and passion, initiative and response, conditioning and creativity. These polarities are somehow transcended in the fusion of Jesus' helpless passion with God's most supremely free action.

This is why, for Ramsey, there is nowhere else for a theologian to begin but with the paschal event (see GC pp. 5–7). The Word made flesh is never an object for theology; the Word on the Cross is the actual condition for the perception, Balthasar's *Sensorium*, of theology's business. Yet it is at the same time the Cross as proclaimed, not as bare event – and so the Cross as the Cross of the Risen One. God's own witness to, God's 'owning' of, the Cross as the place he has made uniquely his place is part of what makes glory visible (which is why Ramsey could never have managed to settle for a mental, internalized account of the Resurrection; its witness is again as non-negotiably mysterious as any other moment in the material world). We do not – as some, including Ramsey, would say a theologian like Rudolf Bultmann does – present the Cross and appeal to some intense inner drive of blind trust and self-projection that allows us to acknowledge the Lordship of the crucified. We are overtaken by the Resurrection as the event that will not allow us to ignore the Cross or mourn it or regard it as a past event of failure and shame. Here again, I suspect Ramsey had in mind some of the most complex and demanding pages of Hoskyns on the Fourth Gospel, where he develops the idea of the Spirit in John as God holding before us, inescapably, the events of Jesus' life and death, as well as the text of Scott Holland that he quotes about the whole earthly life of Jesus being raised in the event of Easter (*The Resurrection of Christ*, pp. 9–10).

The theology that is revealed in the face of Christ, in the perception of glory in humiliated humanity, thus determines that our theology has to be done 'in the face of Christ'. It is necessarily a theology that is rooted in relation to the concrete Christ – the historical figure as held before us through the event of the Resurrection and the continuing action of the Spirit. And for it to be a truthful activity, manifesting somehow in words what it is talking about, it has to be a kenotic activity, a speech that is 'dispossessed' by the encounter with Christ. As such, following through the logic of Ramsey's whole scheme, it does not happen outside the Body of Christ, which is, as *GC* puts it, the 'expression' here and now of the paschal event of death and Resurrection. Theology in the Body does not only talk about this event or seek to understand it; it seeks to embody it.

What precisely this must mean in practice Ramsey does not say – though some would say he succeeds in showing. It is certainly, in intention, a relativizing of theology. 'The Church is pointing beyond theology', as he says in *GC*; the theologian's work and 'ideal' has to be lost in the reality of the Body for it to find its proper meaning. It also demands what *GC* so emphasizes, a penitential clarity about the Church's failings, the sense of a community under judgement as the only credible sign of the true presence of the Body; if theology is in some sense lost in the life of the Body, this is not at all to say that the concerns of an institution are now allowed to absorb or neutralize the asking of unwelcome questions. The unwelcome questions, however, are not speculative but moral and spiritual, questions about whether the paschal mystery is in fact honoured and lived among those who call themselves believers. If theology has a role in this, it is again and again to recover the vision of the Church as it fundamentally must be, as witness to the Cross and Resurrection. Hence Ramsey's surprising and insightful comment (*GC*, pp. 202–3) that Barth and Brunner have restored to Protestant theology a proper understanding of the Church's function – a Church always characterized by 'tribulation' because it is always the meeting place of sin with the love and judgement of God. Ramsey refers to Barth's Romans Commentary on this point, to a passage where Barth insists that we discuss the manifest failings and betrayals of the Church only within a strictly theological context: to see the tribulation of the Church clearly is to see the scope of divine love. It is in fact a sort of echo of Ramsey's own central theme. Seeing God in the middle of Godlessness is to see glory; to apprehend the liberty of God in the Godlessness of the Church is to be at the heart of the one theological mystery, the paschal freedom of God to be where love insists on being, in the depths of what is other.

Gradually some sense of what Ramsey might mean by a 'dispossessed', self-losing theology comes into focus. It is not and cannot be a systematic edifice, constructing a picture of the universe and of God's action in it that could be contemplated as an object (and remember that Barth always denied being a systematic theologian). It is a constantly renewed struggle to keep the paschal reality at work in the Church's language – for praise and thanksgiving (which is why the Eucharist is always a fundamentally theological occurrence) and for self-scrutiny on the part of the community and acknowledgement of failure. Theology has to spell out what it can of how and why the face of Christ is what transforms the human world; having done that, it does not seek any further place or dignity, but stands ready to resurrect the question when the Church's practice and speech have overlaid it. Hence Ramsey's approving reference, at the end of *GC*, to Maurice's description of theology as digging rather than building, removing debris, undermining the partisanships of believers so as to unite at the foundational level where the act of God is at work.

And it is Maurice who gives Ramsey one of his most evocative pictures, in an address delivered in Cambridge for the centenary of Maurice's death. Maurice, he reminds us, believed that theology was everyone's business. Sometimes he allowed this to lead him into rather ambitious generalizations about what the ordinary person knew or believed. But behind this lay a solid awareness that the subject matter of theology is every man, woman and child, so that the struggling and not very articulate awareness of even the poorest and least intellectual Christian living in the face of Christ has as much claim to be theology as the 'professional's' work. On his deathbed, Maurice 'began talking very rapidly but indistinctly . . . about the Communion being for all nations and peoples, for men who were working like Dr Radcliffe (his physician). Something too about it being the work of women to teach men its meaning . . .' (*CTP*, p. 44)

Neither Maurice nor Ramsey is the most obvious recruit to feminist or liberation theology; but the picture of the dying Maurice pouring out those barely intelligible words about those who are able to uncover the meanings of the mystery brings us momentarily into a similar world. It addresses the 'professional' theologian in a way that sobers and challenges. Ramsey very evidently believed that theology needed doing and doing well, with the tools of historical and linguistic and philosophical expertise. But the doing of it well was never to be thought of as the successful polishing of argument or refinement of concepts; whatever of this needed doing was subordinate to the work of the Body – not as a directive and inquisitorial overseer, but as the environment in which the transforming seriousness of God's glory in Christ was definitively at work. Theology would have to begin, just as Luther argued, with the knowledge of the Cross; but the Cross always as that place in creation where we may find God's integrity made plain. And that integrity is made plain only as the theologian's mind is converted – lost to the ambitions of a pattern-making ego or an ideological programme.

It is not, in the nature of things, a job description, a set of conditions that must be met by anyone professing to make contributions to a subject conventionally called theology. It is something recognized in and by the Body, recognized in gratitude for the way in which it digs down to what is alone truly generative of the common life and the common prayer. In the long run, the Church discerns those who are in a particular sense its theologians. Few would doubt that Michael Ramsey has been and still is discerned as such.

This lecture, given at Lambeth Palace, was sponsored by the Trinity Institute of Christianity and Culture.

Michael Ramsey, Transfiguration and the Eastern Churches

GEOFFREY ROWELL

My first encounter with Michael Ramsey was as an undergraduate in Cambridge reading Theology and the Archbishop came to preach at Great St Mary's. In the question and answer session afterwards – at which he was so good – an undergraduate got up and asked him if he believed in the Devil. 'No,' the Archbishop replied, 'but I think I believe in devils, because evil is essentially divisive.' It was a quintessential Ramsey reply, and an appropriate one with which to begin this discussion, which has as one of its major themes Michael Ramsey and the quest for Christian unity, in particular with the Eastern Churches.

A year or so later, in 1964, having joined the Anglican and Eastern Churches Association, I was invited to Lambeth to a reception to mark its centenary[1] and found myself being portentously announced immediately after the somewhat flamboyant Armenian philanthropist, Mr Nubar Gulbenkian, sporting a large purple orchid in his buttonhole. It was my first personal meeting with the Archbishop, who welcomed a nervous undergraduate as warmly as the wealthy Armenian who had preceded me. At about the same time I was commissioned on my undergraduate summer travels to take a letter from the Archbishop to the Metropolitan of Shamisdin, the acting head of the ancient Church of the East, the old Assyrian community with which the Church of England had long and cordial relations. On my one and only visit to Baghdad I found myself smuggled to the house where the Metropolitan was being confined under house arrest, to present the Archbishop's letter.

But enough of personal reminiscence. Let us begin in Cambridge where Michael Ramsey was born at 71 Chesterton Road on 14 November 1904. He was the younger son of Arthur Stanley Ramsey, fellow in mathematics at Magdalene, so his connections with the college went back to his earliest days. His mother, Agnes, was the daughter of a Lincolnshire vicar, and I owe to the present bishop of Portsmouth, Dr Kenneth Stevenson, the story of Bishop Michael visiting Horbling church in which he was baptized, and standing by the font moved to tears, murmuring, 'O font, font, font, in which I was baptized!' His deep sacramental sense and understanding of baptism as being plunged into the death and Resurrection of Christ, which was at the heart of the Church's life, comes out in that moment of time.

With his mother an Anglican and his father a Congregationalist deacon, the unity of the Church was a concern that grew in Michael Ramsey from his earliest days. The Free Church tradition made him suspicious of a bland endorsement of Establishment and, as one who was deeply troubled by the parliamentary refusal of the years of patient liturgical revision that had gone into the 1928 Prayer Book, he rejoiced at the end of his archiepiscopate to see the passing of the Worship and Doctrine Measure which set the Church of England free from that kind of parliamentary veto.

At King's College choir school, where the headmaster, C.R. Jelf, was strict, aloof and unbending, mirroring something of Michael Ramsey's own father, he was deeply influenced by Eric Milner-White, the Chaplain (and soon afterwards, Dean) of King's, who was by contrast, 'smiling, sympathetic, bubbling over with humour, taking the boys for walks and encouraging rather than discouraging them'.[2] Michael Ramsey remembered with joy Milner-White's divinity lessons – 'Milner made it such fun'[3] – and in his last years at St John's Home in Oxford Milner-White's photograph was one of a select group on his walls.[4] He contributed an epilogue to a short biographical memoir of Milner-White that reflects not only Milner-White's theology and churchmanship as one of the Cambridge liberal Anglo-Catholics associated with the Oratory of the Good Shepherd and *Essays Catholic and Critical* (1926) but much of Michael Ramsey's own sympathy and concerns as well. In 1920 Milner-White had spoken at the first Anglo-Catholic Congress on 'Christian Unity: The Church of Rome' in which, as Ramsey noted, he had spoken of a 'true unity between Rome and Canterbury' that already existed.

> There is the unity of many centuries of older history which they share; the dogmatic unity of the Creeds; the unity of sacramental life; the unity of saintly lives 'in the priesthood, in the cloister and in ordinary walks of life'; and a unity of atmosphere which he calls the 'mystical' unity. Theologically, this basic unity which persists

despite divisions of polity, of doctrine, and of many quarrels is to be understood in scriptural terms as the unity of spiritual race, of the people of God.[5]

Milner-White argued for a free, progressive and tolerant Catholicism in which all truth finds its home. He also stressed, as was quite as characteristic of Michael Ramsey, that the true history of the Church can never be written in human books, 'for it has taken place not in courts, curias and councils where power is great and decisions are registered, but in cottages, streets and places where men work and pray'. 'The sacrament to the world (the Church) will only be complete when it becomes the world, and the Royal Priesthood is universal.'[6] Ramsey welcomed Milner-White's contribution to *Essays Catholic and Critical* 'as presenting the Catholic Church less as an institution than as a life, less as a fenced terrain than as a light able to penetrate and pervade'. He went on to note that, although Milner-White was

> never a close student of Eastern Orthodox writers his mind was in this respect akin to some of them. He inclined to a mystical rather than a legalistic approach towards Protestantism and the Free Churches . . . He saw the process [of Christian unity] as one of the sharing of spiritual treasures, and he would make easy rather than hard the acceptance by others of Catholic inheritance.[7]

When Michael Ramsey was enthroned as Archbishop of York in 1956, Eric Milner-White, by then Dean of York, welcomed him with delight that 'My child in the Spirit has become my Father in God.'[8]

When Michael Ramsey went up to Magdalene in 1923 after his years at Repton, as a 'somewhat gangly brown-haired young man',[9] Milner-White remained an influence. Michael Ramsey discovered, through Little St Mary's in particular, the Catholic inheritance of the Church of England, and a deep sense of the sacramental, of mystery, awe and the supernatural. Touched by William Temple's 1926 mission (which he chaired as president of the Union), he offered himself for ordination, and continued to revere Temple's theology and what Adrian Hastings described as 'a mind committed to communicating a vision with infectious enthusiasm – "the magic fascination of the love of Christ" as he called it to the boys at Repton'.[10] Temple's theology of the Incarnation, understood the Incarnation, as did Duns Scotus, as 'the perfect crowning in grace of the whole order of things in created nature'. He had a vision of wholeness that was Johannine in character, and in St John he found the light that shone in a darkness that was cosmic, and where the glory of God is known in the Cross of Christ. Ramsey revered Temple and shared much of his theological passion. He wished to be buried (and his wish was granted) 'not far from William Temple'. But there was also another influence, that of Edwyn Clement Hoskyns, a theological mentor, who addressed for him some of the sharp theological questions from which Milner-White with his primarily pastoral and devotional concerns seemed to be distant.[11] Hoskyns lectured on the New Testament with passion and excitement, as Ramsey later recalled:

> though I never became an uncritical devotee, I learned from him, more vividly than from anyone else, that the study of the New Testament is an exciting adventure, and while it calls for a rigorous critical discipline it is not made less scientific if the student brings to it his own experience of faith.[12]

Words from a sermon that Hoskyns preached at the foundation of Derby convey something of the impact that he had on the shaping of Michael Ramsey's theology:

> The Church exists in the world only to bear witness to the power of God, to his sovereign, regal power and holiness, to his miraculous power and glory, and just in so far as the Church bears her witness, you and I are brought under the judgement of God, stript and naked of all pride in human achievement and human intellect, sinners, miserable sinners. It is not what we think about God that matters, but what he thinks about us; it is not what we think about Christ and the Church and the scriptures which is of any great value, but how we are judged by the word of God and his Son, Jesus Christ.[13]

Or, as Hoskyns powerfully put it elsewhere: 'the Church has always a dagger at its heart, for it cannot long escape from its own theme, the theme which it is bound to proclaim – Christ Crucified'. He urged his hearers to 'make room for the glory of God' for 'the theme of the Church – Crucifixion–Resurrection – is therefore the song which is sung, whether it be recognized or not, by the whole world of men and things, in their tribulation and in their merriment'.[14]

Bishop Kenneth Sansbury judged that Ramsey's first, and perhaps most significant book, *The Gospel and the Catholic Church* (1936), bore the clear imprint of Hoskyns, who had noted how infrequently the word 'Christian' appeared in the New Testament compared with the frequency of the reference to the Christian *ecclesia*. 'The underlying conviction of [Ramsey's] book', Sansbury wrote, 'is that the meaning of the Christian Church becomes most clear when it is studied in terms of the Death and Resurrection of Jesus Christ'. His exposition of this in *The Gospel and the Catholic Church* 'pointed straight back to the Corpus lecture room a decade before', though Sansbury also noted more historical influences, writing that Charles Gore's reasoned defence of sacramental Catholicism 'with its roots in F.D. Maurice and Bishop Westcott provided [Ramsey with] a framework of faith which . . . remained a continuing source of inspiration for his whole life and teaching'.[15]

In the early chapters of *The Gospel and the Catholic Church* Ramsey set out the foundation of the Church in the Cross and Resurrection of Jesus 'and the mysterious sharing of the disciples in these happenings'. What divides Catholics and Protestants in Western Christianity – arguments about Church order, episcopacy, worship, liturgy and creed – can only be rightly addressed by a return to this fundamental perspective. Father Gabriel Hebert, of the Society of the Sacred Mission, later to work with Michael Ramsey on the report *Catholicity*, wrote of how for 'the Christians of the apostolic age, the facts of the death and resurrection of Christ were at once external facts belonging to history, and internal facts ever renewed in their own experience'. The Christian life is a life of incorporation into the Body of Christ, a dying to the 'old self-centred life' and a sharing in a new life of κοινωνια. Baptism and Eucharist are constitutive of the Church.[16] As Owen Chadwick comments in his biography of Ramsey, in *The Gospel and the Catholic Church*, Ramsey 'cried to the Church to be itself; to know that its being rests upon a death and an empty tomb; and to be itself whether modern Britain will listen or close its ears'. At the same time the book has a deep eirenic and ecumenical engagement, coming from Ramsey's own inheritance from his Congregationalist father, and from his own discovery of Catholic Anglicanism:

> He would show the Catholic that the Church is nothing without the Word spoken in the crucifixion. He would show the Protestant that the Church, with its order, and structure, and mission, is a necessary part of the Word spoken in the crucifixion. The book is full of the Bible, and yet is an essay in Church order.[17]

The Gospel and the Catholic Church was written when Michael Ramsey was sub-warden of Lincoln Theological College. It was here that he met one of the first notable Orthodox influences upon him, George Florovsky (1893–1979). Florovsky, who had been a lecturer in philosophy at Odessa University, left Russia in 1920 and in 1926 became Professor of Patristics at the Orthodox Theological Institute of St Sergius in Paris, where he was ordained priest in 1932. He wrote extensively on the Greek Fathers and on Russian religious thought. As Rowan Williams noted at the time of Florovsky's death, his ecclesiology is one in which:

> the Church reflects the life of God-in-trinity because its life is one of active mutuality – a 'catholic' life in which the interests of the particular and the general do not conflict but nourish one another ... his work is a valuable corrective for any who would identify Orthodoxy with mystical or aesthetic vagueness.[18]

Ramsey wrote, when he was called upon as Archbishop of Canterbury to send a greeting for Florovsky's seventy-fifth birthday, of the 'notable part' Florovsky had played 'in the arousing of interest in and knowledge of the Orthodox Church amongst many people in England'. He saluted 'a great friend, priest and doctor' whose 'influence in that way will not be forgotten'. In response Florovsky wrote about visiting Ramsey at Lincoln:

> You reminded me of one of the best periods of my life. I still remember my first visit to Bishop's Hostel, Lincoln, where we first met. I also remember how we went together to Kelham to see our common friend, the late Father Gabriel [Hebert]. I remember our long talks and disputes at that time later. It was more than just a passing episode. I am deeply indebted in my theological and ecumenical function to my contacts with the British divines like you and the late E.C. Hoskyns.[19]

It was clearly a meeting of mutual indebtedness that was to manifest itself later in 1948 in Amsterdam at the first meeting of the World Council of Churches, when the cold war left Florovsky from the Russian diaspora as the major spokesman for Orthodoxy and Michael Ramsey as a Catholic Anglican speaking for a Catholic tradition that was not represented because Rome refused to take part. Karl Barth, whose influence on Hoskyns (the translator of Barth's powerful commentary on Romans) had been significant for Ramsey for a time, was also present, and Roman Catholics noted the strange paradox that the contributions of Florovsky, Ramsey and Barth had led to an ecumenical impasse because none of them was prepared to put up with an idea of Church unity that was simply a Protestant federation.[20]

If Florovsky was the first significant Orthodox theologian Michael Ramsey encountered, it was not his first encounter with Orthodoxy. In his presidential address to the Fellowship of St Alban and St Sergius in 1972, Ramsey recalled how his feel for Orthodoxy went back '45 years, when it was first evoked in me through my friendship with Derwas Chitty when we were fellow students [at Cuddesdon]'.[21] In his Lev Gillet memorial lecture, given ten years later in 1982, he recalled asking Derwas Chitty, 'Why do you kiss the icons?' and 'he said to me, "We are bidding the saints goodnight" '. It was Derwas Chitty who introduced Ramsey to William Palmer's work on Russia and the English Church and the correspondence between Alexis Khomiakov and Palmer, which included Khomiakov's essay on the Church as saints participating with saints.[22] Chitty had first encountered the Orthodox world in Palestine between 1924 and 1927. It left him with a life-long love of Orthodoxy, and particularly of the early monastic tradition of the Desert Fathers.[23] Chitty with, as Owen Chadwick puts it, his 'high-pitched voice, rapid limbs which contorted themselves in the effort to say something that was too mystical for words ... and a religious love of everything eastern, from icons and tall black hats to the beards of the clergy', and his infectious enthusiasm, sparked an interest in Ramsey, who resonated with Chitty's emphasis on '*glory* as the leading idea of Eastern religion' and likewise with Chitty's perspective on Anglicanism as having a special relationship with the Orthodox churches, whom Anglicans 'have not condemned as heretical or schismatic or "Unreformed" ', seeing the Anglican vocation as providing 'a bridge to authentic Catholicity which all Protestants can use'.[24] As Ramsey himself wrote:

> from Derwas first I learned that Orthodoxy meant not true opinion so much as true glory, and that the saints are not isolated, meritorious mediators ... but rather a family in which we may all pray to one another, and pray for one another; a family created by the God-Man through the Holy Ghost and the response of Blessed Mary.

In a tribute to Derwas Chitty Donald Allchin quoted words that

Chitty wrote at the end of the war years, and could also apply to Michael Ramsey:

> I have been babe and child and boy and man, and shall, God willing, go on to old age. In the Resurrection the whole of this physical life that I have lived will be no mere memory, but a present reality restored – only, if the grace of God is such for me, I shall be able to see its evil no longer in a hell of isolation, but transcended, overcome and transformed by the Good of his Cross – his Atoning Process – put in its place in the revealing of God's Atoning Power, as Eternity takes all time within its immediate view. Such is the inconceivable joy of Resurrection for all who have loved Life and loved the human beings around them – nothing is lost of what has been, but all is transfused with new light in the completeness of the picture, in the Heavenly Glory. And yet, when we have it, will it not all appear as worthless as compared with that Glory of God himself, which of his Mercy will be ours.[25]

Ramsey, remembering Chitty and his introduction to Orthodoxy, noted that he thought it continued to be true 'that when West discovers East it is the family of the saints which, after a brief feeling of strangeness, wins and warms the heart'.[26] When, as Archbishop of York, he led an Anglican delegation to Moscow for theological discussion he spoke of the saints and of transfiguration:

> The face of Christ in the transfiguration shone as the sun. The Saints shine not as the sun but with the reflected glory of Christ . . . The family is one: it is filled with the glory of Christ and in this belief we give glory to the Saints . . . We can learn from you more about the one family of the living and departed Saints in Christ. You will patiently learn from us of our care for the unique glory of Christ who shines as the sun.[27]

He rejoiced to remember that Bishop Pearson in his classical Anglican *Exposition of the Creed* in the seventeenth century had emphasized the same deep common life and communion between saints on earth and saints in heaven. He emphasizes that 'the saints participate with those Christians who are far from saintly and indeed somewhat nominally Christian through their sins and imperfections', quoting Pearson's words:

> I am fully persuaded of this as of a necessary and infallible truth, that such persons as are truly sanctified in the Church of Christ, while they live among the crooked generations of men, and struggle with all the miseries of this world, have fellowship with God the Father, God the Son, and God the Holy Ghost, as dwelling with them and taking up their habitations with them: that they partake of the care and kindness of the blessed angels who take delight in the ministration for their benefit, that besides the external fellowship which they have in the word and sacraments with all the members of the Church, they have an intimate union and conjunction with all the saints on earth as the living members of Christ; nor is this union separated by the death of any; but as Christ in whom they live is the Lamb slain from the foundation of the world, so have they fellowship with all the saints which from the death of Abel have ever departed in the true faith and fear of God, and now enjoy the presence of the Father and follow the Lamb whithersoever he goeth. This I believe *the communion of saints*.[28]

He noted also Pearson's Marian devotion, citing with approval his comment that:

> we cannot bear too reverend a regard unto the *mother of our Lord*, so long as we give her not that worship which is due unto the Lord himself. Let us keep the language of the primitive Church: Let her be honoured and esteemed, let him be worshipped and adored.[29]

Encouraged by encounters, not only with Derwas Chitty and George Florovsky, but also by the exiled Russian layman, Nicolas Zernov, General Secretary of the Russian Student Christian Movement, Ramsey joined the Fellowship of St Alban and St Sergius, founded in 1928 at the second Anglo-Russian Conference in St Albans. He attended many of the summer gatherings of the Fellowship, where leading Russian theologians came, mainly from Paris, and Anglicans such as Bishop Headlam, Oliver Quick, V.A. Demant, N.P. Williams, Leonard Hodgson and H.L. Goudge. Michael Ramsey was among the younger theologians in company with Eric Mascall, Eric Abbott, Geoffrey Curtis, CR, Algy Robertson, one of the founders of the Anglican Franciscans, Oliver Tomkins, Gabriel Hebert and Evelyn Underhill.[30]

In 1935 Ramsey published an early paper on 'Reunion and Intercommunion' in the Fellowship's journal *Sobornost*, where the same notes appear as in *The Gospel and the Catholic Church*:

Transfiguration and the Eastern Churches 197

The Church is the Body of Christ crucified and risen. Each single member and each group within the Body, by learning its utter dependence upon the whole, learns to die to self and thus shares in the death and resurrection of Christ. This relation between the Church and Christ's death and resurrection is expressed in the Church's order and sacramental life. Thus (1) Baptism is into Christ's death, and into the one Body . . . (2) The Eucharist proclaims Christ's death, and unites the Christians in the one Body . . . (3) The Episcopate represents the acts of Christ in the flesh and in the universal church, upon which every local community of Christians depends. Every member of the Body glorifies not himself, but by death to self, lives only a life which is the Body's own life.[31]

Concepts of Christian unity, therefore, which make it merely a matter of human feeling, and that treat the Eucharist as the form of Christians feeling fellowship 'rather than the act of Christ in His own body' fall short of the truth.[32] Writing on Eastern Orthodoxy in *The Gospel and the Catholic Church* Ramsey cited with approval St John Chrysostom's image of the two altars, one of stone, the other of human persons: 'when thou seest a poor brother, reflect that thou beholdest an altar'.[33] The same reference occurs many years later in the lecture, 'Constantinople and Canterbury' that he delivered as Archbishop of Canterbury in the University of Athens.[34] There was always an ethical dimension in Ramsey's doctrine of the Church. There, too, is the theme of glory. The Eastern theologians did not expound the Church; they expounded Christ the Redeemer and in such a way that the Church is included in their exposition. 'The glory of the Church is most apparent not when it is buttressed and defended as an institution, but when, without any particular "Church-consciousness", it is seen as the spontaneous glory of the Christ.' Ramsey commends the East for avoiding Western legalism, with its 'externalising' and 'institutionalising' tendency, and reminding us that the word 'Catholic' describes 'not only external universality . . . but also internal wholeness, whereby every member has his share in τo καθολου. Church life and the life of the soul are identical. Orthodoxy is not something imposed but is in reality right glory or worship.[35]

Two years later, in a paper read at the Fellowship Conference at High Leigh in July 1938, Ramsey emphasized that Peter's Confession of faith united doctrine, worship and life. The ethical submission of the will was integral to the response of true faith and worship. Church order is 'part of the outward form which the life takes, and the exercise of the office is one of the ways in which Doctrine is learnt and Worship rises to heaven'. The Lord trains his disciples 'in the inward Catholicity or "wholeness" of doctrine, worship and life: of the mind, the heart and the will . . . Only as this inward Catholicity is present can there be the outward unity of the Church before men.' Αλεθεια – truth – is not correct propositions about God, 'but the activity of God himself; πιστισ – faith – is both binding intellectual assent, *and* the devotion of the will and the affections.' Doctrine without worship results in a cold intellectualism that chills and repels and divides. Worship without doctrine leads to a pietism that repels and divides because it is a self-centred thing. Order divorced from the context of doctrine and worship leads to a prelatism that repels and divides. These are the inward schisms that underlie outward ones.[36] This sense of the close linkage between unity, truth and holiness is a theme that remained constant in Ramsey's theology from its early shapings and throughout his episcopate.

By 1949, when he was Van Mildert Professor at Durham and a canon of the cathedral, Ramsey published another book that, in a different but related way, touched on his appreciation of the Eastern Christian tradition. *The Glory of God and the Transfiguration of Christ* was, Ramsey said at the end of his life, the book he was most glad to have written.[37] Douglas Dales describes it as 'the most abiding monument to the impact that Orthodoxy made upon Bishop Michael's whole theological vision'.[38] As the title implies it picks up the theme of glory, and there can be few books that have as their epigram quotations, one from *Alice through the Looking Glass*, another from the Tractarian biographer of Edward Pusey, Henry Parry Liddon, and the third from E.C. Hoskyns – the last being the pungent words from his *Cambridge Sermons*, 'Can we rescue a word, and discover a universe? Can we study a language, and awake to the Truth? Can we bury ourselves in a lexicon, and arise in the presence of God?'[39] The word for Michael Ramsey was, of course, 'glory' – δοξα in Greek, *kabod* in Hebrew. The book is divided into two parts, the first (and longer) carefully examining the theme of the glory of God and its meaning, in the Old Testament and then in the New, the second turning to the theme of transfiguration. Writing with the clarity that was one of his special gifts, Ramsey shows himself aware of the tensions, contrasts and developments in the understanding of glory in the Bible. Time and again we find profound and piercing sentences that invite us to engage more deeply with that deep pattern of redemption and sanctification that for him, as we have already

Transfiguration and the Eastern Churches 199

seen, was at the heart of the life of the Church. To give just a few examples:

> Nor is it otherwise with the glory. As they worship Jesus the Lord who has been exalted into it, and as they look for the day when it is made visible, they come to realize that it has been disclosed to them and is already near them.[40]

> And the change is from glory to glory. There is no despair, for glory is a present possession: there is no contentment, for a far greater glory is the final goal.[41]

> The sight of God . . . is the transfiguration of man.[42]

> Calvary is no disaster which needs the Resurrection to reverse it, but a victory so signal that the Resurrection follows quickly to seal it.[43]

> By the mission of the Church the judgement and the glory are made known to mankind, and the world can take its choice.[44]

> The Church's claims are ratified by the Church's humility, and the Church's hunger for what she lacks. Torn from this eschatological context the doctrine of the Church becomes the doctrine of an institution among other institutions upon the plane of history. Set in this eschatological context it is the doctrine of a Church filled already with glory, yet humbled by the command to await both a glory and a judgement hereafter.[45]

> The Christian hope is therefore far more than the salvaging of human souls into a spiritual salvation: it is the re-creation of the world, through the power of the Resurrection.[46]

In the latter half of the book, in which Ramsey turns to the theme of transfiguration, he reveals his awareness of the centrality of the transfiguration theme in the theology of the Eastern churches.[47] In the East the cosmic effects of redemption are stressed, and the Christian life is seen in terms of our participation with the new creation. The East has seen the Cross in the light of the Resurrection. The Transfiguration is seen not as 'an event among other events, and a dogma amongst other dogmas', but as 'a symbol of something which pervades all dogma and all worship'. Ramsey cites not only the Orthodox liturgical texts for the Feast of the Transfiguration, but also the theological reflections of Nicholas Arseniev on the cosmic reference of transfiguration. Θεωσισ – deification – is linked with this, though interestingly Ramsey in the short section on 2 Peter does not make the connection between the Transfiguration reference in that letter and the promise that we shall be 'partakers of the divine nature' – a key text for that doctrine. So Ramsey concludes this section:

> What the Baptism is to the public ministry of Jesus, the Transfiguration is to the Passion. In both events the Spirit descends. At Jordan the Spirit comes to Him for the fulfilment of His work as *prophet,* on the mountain the Spirit (symbolized by the cloud) comes to Him for His mission as *priest.* There and then He is glorified, for the glory is His acceptance of the path of suffering and Calvary is anticipated in the decision to suffer. Indeed we may see in the Transfiguration the designation of our Lord as a priest for ever after the order of Melchizedek, 'who through the eternal Spirit offered himself without blemish unto God.' (Heb. ix, 4)[48]

As with most who are called to the ordained ministry Michael Ramsey's theology was shaped by his formative early engagements, in his case with Temple and Hoskyns, and in reaction to the dessicated liberalism that was in the ascendant in the Cambridge Divinity Faculty of his day. His discovery of the Eastern churches and their theology of cosmic redemption and transfiguration and their sense of mystical theology and the close relationship between theology and worship remained important to him. But the Orthodox influence, though mediated through significant encounters with theologians such as Florovsky, was not until his episcopal ministry something nurtured by immediate experience of the Orthodox world and its worship.

When he became a bishop on appointment to Durham in 1952 his world changed, and there were always tinges of regret combined with a deep sense of obedience to the call of God. He wrote to Ronald Williams, the bishop of Leicester, a year later, of how, when the summons came, it so distressed him because of what it meant he had to give up. He read the letters of Mandell Creighton on giving up the Dixie Professorship of Ecclesiastical History to accept the see of Peterborough, and was comforted by Creighton's sense of the loss of his books and his study, and his equal readiness to accept both the burden and the joy of pastoral ministry and the oversight of the Church. He would have felt sympathy for Creighton's lament:

> My wandering career seems to have come to an end. My peace of mind is gone: my books will be shut up: my mind will go to seed: I shall utter nothing but platitudes for the rest of my life, and everybody will write letters in the newspapers about my iniquities.

No less would he have sympathized with Creighton's response to a historian colleague:

> To me the one supreme object of human life is and always has been to grow nearer to God: and I regard my own individual life as simply an opportunity of offering myself to him. All knowledge has been to me merely a further revelation of Him, and my relations to my fellow creatures are dependent on His call.[49]

Henceforth Ramsey was to be in the world of inter-church relations and councils and this undoubtedly had an impact upon him as a theologian. As he told David Paton, looking back on his time as Archbishop of Canterbury:

> People say that my coming to Lambeth meant the end of me as a theologian. They could not have been more mistaken. If I had stayed at York I would have remained a complacent Tractarian. As it is, coming to Lambeth has freed me to think about a whole host of new subjects and I became a theologian.[50]

In his presidential address to the Fellowship of St Alban and St Sergius in 1972 he noted three phases in his relationship with Orthodoxy. The first was an 'excited honeymoon', when the encounter with Orthodoxy 'invoked new insights concerning worship and liturgy, concerning the communion of saints, concerning the nature and mode of theological thinking'. In the second phase, 'my own theological thinking became more Eastern than Western. The New Testament and the Greek Fathers came to be the medium in which I thought, together with such Anglican Divines as had themselves been influenced by Greek theology.' Thirdly, as a professional ecclesiastic in the West, Western themes predominate, yet again and again in times of frustration and perplexity Orthodox insights 'come to the rescue and begin to make sense of the paradoxes and perplexities that would otherwise be baffling'.[51] In the same address Ramsey links the theme of cosmic salvation found in Sergius Bulgakov with the vision of cosmic redemption in Teilhard de Chardin. He also addresses the challenge of the charismatic movement to the institutional churches and again finds Orthodox perspectives helpful.

> [If] 'we think of the world primarily as *that which is being re-created* through the presence within it of the Risen Christ and his Body, then the ecclesiological problem of the Church's boundary becomes much less burdensome because, while the Spirit of God is at work within the Church's fellowship, we shall not be surprised if the Spirit of God is also at work beyond the precise frontiers of that fellowship, working for the world's re-creation, a re-creation in which, finally, all will be gathered in Christ.[52]

Ramsey ends this lecture with some Eucharistic reflections, noting that while the Eucharist 'draws us from the world to share in Christ's sacrifice together with the whole company of heaven, it also draws us to share in Christ's outgoing action to the world for the world's re-creation'.

> If we receive the Sacrament upon our knees, nothing more befits the reverence and adoration in our hearts; if we receive the Sacrament standing . . . nothing more befits our attitude of obedience as men and women ready to go out, to act and to do. For Jesus who is the Word of the Father feeds us so that we may increasingly share with him in the world's re-creation. He does not feed us in order to draw us away with him into a separate realm of religion, but in order to draw us into participation with him in his work of moulding the world into his likeness.[53]

In some ways the move to the world of Church leadership from the world of theology led to a disappointment that Orthodox leaders with whom he shared so great a theological vision did not respond in practical terms with as energetic endorsement as he would have wished. He told David Paton that he had spent a lot of time and energy (and indeed money) on the Orthodox leaders and had got very little in return.[54] But that may have been just the reflection of a particular moment. His addresses on the occasion of the visits of Orthodox leaders to the Church of England and his visits to Orthodox countries both underline the familiar themes of his theology and are warm and courteous. In the Ecumenical Patriarch, Athenagoras, he recognized a Christian leader of great stature, and they formed a close friendship. Athenagoras, who found in the worship of the Church of England 'such a great Liturgy, so beautiful, so reverent . . . in the same spirit as our own',[55] recognized in Ramsey 'a deep theological thinker, a good shepherd, a courageous leader of the Anglican Church, and one of the protagonists for the prevailing of the ecumenical spirit in the Christian world'.[56] Ramsey responded in a tribute to Athenagoras on the twentieth anniversary of the Patriarch's enthronement:

> Through the years he has been a brave shepherd of his own flock of Orthodox Christians in years of trial, he has been among the greatest friends and protagonists of Christian unity, and he has given a moving example of what it means to be a Christian – always sensitive to the stresses of mankind, yet always having a heavenly serenity which fortifies the faith of others.[57]

In a message to mark Michael Ramsey's fortieth anniversary of ordination as a priest Athenagoras called him, in a wonderful phrase, 'you beloved and unforgettable Beatitude',[58] and told him in 1978 'that he had done more than the theological dialogue could do for the rapprochement of our two churches'.[59] When Athenagoras came to London in 1967, following Ramsey's visit to Istanbul in 1962, it was the first visit of an Ecumenical Patriarch to Britain. They exchanged gifts of chalices. Michael Ramsey wrote afterwards to Sir Steven Runciman of how privileged he had been to be present 'at one of the most historic and moving happenings' in which he had shared.[60] The communiqué after the visit encouraged the setting up of an official Anglican-Orthodox Dialogue, building on much work that had been done before. Afterwards Athenagoras wrote of how moved he was by Ramsey's gift of a chalice:

> We remember, Brother, the gift which you have offered to us in Lambeth, that is, the Holy Chalice.
> WHEN, brother shall we reach this?
> OUR people with agony are awaiting.
> EMBRACING you in a holy kiss.[61]

When Patriarch Justinian of Romania came in 1965 Ramsey recalled how the Church of England and the Romanian Church were brought closer together in friendship and in knowledge by the Romanian-Anglican Conference in 1935. He noted how his predecessor, Theodore of Tarsus, had come from the East, so that it was not strange that the Church of England looked to the East as well as to the West. 'Our hopes', he said, 'are for nothing less than the full communion of our Churches within the one Holy, Catholic and Apostolic Church which we profess in the ecumenical Creed.'[62]

> Christian unity [he told the Patriarch] is not in doctrine alone; it is prayer, in friendship, in the call to holiness, in the binding of Christian souls to our Lord Jesus Christ and to one another . . . we shall be nearer to one another if we are nearer to Christ in obeying His will and in loving Him as he loves us.[63]

Once again holiness, the way of obedience to Christ and participation in the life of Christ, is inseparable from unity.

In Athens in 1962 he spoke of the importance of acts of 'economy' in the pilgrimage to unity, and of how Anglicans looked to the Orthodox, as 'the Church of the Resurrection, the Church of the Communion of Saints, and of how Holy Tradition was rightly understood as 'God Incarnate living and moving in the whole life of Christians'. He spoke of the need of engaging with 'modern, scientific, technological culture' in the spirit of the Greek theology of the divine Logos working in all the created world, and no less of responding to the challenge of the homeless and the refugees as 'a very part of our search for unity in Christ'. He concluded with an affirmation that 'the *world* is a place where Christ by His death and resurrection has won a cosmic victory: it is in His hands already, and all unseen His power draws it into unity'. In that Orthodox faith of Christ victorious, the Church lives as 'a body where, amidst its many sinful and fallible members, Christ is present as the Church's inward life; and the portion of the Church on earth is ever one with the Church in paradise and heaven'.[64]

It is in this ecclesial context that the theme of transfiguration is so significant for Michael Ramsey's theology, his personal spiritual pilgrimage and his closeness to the Orthodox churches. At Michael Ramsey's funeral Archbishop Robert Runcie spoke of Bishop Michael's 'unselfconscious awareness of God', and how he saw Christian pilgrimage 'as a single movement towards God and into the world'. If he spoke much of 'the glory of God, the Glory of heaven . . . he always insisted that was the glory of self-giving revealed in the

Cross'.[65] In a Memorial Service at York Minster Archbishop John Habgood took up a similar theme, speaking of three types of transfiguration that were evident in Michael Ramsey's life, theology and ministry. First, there was the transfiguration of suffering, for 'no life can be without suffering. And there was suffering beneath that tranquil exterior – not least in the pain of early bereavement [in the deaths of his mother and his brilliant, atheist brother, Frank]. But it was suffering transfigured, made to shine by the light of the Cross of Christ'. Second, there is the transfiguration of knowledge. The gospel is 'the perfect introduction to all truth' yet it can only be known in its fulness, as we reach out to truths beyond what has already been given to us. 'The earth as well as the heaven is full of God's glory, and his visible glory is but the garment of his truth, so that every addition to truth becomes a fresh opportunity for adoration.' Knowledge is transfigured by worship. Third, Archbishop Habgood said, was the transfiguration of the world. It was a world full of beauty and pain, judgement and resurrection; for Michael Ramsey a world to be hugely enjoyed. Yet the world must not dominate us, and here the key to transfiguration is detachment:

> To see the world aright as the substance through which glory can shine, there has to be a degree of detachment from it; love without possessiveness. Peter on the mount of transfiguration wanted to hold on to the vision. He had to learn to let go.

And so, John Habgood concluded:

> Glory, holiness, adoration, the centrality of the vision of Christ, the glimpse of divine wonder in the midst of the ordinary, the courage to risk change in pursuit of his vision, the sense of assurance of one who had himself been on the mountain top – and *knew*.[66]

In a sermon preached at the Cuddesdon College Festival in 1958 Michael Ramsey spoke on the text from the ninth chapter of St Mark's Gospel: *He bringeth them up unto a high mountain apart by themselves, and he was transfigured before them.* He spoke of the importance of withdrawal and of the transfiguration that that enables, surely mindful of his own dark experiences in a place that was always a holy place for him. When the Lord went up the mountain of transfiguration, taking chosen disciples with him:

it did not mean that He had left behind Him the conflicts of the Galilean ministry which had gone before, or the conflicts of the Via Crucis which were to follow . . . When our Lord went up to be transfigured, he carried with Him every conflict, every burden, both of the days behind and the days ahead, up there to be transfigured with Him. And when we go apart to be with Jesus in His glory, it is so that our frustrations, our limitations and our cares may be carried into that supernatural context which makes all the difference to them. They are not forgotten: they are not abolished: they can still be painful. But they become transfigured in the presence of Jesus, our crucified and glorious Lord. And when we have carried our frustrations up to our Lord in His glory, we find in the days which follow that He so generously brings His glory right down into the midst of our frustrations.[67]

The transfiguration that Michael Ramsey so rightly saw as the consequence of the grace by which we participate in the glory of God, and which was so central to his empathy with the Orthodox churches of the East, is a theme that is also found in the Anglican tradition, not least in the seventeenth-century poet-priest Thomas Traherne, some of whose newly discovered works Michael Ramsey would surely have rejoiced to have known. And for this reason I conclude with three short stanzas from Traherne's 'The Ceremonial Law' as a tribute to the great Archbishop, Anglican theologian and friend of the Orthodox churches who lived and taught the glory of Christian life as participation in God.

> Fill our souls with Vigor, Life and Sence
> For otherwise the very Gospel will
> But be a letter, that being dead doth kill.
> The Vail is done away in Christ, the Skreen
> Remov'd, the Cloud disperst, when He is seen.
> He is the brightness of his Father's glory.[68]

> For then in truth we only are Divine
> When Wisdom, Love and Goodness in us shine.
> And being full of Heavenly Blessedness
> Ourselves, make others with us to possess
> The Glory we enjoy.[69]

O that I could O Lord but feel
The glorious Beams of that fair Sun, and kneel
Adoring ever till I all became
A Living, Loving, and Returning Flame.[70]

It is surely that which Michael Ramsey saw as the Glory of God and the Transfiguration of Christ, and so of Christians in the Body of Christ, the Church.

Given at Magdalene College, Cambridge.

Notes

1 The Eastern Church Association was founded in 1863–4 to pray and work for reunion with the Eastern Church. In 1906 a new society called the Anglican and Eastern Churches Union was formed in London by a group of Anglo-Catholic clergymen. Its work being abruptly ended by the outbreak of the First World War the two societies amalgamated under the name of The Anglican and Eastern Churches Association (Nicolas and Militza Zernov, *The History of the Fellowship: A Historical Memoir*, http://www.sobornost.org/history.htm, 1979).
2 Philip Pare and Donald Harris, *Eric Milner-White 1884–1963: A Memoir*, London, 1965, p. 21.
3 Donald Harris to Owen Chadwick, Correspondence re the Biography of Michael Ramsey, MS 4496, Lambeth Palace Library, f. 342.
4 Ibid., p. 22; Owen Chadwick, *Michael Ramsey: A Life*, Oxford, 1990, p. 397.
5 Pare and Harris, *Eric Milner-White*, pp. 97–8.
6 Ibid., p. 100.
7 Ibid., p. 101.
8 Chadwick, *Michael Ramsey*, p. 93.
9 Bishop Kenneth Sansbury to Owen Chadwick, MS 4496, Lambeth Palace Library, f. 184.
10 Adrian Hastings, 'William Temple', in Geoffrey Rowell (ed.), *The English Religious Tradition and the Genius of Anglicanism*, Wantage, 1992, p. 217.
11 Pare and Harris, *Eric Milner-White*, p. 102.
12 Michael Ramsey, Foreword, to E.C. Hoskyns and F.N. Davey, *Crucifixion–Resurrection: The Pattern of the Theology and Ethics of the New Testament*, ed. Gordon S. Wakefield, 1981, p. xi.
13 Ibid, p. 59, citing Hoskyns, *Cambridge Sermons*.
14 Ibid., pp. 85–6, citing Hoskyns, *Cambridge Sermons*.
15 Bishop Kenneth Sansbury to Owen Chadwick, MS 4496, Lambeth Palace Library, ff. 187, 183.
16 Gabriel Hebert, in *Theology*, xxxii, May 1936, No. 191, pp. 307–9, cited in Geoffrey Rowell, Foreword, to Ramsey, GC, 1990 edn, p. iii.
17 Chadwick, *Michael Ramsey*, p. 48.

18 Rowan Williams, 'George Florovsky (1893-1979): the Theologian', *Sobornost, incorporating Eastern Churches Review*, Vol. 2. No. 1, 1980, p. 72.
19 George Florovsky to Michael Ramsey, 16 November 1968, Ramsey papers, Lambeth Palace Library, Vol. 148, f. 129; E.L. Mascall recalled a lecture by Florovsky on a later visit to Lincoln where his thick Russian accent had led his audience to think he was talking about an Anglican lemon encountering Orthodox zoology, when he was really talking of an Anglican layman encountering Orthodox theology (E.L. Mascall, 'George Florovsky (1893-1979)', *Sobornost, incorporating Eastern Churches Review*, Vol. 2., No. 1, p. 69).
20 Chadwick, *Michael Ramsey*, pp. 66-7.
21 Michael Ramsey, Presidential Address at the Annual General Meeting of the Fellowship of St Alban and St Sergius, 18 March 1972, *Sobornost*, Ser. 6, No. 5, Spring 1972, p. 29.
22 Ramsey, in *Sobornost*, Vol. 3, No. 2, 1981. William Palmer (1811-79), Fellow of Magdalen College, Oxford, visited Russia in 1840 and 1842. After his death his account of this visit was edited by John Henry Newman and published as *Notes of a Visit to the Russian Church* (1882). Alexis Khomiakov (1804-60) was a Russian philosophical theologian, strongly critical of scholastic rationalism, and German Idealism. 'Over against the Roman Catholic ("unity without freedom") and Protestantism ("freedom without unity") conceptions of the Church Khomiakov saw in the Orthodox Church an organic society of which Christ was the Head and the Holy Spirit the Soul and whose essence was "freedom in the spirit at one with itself". Of this Church the essential quality was inward holiness, and those who partook of it could be saved even though not in external communion with her ... His conception of the Church (often summed up in the concept "sobornost") has exercised considerable influence on Orthodox ecclesiology' ('Khomiakov, Alexis Stepanovich', in F.L. Cross and E.A. Livingstone (eds), *Oxford Dictionary of the Christian Church*, 3rd edn, Oxford, 1997).
23 The fruits of many years of study were published in his book, *The Desert a City: An Introduction to the Study of Egyptian and Palestinian Monasticism under the Christian Empire*, Oxford, 1966.
24 Chadwick, *Michael Ramsey*, p. 287; Edward Every, 'Derwas James Chitty, 1901-1971', *Sobornost*, Ser. 6, No. 3, Summer 1971, p. 179.
25 A.M. Allchin, 'D.J. Chitty: a Tribute', *Sobornost*, Ser. 6, No. 3, Summer 1971, p. 181.
26 Michael Ramsey, 'The Communion of Saints', *Sobornost, incorporating the Eastern Churches Review*, Vol. 3, No. 2, 1981, p. 193; cf. also GC, pp. 147-8.
27 H.M. Waddams (ed.), *Anglo-Russian Theological Conference, Moscow, July 1956*, 1957, p. 118.
28 Ibid., p. 196, quoting J. Pearson, *An Exposition of the Creed*, ed. J. Burton, Oxford, 1864, p. 634.
29 Ibid., quoting Pearson, p. 321.
30 Nicolas and Militza Zernov, *The History of the Fellowship*, p. 6; Nicolas Zernov, 'Bishop Frere and the Russian Orthodox Church', in C.S. Phillips, *Walter Howard Frere, Bishop of Truro*, 1947, pp. 185-98.

31 Michael Ramsey, 'Reunion and Intercommunion', *Sobornost*, Vol. 2, NS 1935, p. 15.
32 Ibid.
33 Chrysostom, *Hom*. XX, on 1 Corinthians 9.18. quoted in Ramsey, *GC*, p. 146.
34 Michael Ramsey, *Constantinople and Canterbury: A Lecture in the University of Athens*, 1962, p. 13.
35 Ramsey, *GC*, pp. 146–8.
36 *Sobornost*, Ser. 4, No. 4, 1938.
37 Chadwick, *Michael Ramsey*, p. 63.
38 Douglas Dales, *Glory: The Spiritual Theology of Michael Ramsey*, Norwich, 2003, p. 122.
39 E.C. Hoskyns, *Cambridge Sermons*, 1938, p. 70.
40 Michael Ramsey, *GG*, p. 35.
41 Ibid., p. 54.
42 Ibid., p. 62 (the reference is to Bishop Westcott).
43 Ibid., p. 81.
44 Ibid.
45 Ibid., p. 89.
46 Ibid., p. 90.
47 Ibid., pp. 135–40.
48 Ibid., pp. 139–40.
49 Michael Ramsey to R.R. Williams, 4 October 1953, Lambeth Palace Library, MS 4496, ff. 357–8; [Louise] Creighton, *Life and Letters of Mandell Creighton*, 1913, vol. 1, pp. 401–4.
50 Michael Ramsey to David Paton, MS 4496, Lambeth Palace Library, f. 148.
51 Michael Ramsey, 'Three Phases of the Ecumenical Movement', *Sobornost*, Ser. 6, No. 5, Spring 1972, p. 292.
52 Ibid., p. 295.
53 Ibid., p. 296.
54 Lambeth Palace MS 4496, f. 147.
55 Ramsey MSS, Lambeth Palace Library, 114, f. 267.
56 Ibid., f. 258.
57 Ibid., 157, f. 232.
58 Ibid., f. 233.
59 Patriarch Athenagoras to Michael Ramsey, 24 June 1978.
60 Michael Ramsey to Sir Steven Runciman, 14 June 1972, Ramsey MSS, Lambeth Palace Library.
61 Patriarch Athenagoras to Michael Ramsey, Ramsey MSS, Lambeth Palace Library.
62 Address in Canterbury Cathedral, Ramsey MSS 107, f. 199.
63 Ibid., Westminster Abbey address, 20 June 1968, f. 208.
64 *Constantinople and Canterbury*, pp. 12, 13, 14.
65 Robert Runcie, Sermon at Michael Ramsey's funeral.
66 John Habgood, Address at the Memorial Service for Michael Ramsey, York Minster, July 1988.
67 Michael Ramsey, *CEA*, p. 160, cited in 'The Training of a Priest', in Mark D. Chapman (ed.), *Ambassadors of Christ: Commemorating 150 Years of*

Theological Education at Cuddesdon 1854–2004, Aldershot, 2004, p. 219.
68 Thomas Traherne, 'The Ceremonial Law', MS, The Folger Library, Washington, DC, USA. I owe this, and the two quotations that follow to my graduate student, the Revd Calum Macfarlane, who is researching the theme of transfiguration in Thomas Traherne.
69 Ibid.
70 Ibid., f. 190 v. 2.

The Lutheran Catholic

ROWAN WILLIAMS

In 1948, the first meeting in Amsterdam of the infant World Council of Churches faced major difficulties in producing an agreed text on the theology of the Church: the combined energies of Karl Barth, Georges Florovsky and Michael Ramsey had frustrated some of the more bland and optimistic attempts to draft an ecclesiological basis for the new Council. These three extraordinarily diverse thinkers, whose mutual respect is well documented, were all determined to prevent what might be called a Liberal Protestant concordat between a bundle of Christian organizations, determined to bid for higher stakes. But the higher stakes did not amount simply to a more ambitious human programme; the root issue was about if the Church was actually one in some sense, resting upon 'a unity which is [God's] creation and not our achievement'. That this was the phrasing which finally emerged at Amsterdam owed a good deal to the combined talents, both wrecking and constructive, of the three definitely non-Liberal Protestant figures who had pressed for recognition of the unity of the Church in the act of God rather than unity as a goal for human negotiation.

That last turn of expression deliberately echoes something Ramsey wrote in GC (p. 175): 'Unity, therefore, exists already, not in what the Christians say or think, but in what God is doing in the one race day by day. And the outward recovery of unity comes not from improvised policies, but from faith in the treasure which is in the Church already.' The language of the 'one race' is curiously prominent in many passages of GC; it is meant to underline what is perhaps the single dominant theme of that still remarkable book – that the Church is the 'form' of the gospel. The association of human beings together by faith in Jesus Christ is not an afterthought to the proclamation of the good news of salvation. What the proclamation does is to create relations between human beings comparable to those of ethnic solidarity. The dense and important fourth chapter of GC explains: the Church is a new race, but it is so because of two prior underlying realities – the fact that Christians participate in the one narrative of Christ incarnate, crucified and risen, and the fact that the one God is active in these events, 'including' the tragedies and conflicts of history, not least Christian history, within his single action (pp. 47–50). Ramsey quotes Barth on Romans to the effect that 'the oneness of God triumphs over the whole questionableness of the Church's history'. Here is a form of human solidarity, in other words, whose coherence is given from outside – from the unique history that as a matter of historical fact creates it and from the action and purpose extending from before time to time's end that is God's work. Repeatedly in *GC* Ramsey insists that the unity of the Church is in the fact that 'all have died': in virtue of the self-giving of Christ on the Cross, all believers are drawn into the one event of that self-giving, culminating as it does in Calvary. There is one movement, one dynamic in the Church, which is the Christian's movement in Christ towards the Father through the emptiness of the Cross. Chapters 2 and 3 of *GC* are really a long meditation on 2 Corinthians 4 and 5: those chapters describe the re-formation of the basic structures of human self-understanding that goes on in the baptized life, and thus the foundation for any coherent account of Christian mission. But it is the special insight of Ramsey to point out that here also is the heart of any theology of unity. What is unique about the solidarity of this human group is that it is grounded in an event that is constantly going on in and through all those involved; an event that is at the same time the eternal event of God's self-giving as trinity.

It is this picture of unity as one event going on that should help us see what is at stake in Ramsey's theology of the Church, and why – to pick up the theme in my title – he so illuminatingly uses Luther to reinforce his account of what is central in Catholic theology. The meaning of 'Catholic' in *GC* is something to do with a belief in salvation as a social fact, as incorporation into the new solidarity of the *ekklesia*, the 'Catholic fact', as he puts it (p. 65). There is no such thing as an unstructured, individual experience of the new life, a reality somehow prior to the corporate, so that a person might be brought into union with Christ and then start considering how to negotiate with other believers. 'Catholic' belief is belief that is clear about this, clear about the immediate effect of Christ's work in reconstructing who we are with each other as well as with God. It is thus belief that refuses to see Christian commitment as adequately understood in terms of the simple choice of a satisfying alternative among a number of philosophies. Of course Christian commitment is a free decision to walk with Jesus Christ; there is nothing automatic about it, and Ramsey would certainly have agreed that there are no such beings as hereditary Christians. The seriousness of what is involved in walking with Christ immediately makes it clear that we are not dealing with anything less than a sober self-location within a community of others who have likewise brought themselves to decision. But, an enormous qualification in this connection, two elements enter in that change the terms of the discussion. The first and more important is that any decision made by the believer is to be understood as a response to initiative from outside, not a selection from among static or abstract alternatives. The Christian holds that s/he is chosen before choosing, engaged by divine action before owning the consequences. The second is that because of this the consequences of the human decision are out of the decider's control; it will set up relations not fully understood or foreseen because of its nature as a response to and an involvement in an act that is already (eternally) under way. We have (and the image is an obvious one) immersed ourselves in the event that is going on in the Church, in the unity that stems from the Word of God incarnate. In a sermon of 1969, Ramsey wrote of our 'calling to be saints' (1 Corinthians 1.2) as the ground of unity: 'to have this calling, however poorly we understand it, and to have this goal, however miserably we fall short of it, is to be one with anyone else, with everyone else who has this same call and this same goal'; this is 'a unity not made by us, not chosen by us, but created by Christ' (*CTP*, p. 95).

There is an obvious misunderstanding that Ramsey is well aware of and he attempts to guard against. It is to think that because the model of a reasoned choice of a philosophy of life doesn't fit belonging in the Church, the Church as a visible structure is thereby given rights over the particular person in a way that denies individual freedom and enshrines unaccountable authority. When Ramsey writes about the medieval Church, this is the kind of misapprehension that seems to be most clearly in his sights. The medieval Church, he argues, failed in faithfulness to the gospel because it defined itself increasingly as a system of institutionalized order or control, comparable to the other systems around – or rather, in the early Middle Ages, providing such a system because no other power was able to. And because of this, the primitive notion of a community of unique solidarity defined by God's act was replaced by a society that guaranteed to 'broker' good relations with God: Ramsey has some tantalizing but suggestive remarks about the way in which sacrificial language changed its register in the Middle Ages (*GC*, pp. 168–9) so as to obscure both divine initiative and corporate human response. Whatever he is supporting, there can be no doubt that he is criticizing any institutional framework that suppresses human liberty by executive force.

But Christian commitment demands a transformation of how we understand that liberty. It cannot be imposed, but the ethos of the Catholic Church, in Ramsey's sense, nurtures and deepens another sort of freedom – freedom structured around the freedom of Christ to offer himself to the Father and to human beings, that freedom which Ramsey so often writes about in relation to the glory of Christ (there is a good brief critique of some modern theological accounts of freedom in *GW*, pp. 34–8, and a summary of what is to be learned from Christ's freedom in *FFF*, pp. 11–14). A proper Catholic identity, he implies, is one in which the absorption of what Christ's freedom means is daily sustained by a climate of exposure to the full radical reality of Christ incarnate embracing the Cross – in Scripture and sacrament and contemplative prayer as well as the reality of that kind of service in the world that does not look for success or fashionable reputation but simply does what Christ does. And this is different from a supposed Catholic identity for which what matters is that the Church should be a plausible competitor in the struggle for ideological dominance, power over individuals or societies.

The medieval Church was not Catholic enough; it did not have sufficient trust in its own inner, organic distinctiveness and tried to occupy and defend a portion of the world's territory. The Reformation was needed to restore the Church's Catholicity. Ramsey's presentation of Luther in *GC* has often been noted as one of his triumphs; he is able to seize on the essentials of Luther's protest and show how it reacquainted the Church with the gospel. Luther's movement 'meant the recovery of truths about the Church which are central in the teaching of S. Paul and S. Augustine and in the inner meaning of Catholicism' (*GC*, p. 171), and these include (pp. 188–90) the sense of the Church as a priestly people, the absolute significance of baptism, the focal importance of a ministry of reconciliation and a robust account of the objectivity of Christ's presence in the Eucharist. In various ways, all these affirm the nature of the Church as intrinsic to the gospel and the importance of holding the Church to be what it is in virtue of God's initiative. Luther's passionate attacks on priestly elitism and on the politicizing of clerical power (the Church as a kind of state) are in Ramsey's eyes a campaign for restored Catholicism, since they presuppose that the Church is indeed an organism before it is an institution and that the Church's security cannot rest upon a hierarchical system of control.

Luther in short witnesses to a Church that is truly an organic unity, created by the act of God in Christ; even more significantly, he is absolutely clear about the centrality of the Cross in the Church. For Luther, the induction into a living membership of the Body of Christ is a matter of embarking on the disruptive and self-questioning path that strips us of confidence in our own ability to heal our wounds or make our peace with God. Under the Cross, we find that the will and power of God to heal us is already in action, in a way that no human intellect could have devised. The destruction of our own reasoned plans for reconciliation with God mirrors the self-emptying of God in the apparently Godless terror of the Cross. God gives himself away in the humiliation of Christ's life and death; we can only respond if we are prepared to cast off a theology that delivers any kind of plans for our rescue and any kind of rational comprehension of God's action. The Church is a fellowship of those overtaken by God, in mind and heart.

It would not be too much to say that, for Ramsey, every Catholic must be a Lutheran – at least to the extent of resisting any suggestion that faith is a variety of human choice, the selection of a worldview, or that the Church is a structure for humans to manage, a means to organize or edify or support Christian persons. The Church is not a means to anything except our growth into being sons and daughters of God: it is the form of conversion and discipleship. And Ramsey is, for his time, strikingly bold in his insight that Luther is in no sense an apostle of intellectual liberty in its modern sense, nor of religious individualism. By emphasizing God's priority, Luther in fact repudiates as strongly as anyone could a religious identity resting on human argument or human feeling, as opposed to that 'being overtaken' to which I've referred.

But Ramsey does not stop with this. As his discussion proceeds, we can see that he also wants to say that only a Catholic can be a good Lutheran. He notes (GC, pp. 190–3) that Luther's historical circumstances made it virtually impossible for him to think about the visible structures of the Church in terms beyond those current in his day. No one in the Christian West was thinking about visible ministerial structures in any ways other than those defined by law, focusing on prerogatives and powers. What might be called the symbolic geography of the Church was a closed book. Hence he is cavalier not about the practices of the Church, which are as rigorously visible and corporate as anyone could wish, but about the 'order' that sustains and transmits these practices. In Ramsey's argument, the failure to do justice to this ends up by leaving the door open to just those tendencies to individualism and a misplaced concern with interiority that Luther's theology overall moves us away from. The lack of a theology of the apostolic role leaves a gap in the area of the concrete historical givenness of the Church that seems to suggest there is a whole dimension of the Church's life that is after all amenable to human choice, to a process of devising structures that will function as we want them to. To be absolutely consistent with Luther's fundamental insights, we should have to say that the visible continuities of the ministry, the apostolic function as part of the Church's basic organic anatomy, are hardly less important in the Church's battle to proclaim the priority of God's action than Scripture and sacrament.

This has been Ramsey's theme in the early chapters of GC, and he has already made it clear that he does not wish to turn this into an argument about conditions for any ecclesial body being recognized as a 'true' church (pp. 66–7). But it is certainly an audacious turning on its head of the common Lutheran assertion that a doctrine of apostolic succession is ruled out by the true doctrine of justification. Ramsey is in effect saying that justification by faith really requires something like apostolic succession if it is not to slip into fresh distortion. If we are left to devise our own structuring for the communal organism of the Church, if this is a matter incidental or indifferent for the real identity and integrity of the Body, does this not suggest that there is, so to speak, some bit of our unreconstructed individual ego-existence that remains untouched by incorporation into Christ; and thus that an element of concern about 'works', in Luther's terms, finds its way back into theology? There is something in the Church's organic reality that is not shaped by strict considerations of obedience to God's action, conformity to God's incarnate presence: how can we theologize about ministerial order in this light? But if we can't, then something in the Church is within the scope of our preferences and our convenience, our self-serving and self-justifying.

Lutheran theologians have remained unimpressed by this splendidly counter-intuitive move on Ramsey's part. But there is a point to his argument that still deserves attention. He is perhaps less critical historically than we should now like in his confident assumption that there is a seamless and theologically coherent movement in early Christian thought from apostolic to episcopal ministry; and modern ecumenical theology is far more inclined to treat the question of apostolic continuity as relating to a range of practices and structures

The Lutheran Catholic

in the Church rather than simply to the threefold ministerial order. But he does leave us with a perfectly serious question. If the Church is essentially an undifferentiated community of mutual service, gathered from time to time for a visibly united act of worship, does this not weaken the strong Pauline sense of sharply distinct charisms, gifts that give the community a concrete shape? Mutuality in the Church is not simply a relation between abstract persons, whose identities are interchangeable; nor does a theology of charisms in the Church simply mean that everybody has something generally useful to offer, depending on their temperament. Paul seems to think of sets of functions in the Church, 'locations in the Church, that have to be occupied for the health of the Body; God's grace guarantees that these places will not stand empty. And this is rather different from assuming that the community is really composed of persons whose diverse roles can be sorted out in the housekeeping of the Church as time goes on. To be in the Church at all is to be the recipient of some sort of charism, some place to occupy, not because the community decides that a job needs doing but because God knows what the community will need. 'Perhaps we ought to have a few prophets' is not quite the same as the provision by the Holy Spirit of a necessary (welcome or unwelcome) voice in the economy of a church.

Of course the transition from this to a strict defence of apostolic succession in the classical mode is not nearly as rapid and unproblematic as some have thought. But I think it right to insist that we often face a false set of antitheses in doctrines of the Church, as if we had to settle either for the Church as a flat landscape of interchangeable individuals, bound together by common allegiance to Christ, taking on occasional jobs when it seems desirable, or for the Church as hierarchically ordered by divine command. Neither is biblical, neither sits well with a radical connection between ecclesiology and justification by faith. Ramsey sees this; and in stressing so powerfully the simultaneity of entry into the Church and entry into a set of transformed relations, he suggests a way of looking at the forms of 'apostolic' ministry that might avoid the distortions just outlined. If, say, the visible form and ordering of the celebration of the Eucharist is not a matter of what happens to suit this or that specific group of people at this or that particular time, but somehow embodies a set of structured relations and responsibilities in the Body, it is not a yielding to hierarchical fantasy if we say that something is lost when we stop thinking theologically about who presides and why. And what is lost is not 'validity', let alone the grace of God in word and sacrament, but some dimension of the communicative fullness of the Body in its differentiated gifts. That this applies equally to worship in which, for example, gifts of prophecy (however precisely interpreted) are not manifest is a consequence of my argument that might make us all ponder. But it is this question of the communication of the inner fullness of the Body's reality, I believe, that represents the heart of the theological challenge Ramsey is placing before us, the challenge of conceiving what a Church that is truly dependent on God's act looks like.

Throughout my remarks so far, I have assumed that the idea of a Lutheran Catholic, while paradoxical, is not nonsensical. Before going further, I must turn aside briefly to make some comments on one very serious scholar who has recently argued for a fundamental incompatibility between the two. Daphne Hampson's book of 2001, *Christian Contradictions: The Structures of Lutheran and Catholic Thought*, presents a radical opposition between a Lutheranism defined very strictly in terms of the impossibility of effective 'cooperation' with grace and indeed the impossibility of any theology of growth in holiness, and a Catholicism that supposes a real change in the creature as a consequence of receiving grace. The Lutheran always lives from a centre 'outside' the self, the Catholic from a renewed interiority.

I cannot here do justice to a deeply learned and subtle presentation; but I will remark only on one aspect of Daphne Hampson's case. The Catholic position she presents is one in which the gracious action of God has, you might say, gone native in its entry into the human soul. But there is a fair amount in Catholic theology about the fact that the activating source of grace is always the free and uncreated act of God. And the complex twentieth-century debate about whether or not there is any sense in which grace is 'anticipated' or even presupposed by nature itself shows a sensitivity to just the problem that Hampson identifies – and a general awareness of the risk of making grace 'native' in a trivializing way. I suspect that she might recognize in Ramsey a genuinely Lutheran rhetoric of dialectical insistence on God's sole priority; she might equally suspect that Ramsey's stress on the category of 'glory' reveals a Catholic commitment to seeing rather than hearing as the basis of theological activity. In her summary of her argument (p. 287), Hampson contrasts a hearing model, which necessarily interrupts and acts from outside, with a seeing one, in which the seeing eye retains control of its field and seeks to explore it further. But what this misses is the way in which a theology of vision can talk of being blinded, compelled, absorbed – not being a spectator or even an

The Lutheran Catholic

explorer. Ramsey's theology of God's glory is nothing if not a powerfully interruptive scheme in which to understand what is, incomprehensibly and non-negotiably, before you: you must change and abandon what you thought you grasped. And what Hampson's account also seems repeatedly to sidestep is what it might mean to consider grace as always acting what God enacts, never incorporated in or merged with human agency, even when human agency is transparent to it. Catholic theology shares with Lutheran, after all, a Christology (largely untreated by Hampson) in which these issues are of basic significance. And for all Luther's passionate refusal of any 'synergy' between two agencies, for all his absolute denial that there could be any comparison between divine and human agency, he is clear that, as in the humanity of Christ, divine goodness can be made visible in finite action. If my reading of Ramsey is correct – that he sees the Church as unified by the one thing 'going on' in it, that is the self-offering of Christ in time and eternity, it is hard to maintain that there is no possible bridge between the two admittedly dramatically jarring styles and registers of theology.

But in the last part of what I want to say, I should like to return to the question of what discipleship in the Church looks like when it is serious about God's action and invitation; since I believe that this is the most pressing question that is now before all our churches (not least the Anglican Communion). The challenge is to balance two weighty imperatives. On the one hand, the Church is not the Church unless it is faithful in word and action to the single event that grounds and actively sustains it – the self-gift of God in Christ, with Scripture setting out the full contours of that act in human history and the Church's practice transmitting the form of the reality from generation to generation. It is possible for any group of human believers to lose sight of this, even to misapprehend it drastically; in Ramsey's telling of the story, the medieval Church loses in its thinking and its habits of worship most of the truly distinctive gospel features that ought to characterize it. The Church needs the most relentless critique, and its fidelity is not to be taken lazily for granted. And the implication is that disruption, separation, taking up the stance of *confessio* in Reformation language, are part of the properly theological life of the Church. It is worth pointing to Ramsey's telling quotation from Barth (GC, pp. 202–3) about the 'tribulation' that belongs to the Church's life as it struggles with sin within its history. And yet, on the other hand, if the disruption means a programme of setting up a fresh form of Church identity, attempting to create a pure body of true believers, it is in danger of judging the Church's reality or authenticity by 'works', by the success of Christian performance – and this undermines the very supernatural quality it seeks to safeguard in the Body.

The situation is made harder by our cultural setting. The unhappy irony of the Reformation legacy is the steady slippage from the confessional protest of Luther to the consumer choices of modern Christianity in the West – the search for the Church of your taste and preference. Ephraim Radner, one of the most exacting and rigorous of contemporary American theologians, has outlined the irony in a recent book, *Hope among the Fragments: The Broken Church and Its Engagement of Scripture*, in which he insists that the Church is only itself if it engages with the specific form of Christ as Scripture proclaims it; but also that a movement for reform, purity or separation in the name of this engagement always drifts towards that typically modern pluralism which fails in the long run to do any justice to the utter givenness of God's initiative, fails to think the Church theologically:

> As institutional churches, as formal Christian communities, we now stand in the same condition as that of the first Christians after the resurrection. We have no articulated theology, we have no proven structures of authority, no experienced framework for the reading of Scripture that is common to us as a church. (p. 175)

This may be optimistically presented as great opportunity; but it should first be recognized as 'the judgment of God's history' – that is, as the result of long-engrained habits of unfaithfulness in our practice. We have forgotten how to be churches. Starting new ones will only compound the problem: the traditionalist is in the same boat as the liberal to the extent that both are prisoners of a denominational market (p. 205), even when appeal is constantly being made to the model of Reformation *confessio* – or even early Christian martyrdom. The only theologically honest response is to acknowledge that God's providence has placed us in a divided and in various ways unfaithful Church, and that we have to learn there a form of repentance (individual and corporate) that is our best route towards the form of Christ: 'That God has placed us in this church at this time must mean that he would have us grow in the form of life that bespeaks the Church's repentant readiness to be healed' (p. 208).

Radner goes on to elaborate what is involved, practically and theologically, in 'staying put' – bearing with the contradictions of the

The Lutheran Catholic

visible institution, 'faithfully navigating a hostile church while remaining in communion with it' (p. 212). It is the most accessible contemporary form of being a fool for Christ's sake in a 'Church of fools, filled with waiting, filled with patience, filled with perseverance, filled with prayer, filled with endurance, filled with hope' (p. 214). But at the larger structural level, this means a polity and policy for our churches – and Radner speaks about Anglicanism in particular – that 'hold dependencies in order': we are bound up in so many relations of dependence – to Scripture, to our past, to our present partners and our present members – but we have to find a way of keeping them in tension, not seeking to relieve the pressure by removing whatever ones we currently find hardest or most offensive (p. 229). And this in turn means a call to the churches to discover a form of holiness that effectively challenges the localisms and self-assertive separatisms that are the most effective cultural captivity of the modern Church.

It is no surprise that Radner's last paragraph but one in this difficult and necessary book takes us back to Ramsey, and to GC. The Anglican Church's embrace of incompleteness, which Radner sees as central to Ramsey's vision (p. 218), is grounded in a description of the Church 'in terms of the fate of Christ's body in passion and self-giving – an incompleteness divinely opened to the divine gift of new life' (p. 233). Here is the Church's task, its one task that is truly its task as Church. We may not know where the 'real' Church is in abstract terms – and, if Radner is right, the question itself is going to lead us in the wrong direction in our present climate. But we may still know where the event of Christ is going on, and we may still know what we must do to align ourselves with it. There's the problem, of course: it is more attractive to go in quest of the real Church than to seek for the pattern of Cross and Resurrection in the heart of where we happen to find ourselves. But Ramsey implicitly warns us that the quest can be a way back to the self-defining and self-protective religious institution that always distorts or stifles the gospel. Somewhere in this is a very substantial paradox – that the harder we search for a Church that is pure and satisfactory by our definition, the less likely we are to find it.

Embracing the incompleteness is not a recipe for passive acquiescence in a Church that is corrupt, implicitly heretical or indifferent to the gospel; it is a recognition that the Church is always at best on the edge of all these things and that the self-seeking individual who believes that the Church's problems are always in the souls of others has the capacity to tilt the community further towards its perennial temptations. We have to be Lutherans after all, in the sense of refusing any model of the Church that allows us to think of the Church as a body to which we choose to give our allegiance so long as our individual spirituality is nourished by it – rather than as the very form of our Christian being. As Luther's example shows, this is far from being a passive acceptance of the concrete tyrannies or infidelities of the Church in history; but it demands a theological vision of those failures. And it also requires a difficult spiritual discernment as to how, in an unfaithful Church, we try to live our way into the one event in which the Church actually subsists.

But what we are trying to do is also to become proper Catholics – that is, to live in Christ only in communion with those others whom he has called, and in the differentiated fellowship of complementary gifts and 'positionings' that carries through history a Church that is a visible social phenomenon. Accepting the historical thereness of the Church prevents us from the kind of reinvention of the Church that throws all the emphasis upon our needs and our judgement. In a divided Christendom, the Catholic mindset will not be found only in one institutional structure, and we need to come to terms with what that means; it is fair enough to discuss what structure might best continue to hold the Catholic vision, but we can only approach each other with a measure of humility and recognition of the muddied waters of all our histories.

'Unity exists already', said Ramsey in 1936. He would have ample cause in the years ahead to know what a gap lay between those words and the reality of anxious and proud ecclesiastical bodies negotiating terms of co-operation. But I don't think he would have had second thoughts; indeed, I suspect that he would have thought his vision vindicated. We constantly fail to smooth out the crooked timber of ecclesiastical humanity; if the Church's integrity depended on this, the Church would be an abstraction, an aspiration. But it isn't: there is another timber we are bound to, and it is real even when we are not. 'As [Christ] loses his life to find it in the Father, so men may by a veritable death find a life whose centre is in Christ and in the brethren. One died for all, therefore all died. To say this is to describe the Church of God' (GC, p. 27).

Given at Durham.

'One Body' – the Ecclesiology of Michael Ramsey

DOUGLAS DALES

The Unity of the Body

Michael Ramsey embodied and proclaimed a very distinctive ecclesiology. His sense of the Church was profound, both its unity and its spiritual reality. He believed it to be indeed the Body of Christ, the matrix in which Christians find themselves drawn into the suffering of Calvary and the joy of the Resurrection – one Body with one Head. Michael Ramsey saw himself very much as a priest of the Church of God serving within the Church of England and the Anglican Communion. This distinction between 'Church' and 'church' was fundamental and it appears quite clearly in his first book, *The Gospel and the Catholic Church*, published in 1936, which is among other things one of the most important and prophetic works of Anglican ecclesiology in the twentieth century.

Coming from a Nonconformist background, Michael Ramsey retained a healthy sense of detachment regarding the structures of the Church, but also a dread of religious individualism. No one can be a Christian in a vacuum, for in the words of St Paul, 'what have you that you did not receive?'(1 Corinthians 4.7) He believed instead that the Church is a divine gift, created by Christ, and it is indeed his Body. It is the place of 'living through dying' where Christians, individually and together, are remade in the image and likeness of Christ, and through which divine life flows for the healing of the world. Institutional Church life should ever seek to conform itself to this hidden reality that alone can give life.

He believed that the unity of the Church is a reality to be discovered through prayer and repentance, rooted in the depths of the heart, and to be made manifest in the visible life of the Church. This was his guiding principle in ecumenical relationships, and again his first book proved prophetic of their development during the time when he was

Archbishop of Canterbury. His grasp of history as well as of theology determined his understanding of the Anglican Church, of the Papacy and the role of bishops, and also of the nature of Catholic belief in its relationship to the gospel. His spiritual sympathy with Orthodoxy, and his friendships in this area, reinforced and deepened his debt to Orthodox theology. Indeed, on his own admission he was in some ways an Orthodox among Anglicans. He had no doubt that drawing closer to Christ in prayer enables the Holy Spirit to strengthen unity between Christians: this is the secret of the Church's hidden life – nearer to Christ, nearer to each other.

The Bible and the Church

He was first and foremost a biblical theologian, deeply influenced by the thought of the outstanding bishop of Oxford and theologian, Charles Gore, and nurtured at Cambridge by the Anglican New Testament scholar Edwyn Hoskyns. Michael Ramsey repeatedly looked back also to the biblical scholarship and devotion of Lightfoot, his great predecessor in the see of Durham, as well as of Westcott, both of them scholars of the generation before his own. The ecclesiology that emerges in his first book, *The Gospel and the Catholic Church*, is remarkable for its biblical roots as well as for the clarity of its prophetic insight. His debt to Karl Barth's commentary on the epistle to the Romans is evident and in places explicit: like Barth he anchored the Church's existence in the person of Christ rather than in any institutional order; but unlike Barth he explored the way in which its historic life and liturgy revealed the continuing work of the Spirit of Christ in transforming human lives.

Michael Ramsey's goal was to show how the Catholic structure of the Church is part of the proclamation of the gospel:

> The meaning of the Christian Church becomes most clear when it is studied in terms of the death and resurrection of Jesus Christ. The study of the New Testament points to the death and resurrection of the Messiah as the central theme of the gospels and epistles, and shows that these events were intelligible only to those who shared in them by a more than metaphorical dying and rising again with Christ.

He went on to assert one of his most insistent themes, that:

in this dying and rising again the very meaning of the Church is found; and its outward order expresses its inward meaning, by representing the dependence of its members upon the one Body, in which they die to self. The doctrine of the Church is thus found to be included within a Christian's knowledge of Christ crucified.[1]

This theme of 'living through dying' remained with him throughout all his teaching and writing. He believed that to be a Christian is to be redeemed into the Body of Christ, and that to abide in him is to experience something of his Passion and Resurrection.

The travail and confusion often experienced in a Christian's spiritual life is also reflected in the travail and confusion only too evident in the Church's visible life. Although this inevitably pained him as a priest and bishop, he discerned that it is in fact a sign of the reality of the Passion of Christ working at the heart of the Church's life: what he called 'the hard road of the Cross'. The Church is a place of becoming; and this is not just the preserve of the privileged spiritual few, but of the whole Body as an organic unity. Its divisions are lamentable and historically conditioned; but these too are a sign of divine remaking, for:

> in them is the passion of Jesus, and in them already is the power of God . . . Both divisions and unity remind us of the death and resurrection of Jesus. Division severs his Body: but unity means the one Body, in which every member and every local community dies to self in its utter dependence upon the whole; the structure of the Body thereby sets forth the dying and rising with Christ.[2]

He regarded the visible institutional structure of any particular church therefore as essentially incomplete and provisional.

This conviction about the Church's spiritual reality gave to his preaching and teaching an immediacy that could induce compunction in his hearers, and tongue with fire the words of the New Testament. He wrote of this mysterious and painful dynamic at the heart of Christian life in these words:

> That Christ died and rose, and that Christians share in his death and resurrection and become members of his Body, are historical events which the New Testament records. But history cannot exhaust the meaning of these events, since in them the powers of another world are at work, and the beginnings of a new creation are

present. For God is in Christ reconciling the world to Himself . . . The heavenly status of the Church can hardly be exaggerated, but it is a sovereignty of dying and risen life, its power is known in humiliation, and neither the resurrection of Christ nor the place of the Church beside him can be perceived by the mind of the world.[3]

He firmly believed that 'without the Church a Christian does not grow, since Christ is fulfilled in the totality of all his members'.[4]

The inner unity of Glory

This spiritual growth must begin from within, where the hidden heart of the Church is to be found. His insight here owed much to his early contacts with Orthodoxy, through membership of the Fellowship of St Alban and St Sergius before the Second World War. This affinity with Orthodoxy was already apparent in *The Gospel and the Catholic Church*,[5] and in an address in 1938 to the annual conference of the Fellowship, later published in *Sobornost*, he urged his hearers to attend to the inner schism within Christian life, the fragmentation of thought, worship and behaviour common to all churches and to each individual Christian, asserting that 'doctrine, worship and life utterly interpenetrate one another'. He believed that God calls Christians to 'an inward catholicity or wholeness: of the mind, the heart and the will'. He appealed, not for the last time, to the prayer of Jesus in John 17 to demonstrate the scope of what the Spirit of God intends. For at the heart of every Christian there lies hidden through Baptism the unity of Christ himself, his belief, his worship, his life: 'this orthodoxy lies deep within us all'. Its recovery is the goal of prayer and penitence, as Christian unity is forged deep within the human heart. He went on to declare that although this unity is greater than human language can fully express, the key words of Christian theology in the Greek language of the New Testament and of the Fathers have been inspired by the Holy Spirit to this spiritual end, and to enable participation in that which they describe.

This vision challenges directly each Christian who, consciously or unconsciously, perpetuates division within themselves, or between themselves and other Christians. Michael Ramsey asserted that there is a need for the healing of the rifts 'between our believing, our worshipping and our living. We all have a share in the making and in the perpetuating of these wounds. We all need the inward growth of the one new man'. Meanwhile individual churches have to accept the fragmentary and broken nature of their apprehension of the fullness of faith. 'While our grasp of life is fragmentary, our grasp of truth is fragmentary too; and authority and infallibility lie not in a dogmatic scheme, but in our Lord who dwells with us and is himself the Truth.' From contact with Orthodoxy, Michael Ramsey believed that 'we learn the meaning of that orthodoxy which is within ourselves, and get a vision of its fullness, and its unity of truth and worship and life'.[6]

His personal pilgrimage of spiritual discovery among the Orthodox flowered into his second major work of theology, *The Glory of God and the Transfiguration of Christ*, published in 1949. The Transfiguration came to assume a central position in his thought and spirituality, and he was perhaps the first to communicate the full richness of its significance within the Anglican tradition. The key New Testament word 'Glory' (*doxa*) was often on his lips, and he pronounced it in a very distinctive and memorable way, full of reverence and joy. The book itself is a remarkable study of biblical language and its metamorphosis in response to the experience of God, who is revealed ultimately in the face of Jesus Christ. It represents an amalgam of the influence of Cambridge biblical theology, notably that of Hoskyns, with his own experience of and sympathy towards Orthodox Christianity. It was composed during the Second World War, and it is in part a spiritual response to that tragedy and to the challenges facing the Church as a result.

At the heart of this book there is a discussion of the hidden glory within the Church that is very revealing of Ramsey's thought. Discussing the words of Jesus, 'The glory which thou hast given me, I have given to them; that they may be one, even as we are one' (John 17.22), Michael Ramsey said:

> herein lies the meaning of the Church. It is the mystery of the participation of men and women in the glory which is Christ's . . . Beneath every act in the Church whereby this many-sided work of glory is being wrought, there is the truth about the Church's essential being, namely that the glory of Christ *is there*. The glory which Christians are to grow into and to manifest by the practical response of their Christian life is a glory which *is theirs* already.

He went on to assert that 'the glory in the Church is an invisible glory' for:

though the Church is visible, the glory is not to be confused with earthly majesty and splendour, for it is a glory discernible without and realized within only through faith ... it is hidden even from the members of the Church.

This intimation of divine glory, hidden within the life of the Christian and the Church, is:

but a foretaste of the glory that is to come, and therefore the Church's sense of possession is mingled with the Church's sense of incompleteness ... It follows that the Church's claims are ratified by the Church's humility, and the Church's riches by the Church's hunger for what she lacks. Torn from this eschatological context the doctrine of the Church becomes the doctrine of one institution among other institutions upon the plane of history. Set in this eschatological context it is the doctrine of a Church filled already with glory, yet humbled by the command to await both a glory and a judgement hereafter.[7]

The significance of ecumenism

This vision was already implicit in how Michael Ramsey approached the question of Church Order in his first book, *The Gospel and the Catholic Church*, and it certainly guided how he explored ecumenical relationships as Archbishop of Canterbury. By digging down to the biblical roots of the Church's identity and existence in the New Testament, he was able to establish a framework that would prove instrumental in overcoming some of the historical barriers erected between English-speaking Christians. The deliberations of ARCIC were a direct outcome of the prophetic vision contained within *The Gospel and the Catholic Church,* and their verdict has not been overturned, even if for the time being their implications for Anglican/Catholic relationships have not been fulfilled. His willingness to open participation in Holy Communion to all baptized and communicant Christians was another expression of his belief in the essential unity of the Church that is expressed in the Eucharist. The trust and respect that he received from Orthodox bishops on both sides of the Iron Curtain rested on their sense that he was indeed one with them in his reverence for the hidden glory of Christ within the Church. For his persistent call to participation in that glory was the secret of his own spiritual charisma.

'One Body': the Ecclesiology of Michael Ramsey

Michael Ramsey's belief about the nature of Christian unity may be summed up thus: the Church's unity is connected with the truth about Christ himself. It is the unity of his own Body, springing from the unity of God, uttered in the Passion of Jesus, and expressed in the order and structure of the Church. The one race of men and women united to Christ exists first; it precedes the local church and is represented by it. The one universal Church is primary, and the local congregation expresses the life and unity of the whole Church. This unity is between men and women who, dying to themselves, give glory to Christ's one redemption in history and are drawn into the one Body. The Eucharist is a sharing in the body and blood of Christ, and the means whereby Christians become 'one bread, one body', because it brings them very near to his actual death in the flesh. The New Testament leads us still more deeply into the meaning of unity. It takes us behind the one race, and behind the historical events, to the divine unity from which they spring: 'One Lord, one faith, one baptism, one God and Father of all' (Ephesians 4.5). The unity that comes to men and women through the Cross is the eternal unity of God himself, a unity of love, which transcends human utterance and understanding. Before and behind the historical events there is the unity of the one God. Unity is God's alone, and in him alone can anything on earth be said to be united.[8]

Upon this foundation he constructed his understanding of the visible manifestations of Church Order – Baptism, Eucharist, creeds, episcopacy. About this order he was never indifferent, even though he saw it as pointing beyond itself to the spiritual reality of the Church that alone gave it life and meaning:

> The outward order of the Church therefore is no indifferent matter; it is, on the contrary, of supreme importance since it is found to be related to the Church's inner meaning and to the gospel of God itself... For every part of the Church's true order will bear witness to the one universal family of God, and will point to the historic events of the Word-made-flesh. Thus Baptism is into the death and resurrection of Christ, and into the one Body; the Eucharist is likewise a sharing in Christ's death and a merging of the individual into the one Body; and the apostles are both a link with the historical Jesus and also the officers of the one Church (*ecclesia*) whereon every local community depends. Hence the whole structure of the Church tells of the gospel; not only by its graces and its virtues, but also by its mere organic shape it proclaims the truth... The structure of Catholicism is an utterance of the gospel.[9]

His view of the Church was less institutional than organic, with its fullness of life still developing and unfolding. 'The Church therefore is defined not in terms of itself, but in terms of Christ, whose gospel created it and whose life is its indwelling life.'[10]

His Nonconformist background made him sensitive to the history and structure of the Protestant churches, not all of which retain the historic episcopate, and relations with them was a lively issue for Anglicans throughout his life and ministry. He had no doubt about the importance of the episcopate as embodying, though not monopolizing, the apostolic succession, and as representing the universal nature of the Church in its historical continuity. But he saw the whole matter *sub specie aeternitatis*, saying:

> The Church's Order does not imply that those who possess it are always more godly than those who are without it. For it does not bear witness to the perfection of those who share it, but to the gospel of God by which alone, in the one universal family, mankind can be made perfect. It is not something Roman or Greek or Anglican; rather does it declare to men and women their utter dependence upon Christ, by setting forth the universal Church, in which all that is Anglican or Roman or Greek, or partial or local in any way must share an agonizing death to its pride. Many fruits of the Spirit will be found apart from the full Church Order; yet those fruits and all others will grow to perfection only through the growth of the one Body, in which Christ is all and in all fulfilled; it is the Church Order that in every age bears witness to this one Body, of which every movement, experience, achievement, and institution must know itself to be a fragmentary part.[11]

In his ecumenical vision in the 1930s Michael Ramsey anticipated many of the judgements of Vatican II thirty years later. It is perhaps significant that the prophetic Catholic theologian Hans Küng dedicated his great book *The Church*[12] to Michael Ramsey while he was Archbishop of Canterbury.

Episcopacy and primacy

He applied the same insight to his understanding of episcopacy, in which he believed strongly:

We are led to affirm that the episcopate is of the *esse* of the universal Church; but we must beware of mis-stating the issue. All who are baptized into Christ are members of his Church, and Baptism is the first mark of churchmanship. Yet the growth of all Christians into the measure of the stature of the fullness of Christ means their growth with all the saints in the unity of the one Body; and of this unity the episcopate is the expression. The episcopate speaks also of the incompleteness of every section of a divided Church, whether of those who possess it or of those who do not. Those who do possess it will tremble and never boast, for none can say that it is 'theirs'. For it proclaims that there is one family of God before and behind them all, and that all die daily in the Body of him who died and rose.[13]

In this spirit he could accept the idea that in a united Church there might be a role for some kind of universal primacy. Surveying the development of Western Catholicism, he wrote:

It may well be argued that a primacy of a certain kind is implied from early Church history and is ultimately necessary to Christian unity; but there is all the difference between a primacy which focuses the organic unity of all the parts of the Body, and a primacy which tends to crush the effective working of the other parts.[14]

These words were of course written before 1936, the year of publication of *The Gospel and the Catholic Church*; but again they anticipate many of the debates within Catholicism that led up to and dominated Vatican II and its aftermath. His critique of the Papacy was typical of Anglicanism at that time, and it was both sympathetic and stern. He believed that the Papacy, like the episcopate, was subject to certain criteria of true development in Christianity:

The tests of a true development are whether it bears witness to the gospel, whether it expresses the general consciousness of Christians (*sensus fidelium*), and whether it serves the organic unity of the Body in all its parts. These tests are summed up in the scriptures, wherein the historical gospel, the experience of the redeemed, and the nature of the one Body are described ... The question at once arises whether the Papacy is a legitimate development, growing out of a primacy given by our Lord to St Peter and symbolizing the unity of the Church. The answer must be found in these same tests. A Papacy, which expresses the general mind of the Church in doctrine, and which focuses the organic unity of all the bishops and of the whole Church, might well claim to be a legitimate development in and through the gospel. But a Papacy, which claims to be a source of truth over and above the general mind of the Church, and which wields an authority such as depresses the due working of the other functions of the one Body, fails to fulfil these tests.[15]

His view was close to that of someone he greatly revered, St Gregory the Great, who was deeply opposed to the idea of universal primacy.[16]

Michael Ramsey was deeply committed to the pursuit of Christian unity and he gave ecumenism great leadership throughout his time as Archbishop of Canterbury. Although he gave much effort to relationships between churches as institutions, and cultivated strong friendships with Christian leaders of other traditions, he believed that:

it is on the plane of spirituality that we can with great profit search for Christian unity, less in the thoughts and formulations of the mind than in the depths of the soul, and those actions that are controlled from it . . . Wherever there is Christian spirituality there is already a link between souls on earth and the very life of heaven, and there is already a recovery of the inner soul of Christendom.[17]

In this work, he believed that the theologian has an important role to play in clearing the ground for the recovery of the hidden unity of the Church.[18] A good example of this in his own lifetime was liturgical scholarship that established a historical basis to the celebration of the Eucharist, which could be appropriated across the churches, so that the common form of the Church's central act of worship could emerge more clearly than ever before, thus paving the way for a deeper unity in communion that is still in the future.

Solidarity in suffering

'One Body' is closely allied in Michael Ramsey's thought to 'One flesh': the Pauline and the Johannine language coalesce in the implications of the Incarnation of Christ. 'Flesh' (*sarx*) had for him associations of fragility, vulnerability and sensitivity, and of all these aspects of human existence he was very much aware. For he was a pastor of more than usual sensitivity himself, whose vocation to the ministry had been forged in deep personal suffering. The social aspects of his theology sprang from his deep conviction that Christ assumed humanity in its entirety, and that through him the love of God engages with the suffering of men and women.

He used to the full his position as Archbishop of Canterbury to advance reform of the law dealing with abortion and homosexuality, defending the rights of immigrants and giving active leadership to better race relations in Britain. He upheld the rights of prisoners and was opposed to the death penalty. In all this he was a true disciple of Archbishop William Temple, whom he greatly revered. His worldwide position as leader of the Anglican Communion gave him ample scope to contend against apartheid in South Africa and human rights abuse in Chile, and he was active in championing the cause of Christians under persecution by communist governments. He was not afraid to go into situations of conflict like Northern Ireland and South Africa because he believed that the light of the gospel of Christ has to shine in the darkness, and at times be directed into the darkness, and that Britain and its Church was in a strong position to give a lead. He gave great encouragement and support to Anglican bishops in former colonial countries in Africa and elsewhere as they sought to uphold the values of the gospel in difficult conditions.

His public leadership of the Church in these matters was underpinned by his spiritual response to suffering, and his understanding of its significance at the heart of the Church's life. In *The Gospel and the Christian Church* he wrote:

> Like Christ, the Church is sent to accomplish a twofold work in the face of human sufferings: to seek to alleviate, heal and remove them, since they are hateful to God; yet when they are overwhelming and there is no escape from them, to transfigure them and to use them as the raw materials of love.[19]

This is not just an individual struggle, however, even though it will often be borne by individuals; for it is a share in the travail at the heart of the Church's life as the Body of Christ:

> This unity in pain is very significant; it is not only a unity by similarity and imitation, but also the unity of one single organism in joy and sorrow. Suffering in one Christian may beget life and comfort in Christians elsewhere: 'so then death works in us, but life in you.'

Thus the sorrows of a Christian in one place may be all powerful for Christians elsewhere.[20]

His own teaching about prayer mirrored this vision: 'In contemplation you will reach into the peace and stillness of God's eternity; in intercession you will reach into the rough and tumble of the world of time and change.'[21] It was this deep belief, reinforced by so many encounters with suffering throughout the world, which convinced him that the Church is indeed one, and that its apparent divisions are relative and not absolute. He respected also the fact that there might be a spiritual link between widespread persecution of Christianity and the recovery of Christian unity. He perceived that his was a time when some things were being shaken in order to reveal more clearly the nature of the kingdom of God that is unshakeable.

There can be no appreciation of the ecclesiology of Michael Ramsey, therefore, that does not take into account its essentially interior character. He was heir to English Nonconformity, and to the Congregational tradition that sat light to the visible structures of the historic Church, in order to affirm the priesthood of all believers in living communion with their Lord. This evangelical and puritan inheritance was not set aside when Michael Ramsey became an Anglican. Instead his nurture within the Tractarian and Catholic tradition of the Church of England, coupled to his study of the New Testament and his debt to the liberal Catholicism of Charles Gore, gave this sense of the Church's spiritual nature a new direction. For him the visible structure of the Church, in all its imperfections, always pointed beyond itself to an inner spiritual perfection to which each Christian was called as a member of the Body of Christ. He refused to accept therefore that the life of any institutional church was an end in itself; indeed he was sure that these forms would one day have to die in order for the Church to be revealed in all its fullness. He wrote at the end of his first book about the Anglican Church 'pointing through its own history to something of which it is a fragment', for:

> its credentials are its incompleteness, with tension and travail in its soul. It is clumsy and untidy, it baffles neatness and logic; for it is sent not to commend itself as 'the best type of Christianity,' but by its very brokenness to point to the universal Church wherein all have died.[22]

Eucharist and communion

The bond that unites the visible Church with its inner spiritual reality is the Eucharist, and that reality is entered through Baptism, by which individual Christians become members of the Body of Christ. The Eucharist lay at the heart of Michael Ramsey's own spiritual life and ministry.[23] He also believed that it lies at the heart of what constitutes the Church's life across the world and throughout history. 'In Christian thinking about the Body of Christ, the Eucharist and the Church are inseparable.'[24] In an introduction to Christianity he wrote eloquently and simply about how 'Jesus wills that his death shall somehow become within us'. His gift of the sacrament is 'so that united with him and nourished by him we may offer ourselves in him and through him. For he who gave himself on Calvary, gives Calvary to us, that we may give back our all to him.'[25] His understanding of the essentially sacrificial character of the Eucharist lay close to his understanding of the nature of the Church: 'The Body of Christ shares in his priesthood, for in his Body he lives his life of utter self-giving in the midst of pain and sin.'[26]

This vision of the Eucharist, as constituting the inner nature of the Church in every time and place, was the framework in which he understood the ordained ministry. It was a priesthood inasmuch as it came to share in the priestly self-offering of Jesus the High Priest. To express this, Michael Ramsey married the language of the letter to the Hebrews with the language of St John's Gospel, and together they permeated his writing and his preaching. 'The priest finds that at the altar he is drawn terribly and wonderfully near not only to the benefits of Christ's redemption but also to the redemptive act itself.'[27] To those whom he was ordaining he could write:

> The Eucharist is the supreme way in which the people of God are, through our great high priest, with God with the world on their hearts ... The priest will show them that they are brought near to the awful reality of the death of the Lord on Calvary as well as to his heavenly glory ... As Christ's own minister, in the words and acts of the consecration, the priest is drawn closer to Christ's own priesthood than words can ever tell.[28]

The Eucharist was central to Michael Ramsey's own prayer to the very end of his life, and the way in which he used to celebrate it embodied the teaching contained in his words. His teaching about prayer indicated how contemplation and intercession are two sides of human self-giving to God in response to his love for the world expressed in Jesus Christ.

Michael Ramsey had a lively sense of the communion of saints. He appreciated great figures like St Benedict, St Gregory the Great, St Anselm, Mother Julian of Norwich, and also the theologians who created the Anglican Church after the Reformation and renewed it in the Oxford movement of the nineteenth century. He revered too more recent Anglican scholars and leaders, some of whom have already been mentioned. In this appreciation the historian and the theologian were united in the person of prayer, who sensed that the worship experienced in the Eucharist and in contemplation points beyond itself to the heavenly dimension of the Church's existence:

> Every Christian church was built because there exists the other hidden Church . . . Through the centuries this other Church has stood: human lives united to Jesus, receiving his presence, and showing his goodness, his love, his sacrifice, his humility and his compassion.[29]

Like Pope John XXIII, Michael Ramsey believed that Church unity is inseparable from spiritual renewal:

> true Christianity will hold together the faithful of today with the saints of past ages only as the Church witnesses to truth that is timeless, and to those things that are not shaken. The saints of Europe now in heaven are near to us, and their prayers help us in our conflict.[30]

In one of his last books about the nature of prayer, he asserted that 'deep renewal is needed today if the communion of saints is to be realised in its ancient meaning and power'.[31] As his life drew to its close, Michael Ramsey used to speak fervently about the reality of heaven as the true goal of Christian life and prayer, and also as the perspective in which the life of the Church should always be seen. Blindness to this undermines the confidence and witness of Christians and the sense of the Church's integrity and purpose for, in the words he used to quote from St Augustine, 'God is the country of the soul'.[32] So for him life in the Church was the experience of a living past nurturing a living present, open to the presence and Spirit of Christ, for his Body in heaven and on earth is one. Thus these words encapsulate in a characteristic way his vision and conviction:

'One Body': the Ecclesiology of Michael Ramsey

The deepest significance of the past is that it contains reflections of what is eternal. Saintly men and women of any age belong to more than their own era: they transcend it. Therefore openness to heaven is necessary for a Christian. Heaven is the final meaning of human beings, created in God's own image for lasting fellowship with him. Openness to heaven is realized in the communion of saints, and in deliberate acts of prayer and worship. But it is realized no less in every act of selflessness, humility or compassion: for such acts are already anticipations of heaven in the here and now.[33]

The ecclesiology of Michael Ramsey emerges as a profound distillation of Anglican tradition, enriched by Nonconformist Christianity as well as by more obvious affinities with Orthodoxy and Catholicism. As such it is still able to speak prophetically across the historical and visible divisions in the Church, while encouraging a deeper sense of its essential unity. It is an ecclesiology that sits light to the institutional expressions of Church life, while offering guidance as to their true meaning and spiritual significance. His sense of the Church was of an organic and palpable, if hidden, reality, which becomes clearer the further along the path of repentance and renewal a Christian goes. To this path each and all are called: for it is in the broken heart of men and women that the unity of the Church is revealed, as humanity is made whole by the Holy Spirit. Thus his ecclesiology was essentially about becoming as well as being, tender towards the imperfections of Church life that mask its hidden perfection and glory. Prayer and friendship constitute the bonds of its worldwide life, and contemplation and intercession are two aspects of the same work of love. The Eucharist sets forth to Christians that which they are called to become, both individually and together, and never otherwise. Pain and vulnerability are often the Church's lot in this life, but these can become life giving, for the Church is supported and sustained by the life and prayer of the saints and of the whole company of heaven. Thus what God can achieve through the transformation of the individual person becomes an epitome of what he is achieving in the 'living through dying' of the Church, whose unity transcends time and space; for as St Paul said: 'You died, and now your life lies hidden with Christ in God' (Colossians 3.3). Michael Ramsey embodied what he taught, both in his public ministry and also privately by the person that by God's grace he became: for he was someone who made God real, and so the words of his teaching are tongued with the fire.

Given at Fairacres, Oxford.

Notes

1. Preface, GC, 1990 edn.
2. GC, p. 7.
3. GC, p. 39.
4. GC, p. 38.
5. GC, pp. 148–9.
6. Douglas Dales, *Glory: The Spiritual Theology of Michael Ramsey*, Norwich, 2003, pp. 118–20.
7. GG, pp. 87–9.
8. GC, pp. 47–50.
9. GC, pp. 50 and 54.
10. GC, p. 66.
11. GC, p. 66.
12. Hans Küng, *The Church*, London, 1971.
13. GC, 84–5.
14. GC, p. 163 (cf. Appendix I).
15. GC, pp. 64–5.
16. St Gregory the Great, *Letters* V.18 and 43; VIII.30.
17. CEA, p. 30.
18. GC, p. 221.
19. GC, p. 41.
20. GC, p. 46.
21. CP, p. 14.
22. GC, p. 220.
23. Kenneth Stevenson, 'Michael Ramsey on the Eucharist', *International Journal for the Study of the Christian Church*, 2.1, 2002, pp. 38–49.
24. GC, p. 105.
25. IC, pp. 73–4.
26. GC, p. 114.
27. CP, p. 10.
28. CP, p. 16.
29. Sermon preached at Lincoln Minster 28 June 1972, in CTP, p. 83.
30. 'Europe and the Faith', in CTP, p. 119.
31. BS, p. 114.
32. CP, p. 92.
33. GW, p. 115.

Part Three
Epilogue

True Glory

ROWAN WILLIAMS

It's always entertaining to divide the human race into two categories and decide which group particular people belong to. You're either a little Liberal or else a little Conservative, according to W.S. Gilbert. You're a Roundhead or a Cavalier, a Platonist or an Aristotelean, a Greek or a Hebrew. You belong with Tolstoy or Dostoevsky, Bach or Mozart. You're an optimist or a pessimist – bearing in mind the definition that an optimist believes that this is the best of all possible worlds and the pessimist is afraid he's right . . .

And the game can be played with theologians, of course, not least with Anglican theologians. Do you stand with those who see the world as basically God's good creation, with human beings radiating God's image, or with those who assume that our fallen state is so extreme that the first thing we are aware of is always sin and failure and our need for help from outside? Can we properly use nature and culture to find out about God, or do we depend absolutely on what God tells us in the events of revelation and the pages of the Bible? The former picture is associated with people like Erasmus on the eve of the Reformation, with the great poets and preachers of the seventeenth century, with the Cambridge Platonists and Bishop Westcott and F.D. Maurice and William Temple; the latter with Calvin and the Puritans, with the Evangelical Revival, or with Kierkegaard's pushing towards the edge of what can be understood by reason and ethics, and with Karl Barth, greatest of all Reformed thinkers in our age.

'Christian humanism' is what people tend to call the first picture; the second is sometimes referred to as a 'revelationist' or 'redemptionist' view. But we encounter some obvious problems as soon as we start thinking through both the words used for these views and the actual thinking of the people involved. Calvin had a staggeringly high doctrine of human nature – that's why the failure of human nature was so appalling to him. Bishop Westcott had a profound sense of the evil and corruption in the human heart; that's why the possibility of restoration was so exhilarating. George Herbert is aware of God in the world around, yet he is one of the most searching analysts of human self-deceit and of the need to read the world through the Cross of Christ. Karl Barth believed that, in a world where unspeakable tyranny and violence tried to justify itself by appealing to the pattern of creation itself, it was essential to deny that there was any road from the world to God. But the miracle was that God had opened a road from himself to the world and had said 'Yes' to it, out of his unforced free grace, and everything in consequence was alive with his possibilites.

Michael Ramsey wrote a good deal about Christian humanism, one way or another. He produced a very good book on trends in Anglican theology at the end of the nineteenth and the beginning of the twentieth century; he delivered in Cambridge an extraordinary tribute to F.D. Maurice; in 1968, he reviewed for the *Spectator* a collection of essays on 'The Humanist Outlook', defending what he considered a true humanism. And in his Scott Holland Lectures, published under the title of *Sacred and Secular* in 1965, he discussed the 'long and honourable history' of Christian humanism, and the challenges it faced. After a flowering in the Middle Ages, and a huge new opportunity at the Renaissance, this tradition foundered on the rocks of a controversy between religion and science – or rather between 'a religion which distorts its own true character and a scientific theory negligent of science's own manysidedness' (p. 69).

You might think, then, that if there is anything at all in the polarity between humanism and redemptionism, Ramsey is pretty much on one side of it. Yet in fact he offers as much evidence as a Barth or a Westcott of the relative uselessness of the parlour game we started with. For Ramsey, there is in fact no easy cross-over between the wisdom of human culture and the wisdom of God, for the simple reason that God's wisdom is made plain only in the Cross. 'In Jesus the human race finds its own true meaning', he writes in 1969 (*GW*, p. 100); the Cross represents the fact that this meaning is rejected by human beings, but the rejection itself is exactly what makes possible the manifestation of the true glory of humanity and God together. The Cross is the ultimate sign of a love that will not protect itself or hold back; precisely in letting itself be wholly rejected it can appear as supremely free. When no advantage of power or security is involved, then love can appear as a total giving-away, utterly independent of the world's conditions. A human event becomes the carrier of God's own character, and in that event humanity is shown to be, and enabled to be, the mirror of divine life.

So when Christians engage with the world and with their culture, they don't do so in the hope that they will be readily accepted and that Church and society will flow together in a seamless unity, with no clash of values. Rather, they engage, listen, co-operate, because it is only in the service offered to the world by disinterested love that the action of God becomes manifest. If the world rejects what the Church offers, so be it; love without conditions means that this has always to be reckoned with as a possibility and even as a gift. To be the servant of the world does not mean being a slavish imitator of the world: quite the contrary. It is to be so free from the world's definitions that you're free to offer God's love quite independently of your own security or success. Sometimes the world may be in tune and sometimes not, sometimes there is a real symbiosis, sometimes a violent collision. But the labour continues simply because the rightness of the service does not depend on what the world thinks it wants and if the world believes it has got what it needs from the Church.

This is to do no more than to paraphrase the Beatitudes. To be 'blessed' is simply to be where God would have you be: if you are aware that there is a place where God would have you be, then your state of mind, your achievement in occupying that place, the effects of your labours all become irrelevant. 'Rejoice and be exceeding glad': you are where God is, in the place of poverty, humility, peacemaking, suffering, longing for justice, and what matters is to be there faithfully.

'Humanism'? Yes, but a strange variety, we might well say. The final point of human liberty, the ultimate assertion of human dignity, is to be free with God's freedom. What greater affirmation of the dignity of the human creation could there be? But that freedom is the freedom to empty yourself of self-defence and self-deceit; to be there where God is whatever happens. 'Let us also go, that we may die with him', says Thomas in John's Gospel. You can only be a 'humanist', in Ramsey's sense, if you are willing to let go of quite a lot of what you think is bound up with your 'human flourishing' – to be converted, in fact, brought into the presence of God's glory in the Cross so that in the Holy Spirit the true glory of the human creature may be born in you. 'Man's true glory is the reflection in him of the divine glory, the self-giving love seen in Jesus' (*GW*, p. 100).

The theme is already there in that first great work of Ramsey's, *The Gospel and the Catholic Church*, where he writes – in words of some contemporary relevance – that the real battle over belief in the Creed is the struggle between a word of sin and salvation and mediation by Christ and 'a humanistic view of Christ who is called Divine because

He is admired as Perfect Man' (p. 134). It is an unusually negative use of the word 'humanistic', but it brings out very plainly Ramsey's conviction that we do not actually know what humanity is when we are out of sight of Christ's Cross, we do not know either the glory or the horror. And he continues with a surprising quotation from F.D. Maurice – surprising for those who think of Maurice as the supreme example of harmonious convergence between Church and culture:

> In that day when the intellect and the will shall be utterly crushed upon the car of the idol which they have set up; in that day when the poor man shall cry and there shall be no helper; may God teach his saints to proclaim these words to the sons of men. He was born of the Virgin, He suffered under Pontius Pilate, He was crucified, dead and buried, and went down into hell. He rose again the third day, He ascended on high, He sitteth at the right hand of God, He shall come to judge the quick and the dead. May they be enabled to say, This is our God, we have waited for Him. (GC 134)

Humanism? Yes, the only kind worth believing for a Christian. Divorce your human aspiration from this, and you will never reach the heart of what it is to be human. The great Jesuit thinker, Henri de Lubac (how close to Ramsey in so many ways!) observes in his wonderful *Paradoxes of Faith* what a mistake it is to think in terms of trying to humanize the world before Christianizing it. 'If the enterprise succeeds, Christianity will come too late: its place will be taken. And who thinks that Christianity has no humanizing value?'(p.69). But this cannot mean that we as believers do not struggle for justice, for liberty and peace; rather it says that justice, liberty and peace sought in human terms alone will be empty and fragile, and that even their attainment in the terms most people think of them will not deliver that fullness of humanity which is holiness.

Michael Ramsey had no interest in dictating to the world what to do or frustrating the aspirations of reformers. He simply reminded believers of what they had seen and learned in Christ crucified. There is no alibi for service, for being at the disposal of a world full of terrors. There is no promise of a welcome for this service. There is only the twofold Johannine conviction that we must be where he is and that he has promised to be where we are. In this dark meeting of wordless loves, the glory of God and of God's human image is uncovered. The kingdom is there, given, the inheritance is handed over. 'Behold the Man': this is our God, we have waited for him.

Given at Magdalene College, Cambridge.

'Made Like Him':
Transfiguration in the Spirit

DOUGLAS DALES

The glory of God is the living man: and the life of man is the vision of God.

(St Irenaeus)

These words of St Irenaeus are inscribed on the memorial stone set up in the cloister of Canterbury Cathedral that commemorates the life and ministry of Bishop Michael and Lady Ramsey. If the word 'man' is adjusted to 'person', this saying becomes a master key to penetrating the heart of the New Testament experience of the glory of God revealed in the face of Jesus Christ. The word 'glory' – in Greek *doxa* – was used by Michael Ramsey in a very distinctive way, and for those privileged to know him its hidden spiritual meaning will forever be associated with his memory. He himself devoted one of his most significant books to understanding the unique way in which its biblical meaning is metamorphosed in relation to Christ in the Gospels and also in the writings of St Paul. *The Glory of God and the Transfiguration of Christ*, first published in 1949, remains one of Michael Ramsey's most decisive contributions, not only to New Testament scholarship, but also to penetrating a central theme of Christian spiritual experience. In this book, his debt to Cambridge biblical theology and to Orthodox Christian witness as he had experienced it came together. For Anglicans, the Transfiguration of Christ would forever after assume a central importance in their understanding of the Incarnation. It is therefore highly appropriate that the solemn centenary commemoration of the anniversary of Michael Ramsey's death on 23 April 2004 should have occurred in the particular American Episcopal church in New York, dedicated to the Transfiguration, where it is said that he felt the decisive call in 1925 to the Christian ministry within the Anglican Communion.

As we give thanks for his life and ministry and for his luminous spiritual teaching, Michael Ramsey would have us turn afresh to the source of it all in Jesus Christ, revealed in the pages of the Gospels, and supremely in the Fourth Gospel which he loved and of which he spoke so often. The Gospel of St John is the Gospel of the transfigured Christ although the story of the Transfiguration as such is not included in its pages. Its theme is how 'the Word became flesh and dwelt among us, and we saw his glory, the glory of the only-begotten of the Father, full of grace and truth'. Its pivot is the story of how Jesus stooped to wash his disciples' feet, and the climax of the Lord's ministry is revealed in his own prayer of consecration to his Father in chapter 17. This great prayer provides a vantage point for seeing the inner meaning and character of the whole ministry of Jesus, and also for discerning the way in which God's love and power are revealed in the Passion and the Crucifixion. Long reflection on the meaning of this moment of divine self-disclosure lay at the heart of Michael Ramsey's own spiritual theology and preaching. In his discussion of it in *The Glory of God and the Transfiguration of Christ*, his debt to teachers whom he revered is evident: to the Catholic modernist, the Abbé Loisy, and to the Anglican biblical theologians Hoskyns and Westcott. His handling of the Gospel text is also influenced by the homilies of St Augustine, which he knew so well. This prayer of Jesus is anchored in the traditions found elsewhere in the Synoptic Gospels, which record how he prayed: in many ways it can be seen as an exposition of the Lord's Prayer itself. In Michael Ramsey's own words: 'Jesus speaks to the Father as the Father's eternal Son, and yet he speaks from the midst of an historical crisis of human flesh and blood.'

> This is eternal life, that they should know thee the only true God, and him whom thou didst send, Jesus Christ.
>
> (John 17.3)

Human beings are called to know God as he is revealed in Jesus Christ: that is the heart of the Christian faith. How do they come to know him? They do so as they embrace the life and love held out to them in the person of Jesus, because knowledge of God and eternal life are two sides of the same reality: as Westcott said: 'Eternal life lies not so much in the possession of a complete knowledge as in the striving after a growing knowledge.' Knowledge and life are held together in a relationship, and that is mediated to us through Jesus Christ. 'The true God is the Father who is made known in and by the Son. This revelation of God as love in Himself involves at the same time the knowledge of the Holy Spirit' (Westcott). Or in the epigram of St Augustine: *ubi amor ibi Trinitas* – where there is Love there is the Trinity. So in this prayer, Jesus prays that 'where I am, they also may be with me' (John 17.24) echoing his teaching about how he and the Father would come to indwell those who love him. The goal of Christian life is to experience the love between the Father and the Son, 'that the love wherewith thou lovedst me may be in them, and I in them' (John 17.26). Or again in words of St Augustine: *amet se teipso* – 'Let God love Himself through you.'

> Now, O Father, glorify thou me with thine own self, with the glory which I had with thee before the world was . . . All things that are mine are thine, and thine are mine: and I am glorified in them.
>
> (John 17.5, 10)

It is to St Paul that we must turn first for an exposition of the mystery contained in these words, in his 'Song of Christ's Glory' in Philippians 2. For Paul's words describe a self-emptying or *kenosis,* of one who did not cling to his equality with God but who stooped to become a servant, obedient even to death on the Cross. Thus in this Gospel the act of Jesus washing his disciples' feet discloses the whole dynamic of self-giving love that constitutes the heart of the relationship within God the Trinity. St John, however, sees deeper still, indicating how every act of Jesus is pregnant with the hidden glory of God. As Michael Ramsey said:

> Nowhere does St John tell us that this glory was veiled or laid aside during the Son's incarnate life, but the Son took upon Him a truly human life in order to win by the road of a human life and death a glory that was always his own. Now he asks that the human nature in which he prays may be exalted into union with God.

Divine glory is revealed most fully in the humility of the servant who is the Son. This has important implications for the whole Christian understanding of the meaning of human life, of unique persons capable of bearing a divine relationship. Self-emptying makes space for God to be within each unique person made in his image and likeness. The restraint of self-giving love gives, sustains and perfects life: and this is the key to all other human relationships caught up within the divine dynamic that this prayer reveals.

Holy Father, keep them in thy name which thou hast given me, that they may be one, even as we are one . . . Consecrate them in the truth: thy word is truth.

(John 17.11, 17)

The middle part of this great prayer addresses the relationship that Jesus has created with his disciples, the apostles who will be the human ambassadors and links between himself and those who will come to believe in him. Both the Eucharist and the text of the Gospel itself are the embodiment of this extraordinary act of divine trust, that is summed up in the words of St Paul: 'Christ within you, the hope of glory to come' (Colossians 1.27). As we face profound divisions within the life of the Church worldwide, and within particular denominations not least our own, these words of Michael Ramsey commenting on this passage ring true:

> The connection between sanctification and truth is of the utmost consequence. The disciples in their mission in the world are required to be 'not of this world' in two ways. They are to be consecrated to God in opposition to the world's self-pleasing, and they are to represent the truth of God in opposition to the world's errors. The two requirements are inseparable, even as grace and truth are inseparable in the mission of Christ . . . Therefore Jesus prays 'sanctify them in the truth': for there is no holiness apart from the theology that he reveals, and there is no imparting of this theology except by consecrated lives.

> As thou didst send me into the world, even so sent I them into the world. And for their sakes I consecrate myself, that they themselves also may be consecrated in truth.
>
> (John 17.18–19)

Christianity is a dynamic human and spiritual reality whose centre is found in the Eucharist wherever it is celebrated. To this reality the institutional expression of any church life must bear witness, for it is never an end in itself. The little word 'as' stands for so much in the call of the gospel: 'love one another *as* I have loved you' says the one who came because God so loved the world. If it is true, in words of William Temple that Michael Ramsey often liked to quote, that 'God is Christ-like, and in Him is nothing un-Christ-like at all', then the challenge is how those called by his name become Christ-like themselves. 'The consecration of the disciples depends upon the consecration of the Son of God: they are consecrated, but he consecrated himself first, and his consecration must precede theirs' (Hoskyns). Thus in the Eucharist we are bidden to look again at him whom we pierced, and in so looking to live. For in words of Westcott about this passage:

> The work of the Lord is here presented under the aspect of absolute self-sacrifice. He showed throughout his life how all that is human might be brought wholly into the service of God . . . Now the sacrifice of his life was to be consummated in his death, whereby the last offering of self was made. But the fruits of his victory are communicated to his disciples, for Christ does for himself first that which will be done for them.

> And the glory which thou hast given me I have given unto them; that they may be one, even as we are one; I in them, and thou in me, that they may be perfected into one.
>
> (John 17.22–3)

This prayer is suffused with a note of victory, and through it there breathes the hidden life of the Spirit who will make all things new. If it anticipates the Passion and the Cross, it points forward also to the age of the Resurrection, of which the Church, comprising the disciples of Jesus, is the visible sign. Once again, Westcott is a sure guide here:

> There is, so to speak, an interchange of energy within the divine life that is mirrored in the harmony of relations between the members of the Church. The true unity of believers, like the unity of persons within the Holy Trinity with which it is compared, is offered as something far more than a mere moral unity of purpose, feeling or affection. It is in some way a mysterious mode of existence that we cannot fully apprehend, a vital unity, a symbol of a higher type of life, in which each constituent being is a conscious element in the being of a vast whole. Only in this 'eternal life' can each individual life attain its perfection.

For the secret now revealed, as the measure of human destiny, is that the individual has to become a person, 'perfected into one' by being held within the love of God, Father, Son and Holy Spirit. This metamorphosis, this transfiguration into an image of divine love, creates the unique ethic that sustains Christianity and that redeems the world. For Christ's prayer is that in each and in all, 'the love wherewith thou lovedst me may be in them, and I in them' (John 17.26).

I will that, where I am, they also may be with me; and that they may behold my glory, which thou hast given me: for thou lovedst me before the foundation of the world.

(John 17.24)

We remember with great affection and gratitude someone whose life made God real for so many people, and whose life, ministry and teaching demonstrated the truth of this divine promise. Michael Ramsey's life was founded on prayer, on time spent with Jesus whom he loved in a deeply personal way. His ministry pointed beyond itself towards a vision and fulfilment that for him was summed up in the awesome word 'Glory'. His teaching rested upon the simple conviction that human love of God and of others is a response to the divine self-giving revealed in Jesus in his Incarnation, Cross and Resurrection. To be a Christian is to be drawn within the life of God Himself, and to witness to 'life in all its fullness' as demonstrated by Jesus and given by the indwelling of the Holy Spirit. The sanctity of Michael Ramsey vindicates the timeless words with which we began: that 'the glory of God is found in the living person, and that the true life of a person is the vision of God', Father, Son and Holy Spirit, to whom be the glory. Amen.

Given at New York.

Note

All references to Westcott are from his commentary on John 17: *The Gospel According to St John*, published in 1892.

Bibliography

(Place of publication London unless stated otherwise)

PUBLISHED WORKS BY MICHAEL RAMSEY

'Reunion and Intercommunion', *Sobornost*, Vol. 2, NS, 1935
The Gospel and the Catholic Church, 1936/1956, reprinted 1990
'The Significance of Anglican-Orthodox Relations', *Sobornost*,1938
The Resurrection of Christ, 1945, revised edition, 1961
'What is Anglican Theology?', *Theology*, 1945
The Church of England and the Eastern Orthodox Church: Why their Unity is Important, 1946
The Glory of God and the Transfiguration of Christ, 1949, revised edition, 1967
F.D. Maurice and the Conflicts of Modern Theology, 1951
Charles Gore and Anglican Theology, 1955
Durham Essays and Addresses, 1956
From Gore to Temple: The Development of Anglican Theology between 'Lux Mundi' and the Second World War 1889–1939, 1960
Introducing the Christian Faith, 1961
'The Authority of the Bible', in Black, M. (ed.), *Peake's Commentary on the Bible*, 1962
Constantinople and Canterbury: A Lecture in the University of Athens, 1962
The Narratives of the Passion, 1962
Image Old and New, 1963
Canterbury Essays and Addresses, 1964
Christ Crucified for the World, 1964
The Meaning of Prayer, 1964
Sacred and Secular, 1965
Jesus the Living Lord, 1966 (Oxford: SLG Press, 1992)
Problems of Christian Belief, London: BBC Publications, 1966
Rome and Canterbury, 1967
God, Christ and the World: A Study in Contemporary Theology, 1969
Freedom, Faith and the Future, 1970
The Future of the Christian Church, 1971
The Christian Priest Today, 1972, revised edition 1985
Presidential Address at the Annual General Meeting of the Fellowship of St Alban and St Sergius, 18 March 1972, *Sobornost*, Ser. 6, No. 5, Spring 1972
Canterbury Pilgrim, 1974
The Charismatic Christ, 1974

The Christian Concept of Sacrifice, Oxford: SLG Press, 1974
'The Mysticism of Evelyn Underhill', 1975, in Ramsey, A.M., and Allchin, A.M., *Evelyn Underhill – Anglican Mystic*, Oxford: SLG Press, 1996
Come Holy Spirit, (New York) 1976
The Holy Spirit, 1977
'Bruising the Serpent's Head: Father Benson and the Atonement', in M. Smith (ed.), *Benson of Cowley*, 1980
The Cross and this World, 1980
Jesus and the Living Past, (Oxford) 1980
Lent with St John, 1980
'The Communion of Saints', *Sobornost, incorporating Eastern Churches Review*, Vol. 3, No. 2, 1981
Foreword to Gordon S. Wakefield (ed.), E.C. Hoskyns and F.N. Davey, *Crucifixion–Resurrection: the Pattern of the Theology and Ethics of the New Testament*, 1981
Be Still and Know, 1982

Works by Other Authors

Allchin, A.M., *The Silent Rebellion: Anglican Religious Communities 1845–1900*, 1958
—— 'D.J. Chitty: a Tribute', *Sobornost*, Ser. 6, No. 3, Summer 1971
—— *The World is a Wedding*, 1978
—— *The Kingdom of Knowledge and Love*, 1979
—— *The Dynamic of Tradition*, 1981
—— *The Joy of All Creation*, 1984
—— *Participation in God*, 1988
Allison Peers, E. (tr.) *The Living Flame of Love – St John of the Cross*, 1935/1977
Andrewes, Lancelot, *Preces Privatae*, ed. F.E. Brightman, 1903
ARCIC, *The Final Report*, 1982
Baker, J.A., *The Foolishness of God*, 1970
Baillie, D.M., *God Was in Christ*, 1948
Barrington-Ward, S., *The Jesus Prayer*, (Oxford) 1996
Barth, K., *Commentary on Romans*, (Oxford) 1933
Bouyer, L., *A History of Christian Spirituality*, Vol. 3, 1968
Brown, D., 'God in the Landscape: Michael Ramsey's Theological Vision', *Anglican Theological Review*, 83, 2001, pp. 775–92
Burnaby, J., *Amor Dei*, 1938
—— *The Belief of Christendom*, 1959
Carpenter, J., *Gore: A Study in Liberal Catholic Theology*, 1960
Chadwick, O., *The Founding of Cuddesdon*, (Oxford) 1954
—— *The Mind of the Oxford Movement*, 1960, third edition, 1971
—— *Michael Ramsey – A Life*, (Oxford) 1990
Chapman, Mark D. (ed.), *Ambassadors of Christ, Commemorating 150 Years of Theological Education at Cuddesdon 1854–2004*, (Aldershot) 2004
Chitty, Derwas, *The Desert a City: An Introduction to the Study of Egyptian and Palestinian Monasticism under the Christian Empire*, (Oxford) 1966

Church, R.W., *The Oxford Movement*, (Chicago) 1970
Clare, Mother Mary, *Encountering the Depths*, 1981
Clement, O., *On Being Human – A Spiritual Anthology*, (New York) 2000
Coleman, D. (ed.), *Michael Ramsey: The Anglican Spirit*, 1991
Court, John, 'Michael Ramsey and biblical theology' in Gill, R. and Kendall, L., *Michael Ramsey as Theologian*, 1995
Creighton, [Louise], *Life and Letters of Mandell Creighton*, 1913, vol. 1
Curtis, G., *William of Glasshampton*, 1947
Dales, D.J., *Living through Dying – The Spiritual Experience of St Paul*, (Cambridge) 1993
—— *Glory: The Spiritual Theology of Michael Ramsey*, (Norwich) 2003
Dix, G., *The Shape of the Liturgy*, 1945
Duggan, M., *Through the Year with Michael Ramsey*, 1975
Dunn, J.G.D., *Jesus and the Spirit*, 1975
Every, Edward, 'Derwas James Chitty, 1901–1971', *Sobornost*, Ser. 6, No. 3, Summer 1971
Florensky, P., *Iconostasis*, (New York) 1996
Forsyth, P.T., *The Church and the Ministry*, 1917
Gill, R., and Kendall, L. (eds.), *Michael Ramsey as Theologian*, 1995
Gore, C. (ed.), *Lux Mundi*, 1889
—— *The Incarnation of the Son of God*, 1898
—— *The Body of Christ*, 1901
—— *Can We Then Believe?*, 1926
—— *The Reconstruction of Belief*, 1926
Hampson, Daphne, *Christian Contradictions: The Structures of Lutheran and Catholic Thought*, (Cambridge) 2001
Hastings, A., *A History of English Christianity 1920–1985*, second edition, 1987
—— 'William Temple', in Geoffrey Rowell (ed.), *The English Religious Tradition and the Genius of Anglicanism*, (Wantage) 1992
Hooker, R., *Of the Laws of Ecclesiastical Polity*, 1907, repr. 1965
Hoskyns, E.C., *Cambridge Sermons*, 1938
—— with Davey, F.N., *Fourth Gospel*, 1940
Iremonger, F.A., *William Temple, Archbishop of Canterbury*, (Oxford) 1948
Kendall, L., *Gateway to God – Daily Readings with Michael Ramsey*, 1988
—— *The Mind in the Heart – Michael Ramsey: Theologian and Man of Prayer*, Oxford: SLG Press, 1991
Ker, I., *Healing the Wound of Humanity – The Spirituality of John Henry Newman*, 1993
—— *Newman and the Fullness of Christianity*, (Edinburgh) 1993
Kierkegaard, S., *Philosophical Fragments*, Hong, H.V. and Hong, E.H. (ed. and trs), (Princeton) 1985
Kirk, K.E., *The Vision of God*, 1931
Küng, H., *The Church*, 1971
Lloyd, R., *The Church of England 1900–1965*, 1966
Lossky, N., *Lancelot Andrewes – The Preacher*, (Oxford) 1991
Lossky, V., *The Mystical Theology of the Eastern Church*, 1957
—— *The Vision of God*, 1963
—— *In the Image and Likeness of God*, 1975

Loyer, O., *L'Anglicanisme de Richard Hooker*, (Paris) 1979
Lubac, Henri de, *Paradoxes of Faith*, (San Francisco) 1987
McAdoo, H.R., *The Spirit of Anglicanism*, 1965
—— *Anglican Heritage: Theology and Spirituality*, (Norwich) 1991
Mascall, E.L., *He who Is – A Study in Traditional Theism*, 1943
—— 'George Florovsky (1893–1979)', *Sobornost, incorporating Eastern Churches Review*, Vol. 2., No. 1
Miller, E.C., *Toward a Fuller Vision*, (Wilton, Connecticut) 1984
Milner-White, E., *My God, My Glory*, 1954
Moberly, R.C., *Ministerial Priesthood*, 1897
—— *Atonement and Personality*, 1901
More, P.E., and Cross, F.L. (eds.), *Anglicanism*, 1962
Moorman, J.R.H., *A History of the Church of England*, 1953
Newton, J.A., *Search for a Saint: Edward King*, 1977
Oakes, E.T., *Pattern of Redemption: The Theology of Hans Urs von Balthasar*, (New York) 1994
Palmer, William, *Notes of a Visit to the Russian Church*, John Henry Newman (ed.), 1882
Pare, Philip, and Harris, Donald, *Eric Milner-White 1884–1963, a Memoir*, 1965
Pawley, B. and Pawley, M., *Rome and Canterbury through Four Centuries*, 1981
Prestige, G.L., *Life of Charles Gore*, 1935
Quick, O.C., *Doctrines of the Creed*, 1938
Radner, Ephraim, *Hope among the Fragments: The Broken Church and Its Engagement of Scripture*, (Grand Rapids, Michigan) 2004
Rowell, G., *The Vision Glorious*, (Oxford) 1983
—— et. al. (eds.) *Love's Redeeming Work is Done*, (Oxford) 2001
Russell, G.W.E., *Edward King – Bishop of Lincoln*, 1913
Selwyn, E.G. (ed.), *Essays Catholic and Critical*, 1926
Smith, B.A., *Dean Church, the Anglican Response to Newman*, 1958
Smith, M. (ed.), *Benson of Cowley*, (Oxford) 1980
Sophrony (Sakharov), Archimandrite, *Saint Silouan the Athonite*, (Essex) 1991
—— *Prayer*, (Essex) 1996
Southern, R.W., *St Anselm – A Portrait in a Landscape*, (Cambridge) 1990
Story, G.M. (ed.), *Lancelot Andrewes: Sermons*, (Oxford) 1967
Stevenson, Kenneth, 'Michael Ramsey on the Eucharist', *International Journal for the Study of the Christian Church*, 2.1, 2002, pp. 38–49
Sykes, S.W., *The Integrity of Anglicanism*, 1978
—— et. al., *The Study of Anglicanism*, revised edition, 1998
Temple, W., *Christus Veritas*, 1924
—— *Nature, Man and God*, 1934
—— *Readings in St John's Gospel*, 1945
Thornton, L., *The Incarnate Lord*, 1928
Traherne, Thomas, MS 'The Ceremonial Law', The Folger Library, (Washington, DC) c. 1670
Underhill, E., *Worship*, 1936
Von Balthasar, H.U., *Herrlichkeit, The Glory of the Lord*, (Einsiedeln) 1962, (Edinburgh) 1982
—— *Love Alone is Credible*, Schindler, D.C. (trans.) (San Francisco) 2004

Bibliography

Von Hügel, F., *The Mystical Element of Religion*, 1908
—— *Essays and Addresses on the Philosophy of Religion*, 1924
Waddams, H.M. (ed.), *Anglo-Russian Theological Conference, Moscow, July 1956*, 1957
Wakefield, G. (ed.), *Crucifixion-Resurrection*, 1981
—— 'Michael Ramsey: A Theological Appraisal', *Theology*, November 1988
Ward, B., *The Prayers and Meditations of St Anselm*, 1973
Ware, K., *The Orthodox Church*, 1963
—— *The Power of the Name – The Jesus Prayer in Orthodox Spirituality*, Oxford: SLG Press, 1974
Welsby, P.A., *A History of the Church of England 1945–1980*, (Oxford) 1984
Westcott, B.F., *The Gospel of St John*, 1892
Williams, R. (ed.), *Sergii Bulgakov – Towards a Russian Political Theology*, (Edinburgh) 1999
—— 'George Florovsky (1893–1979): the Theologian', *Sobornost, incorporating Eastern Churches Review*, Vol. 2. No. 1, 1980
Zernov, Nicolas, 'Bishop Frere and the Russian Orthodox Church', in C.S. Phillips, *Walter Howard Frere, Bishop of Truro*, 1947, pp. 185–98
—— and Militza Zernov, *The History of the Fellowship: a Historical Memoir*, http://www.sobornost.org/history.htm, 1979

Index of Biblical Quotations

Old Testament

Genesis 49.6	177
Leviticus 9.6	178
Leviticus 9.23	178
Ruth 1.16	36
2 Chronicles 5.13–14	177, 183
2 Chronicles 6.1	183
Psalm 8	70, 84
Psalm 16	177
Psalm 19.1	79
Psalm 19.12	23
Psalm 22	11, 47
Psalm 37.1	121
Psalm 63.1	132
Psalm 101.1	10
Psalm 106.15	10
Psalm 108	177
Psalm 119.75	55, 121
Isaiah 6.1–4	67, 177
Isaiah 53	11
Isaiah 53.2	73
Isaiah 58.7–8	68
Isaiah 60.1–3	68
Jeremiah 23.23	68
Ezekiel 11.22–3	177
Daniel 7	70

New Testament

Matthew 5.1–11	90
Matthew 5.16	20
Matthew 11.25	88
Matthew 16.18–19	106
Matthew 18.20	88
Matthew 25.31–46	24
Mark 1.15	38
Mark 10.32–45	49, 70
Mark 14.21	7
Mark 14.36	36
Mark 15.34	18, 36, 99
Luke 10.29	24
Luke 10.38–42	28
Luke 12.35–46	23
Luke 14.11	35
Luke 18.13	95
Luke 18.14	120
Luke 22.37	7
Luke 22.42	87
Luke 23.34	87
Luke 23.42	95
Luke 23.46	18, 87
John 1.1–18	4, 9, 72, 109, 172
John 1.14	80
John 3.19	10
John 3.34–5	73
John 5.30	73
John 5.44	73, 74
John 6	41
John 6.51	81
John 6.57	73
John 6.63	44
John 7.18	73
John 7.37	64
John 7.39	38, 77
John 8.28	73
John 8.32	110
John 8.54	73
John 10.17–18	73, 81
John 12.23–4	77, 151
John 12.27	47
John 12.32	11
John 12.41	17
John 13.1–5	73, 99

Index of Biblical Quotations

Reference	Pages	Reference	Pages
John 13.13–14	74	1 Corinthians 2.8	38, 80
John 13.31–5	19, 87	1 Corinthians 3.16–18	82
John 14.6	7	1 Corinthians 4.7	223
John 14.16–18	63, 74	1 Corinthians 10.16–17	18, 19, 104, 105
John 14.26	74		
John 15.8	82	1 Corinthians 11.1	71
John 15.15	75	1 Corinthians 11.26	18, 19, 104, 105
John 15.26–7	74		
John 16.8–13	74, 75	1 Corinthians 12.13	105
John 16.14	82	1 Corinthians 13.12	71, 83
John 16.22–4	135	2 Corinthians 1.20	18
John 17	245–50	2 Corinthians 3.18	82
John 17.1	81	2 Corinthians 4.2–6	19, 71
John 17.5	73	2 Corinthians 4.6	176
John 17.11	104	2 Corinthians 4.8–10	35, 72
John 17.17	77	2 Corinthians 4.12	53
John 17.19	81	2 Corinthians 4.16–18	72
John 17.20–2	82, 104	2 Corinthians 5.14–17	38, 39
John 17.22	19, 51, 227	2 Corinthians 5.21	36
John 17.24	104	2 Corinthians 6.10	135
John 17.26	74	2 Corinthians 6.16	82
John 19.14	81	2 Corinthians 13.14	61
John 19.30	178	Galatians 2.20	28, 103
John 19.34	64	Galatians 3.1–2	38
John 19.36	81	Galatians 3.28	11
John 20	64	Galatians 4.6	79
John 20.19–23	74, 121	Galatians 4.19	71
John 20.29	59	Galatians 5.22–4	38
Acts 1.21–2	165	Ephesians 1.23	39, 102
Acts 2	62	Ephesians 2.13–14	11
Acts 2.25–8	7	Ephesians 2.18	61
Acts 4.13	165	Ephesians 2.21–2	82
Acts 8.32–3	7	Ephesians 4.5–6	104, 229
Romans 1	70	Ephesians 4.13	8, 109
Romans 1.20	79	Ephesians 4.15	102
Romans 3.23	36	Philippians 1.9	8
Romans 5.1–8	64	Philippians 2.1–11	16, 37, 55, 73, 120, 247
Romans 5.14	36		
Romans 5.21	36	Philippians 3.10	56
Romans 6.2–11	38, 105	Philippians 3.21	84
Romans 8.15–17	38, 88, 90	Colossians 1.24	99
Romans 8.18–23	54, 78, 84	Colossians 1.27	38
Romans 8.30	82	Colossians 3.3	115, 237
Romans 8.38–9	71	2 Timothy 2.11–13	49
Romans 12.2	71	Hebrews 2.8–9	11, 84
1 Corinthians 1.2	129, 213	Hebrews 2.10	84
1 Corinthians 1.18–23	8	Hebrews 5.7–10	36, 47, 55
1 Corinthians 1.28	58	Hebrews 6.5	22, 83

Hebrews 7.25	17, 117	1 Peter 2.4–5	7, 82, 129
Hebrews 9.4	200	1 Peter 2.9	7, 43
Hebrews 9.24	17	1 Peter 4.17	10
Hebrews 10.5–10	87	1 Peter 5.6–7	120
Hebrews 10.19–20	13	1 John 1.1	4
Hebrews 13.8	103	1 John 3.2	73, 83, 100, 130
Hebrews 13.15	18		
1 Peter 1.11	7	1 John 5.4–5	49, 58

Index of Names

Allchin, Donald, *Contemporary Anglican theologian* 125
Andrewes, Lancelot *(1555–1626) Anglican bishop and theologian* 126
Anselm *(1033–1109) Archbishop of Canterbury and theologian* 124
Augustine of Canterbury *(died: c.605) First Archbishop of Canterbury in 597* 123
Augustine of Hippo *(354–430) Bishop and theologian* 43, 110, 122, 132, 133–4
Benedict *(c.480–c.550) Abbot and author of monastic Rule* 32, 123, 126
Benson, R.M. *(1824–1915) Contemplative founder of SSJE* 127–9
Columba *(c.521–97) Abbot of Iona in Scotland* 126
Figgis, J.N. *(1866–1917) Anglican historian and theologian* 127
Gore, Charles *(1853–1932) Anglican bishop and theologian* 6, 14
Gregory the Great *(c.540–604) Pope and apostle of the English* 124
Hoskyns, Edwyn *(1884–1937) Anglican biblical theologian* 65, 67
Irenaeus of Lyons *(c.130–c.200) Bishop, theologian, and martyr* 245
John XXIII *(1881–1963) Pope who summoned Vatican II* 130
John of the Cross *(1542–91) Spanish monk and mystic* 123
Julian of Norwich *(c.1342–1413) English mystic* 125
Kirk, Kenneth *(1886–1954) Anglican theologian and bishop* 126
Maurice, F.D. *(1805–72) Anglican theologian and socialist* 10
Temple, William *(1881–1944) Archbishop of Canterbury and theologian* 6, 14, 126, 127
Underhill, Evelyn *(1875–1941) Anglican teacher of mysticism* 126
von Hügel, Friedrich *(1852–1925) Catholic theologian and philosopher* 63, 126

Index of Subjects

Anglicanism	6, 44, 112–14	Marriage	31
Atonement	12, 51, 81	Miracle	14, 21–2, 60
		Monasticism	31–2
Biblical theology	3–14	Mysticism	92–4
Catholicism	107–8, 109–10, 112	Orthodoxy	111
		Other faiths	9
Church Order	105		
Confession	29–30, 119–20	Papacy	106–7
Contemplation	89, 117–18	Prayer	45–6, 86–96
Cross	34–9, 46–51	Priesthood	116–23
Episcopacy	108–9	Repentance	28–30
Eucharist	40–6	Resurrection	38–9, 57–60
Fathers	110	Sacrifice	36–7, 42–4
		Saints	123–32
Glory	19–20, 65–86	Secularism	26–7
		Silence	93–4
Heaven	132–5	Simplicity	15–16
Holy Spirit	61–5	Suffering	11, 35, 51–6
Humility	46, 54–5, 73–4, 120	Trinity	90
Incarnation	14–20, 80–1	Unity	97–104, 114–16, 129–30
Individualism	103		
Intercession	22, 89, 117–18	Vocation	28
Jesus Prayer	91	Worship	16–19, 87–8, 95–6
Judgment	9–10		
Koinonia	16		

www.ingramcontent.com/pod-product-compliance
Lightning Source LLC
Chambersburg PA
CBHW050433240426
43661CB00055B/2373